AVR Microcontrollers Mas

Build Electronics Projects from Scratch

By Sarful Hassan

Preface

Welcome to *AVR Microcontrollers Masterclass: Build Electronics Projects from Scratch*. This book is designed to be your complete companion on the journey of learning AVR microcontrollers and building practical electronics projects. Whether you are a student, a hobbyist, or an aspiring engineer, this book will guide you step by step from the basics to advanced applications.

Who This Book Is For

This book is for anyone who wants to learn about AVR microcontrollers, regardless of their current skill level. If you are:

- A student learning microcontrollers for the first time

- A hobbyist looking to build exciting electronics projects

- An engineer who wants to refresh or enhance your AVR skills

- A maker aiming to prototype smart systems

This book is written in a beginner-friendly tone but gradually covers advanced topics as well.

How This Book Is Organized

The book is structured into clear, progressive chapters, starting from an introduction to AVR microcontrollers, understanding the hardware, learning C programming essentials, and advancing to building real-world projects like home automation, sensor systems, and wireless communication.

Each chapter includes explanations, diagrams, and code examples to support your learning.

What Was Left Out

While this book covers a wide range of AVR topics, it does not delve deeply into ARM-based microcontrollers, RTOS, or advanced PCB design. The focus remains on practical AVR microcontroller learning and hands-on projects.

Code Style (About the Code)

All code examples in this book are written in clean, readable C for AVR microcontrollers. Comments are included to explain important sections, and the code is designed to be copy-paste friendly for your experiments.

Release Notes

This is the first edition of *AVR Microcontrollers Masterclass*. Future editions will include additional projects, IoT integrations, and updates based on reader feedback.

Notes on the First Edition

This first edition was created to fill the gap for a hands-on, practical guide to AVR microcontrollers. Every effort has been made to ensure accuracy, but if you spot errors or have suggestions, please let us know!

MechatronicsLAB Online Learning

Extend your learning beyond this book by visiting MechatronicsLAB:
Website: mechatronicslab.net
Email: mechatronicslab.net@gmail.com

Here, you'll find tutorials, project ideas, and updates related to microcontrollers and embedded systems.

How to Contact Us

For questions, feedback, or collaboration opportunities, reach out anytime:

- Email: mechatronicslab.net@gmail.com

- Website: mechatronicslab.net

We value your feedback and are always excited to hear from our readers!

Acknowledgments for the First Edition

A heartfelt thank you to all our readers, early reviewers, and the MechatronicsLAB community for their invaluable support and encouragement. Special thanks to those who inspired the practical projects shared in this book.

Copyright (MechatronicsLAB)

Disclaimer

Table of Contents

Chapter 1: Introduction to AVR Microcontrollers

Microcontrollers are the backbone of modern embedded systems, used in various applications from home appliances to industrial automation. Among the many microcontroller families available today, AVR microcontrollers, developed by Atmel (now part of Microchip Technology), are known for their efficiency, performance, and ease of use. AVR microcontrollers are widely used in applications that require low power consumption, high speed, and reliable performance.

This chapter provides an overview of AVR microcontrollers, their architecture, features, and advantages, setting the foundation for understanding their programming and applications.

History and Evolution of AVR

Year	Development Milestone
1996	Atmel introduced the AVR microcontroller family.
1997	The first AVR microcontrollers were launched, using RISC architecture.
1998	Introduction of in-system programmable Flash memory.
2003	Development of MegaAVR series with enhanced features.
2006	Introduction of XMEGA series with advanced peripherals.
2016	Atmel acquired by Microchip Technology.
2020	AVR family continues to evolve with newer models for IoT and automation applications.

What is a Microcontroller? A microcontroller is a compact integrated circuit (IC) that contains a processor (CPU), memory (RAM, ROM/Flash), input/output (I/O) ports, timers, and communication interfaces. Unlike microprocessors, which require external components for functioning, microcontrollers are self-contained and designed for specific control applications.

A microcontroller typically consists of:

- **CPU (Central Processing Unit):** Executes instructions from memory.
- **Memory:**
  - **RAM (Random Access Memory):** Temporary storage for data and variables.
  - **ROM/Flash Memory:** Stores the program (firmware).
- **I/O Ports:** Interfaces for sensors, actuators, displays, and communication devices.
- **Timers & Counters:** Used for timing operations, event counting, and PWM (Pulse Width Modulation).
- **Communication Interfaces:** UART, SPI, I2C, and USB for external communication.
- **ADC (Analog-to-Digital Converter):** Converts analog signals to digital values.

Overview of AVR Microcontrollers AVR is a family of microcontrollers developed by Atmel in 1996. The AVR architecture is based on the **Harvard architecture**, where program and data memory are separate, enabling faster processing. AVR microcontrollers use **RISC (Reduced Instruction Set Computing)** architecture, which allows execution of most instructions in a single clock cycle.

Key Features of AVR Microcontrollers

- High-speed performance (1 MIPS per MHz, meaning a 16 MHz AVR can execute 16 million instructions per second).
- Flash memory for program storage (reprogrammable up to 100,000 times).
- Built-in EEPROM for data storage.
- Wide range of I/O capabilities (PWM, ADC, serial communication, etc.).
- Low power consumption with power-saving modes.
- Supports multiple programming methods (ISP, JTAG, bootloader).
- On-chip debugging capabilities.

AVR vs Other Microcontrollers

Feature	AVR	PIC	8051	ARM
Architecture	RISC	RISC	CISC	RISC
Speed	1 MIPS per MHz	0.5 MIPS per MHz	Slower due to CISC	High (Depends on core)
Memory	Flash, EEPROM, SRAM	Flash, EEPROM, SRAM	ROM, RAM, External	Flash, SRAM, ROM
Power Consumption	Low	Medium	High	Very Low
Programming Ease	Easy (C, Assembly, Arduino)	Moderate	Difficult	Moderate to Difficult
Peripherals	Rich (PWM, ADC, USART, SPI, I2C)	Moderate	Limited	Extensive
Cost	Low	Moderate	Low	High

Advantages of AVR Microcontrollers

1. **High Processing Speed:** Executes most instructions in one clock cycle.
2. **Low Power Consumption:** Ideal for battery-powered applications.
3. **Ease of Programming:** Supports C and Assembly languages.
4. **Rich Peripheral Set:** Includes ADC, PWM, Timers, and communication interfaces.
5. **Cost-Effective:** Widely used in educational, industrial, and commercial projects.
6. **Community Support:** Extensive documentation and resources available.

Applications of AVR Microcontrollers AVR microcontrollers are used in various applications, including:

- **Embedded Systems:** Home automation, smart appliances.
- **Robotics:** Motor control, sensor interfacing.
- **Industrial Automation:** Process control, instrumentation.

- **Automotive Electronics:** Engine control units (ECU), car security systems.
- **Consumer Electronics:** Remote controls, gaming devices.
- **Medical Devices:** Heart rate monitors, glucose meters.
- **IoT (Internet of Things):** Smart sensors and networked devices.

Summary In this chapter, we introduced AVR microcontrollers, their architecture, classifications, and key features. AVR microcontrollers, with their RISC-based architecture, high-speed performance, and low power consumption, are widely used in embedded systems and automation projects. We also explored development tools, advantages, and applications.

Chapter 2: AVR Architecture

AVR microcontrollers are based on the Harvard architecture and use RISC (Reduced Instruction Set Computing) principles. They are designed for high-speed performance, low power consumption, and ease of use in embedded systems. This chapter explores the internal architecture of AVR microcontrollers, including their memory organization, CPU structure, and peripheral interfaces.

Harvard Architecture in AVR AVR microcontrollers follow the Harvard architecture, where program memory (Flash) and data memory (SRAM) are separate. This allows the microcontroller to fetch instructions and data simultaneously, improving execution speed.

Block Diagram of AVR Architecture The following block diagram represents the internal structure of an AVR microcontroller:

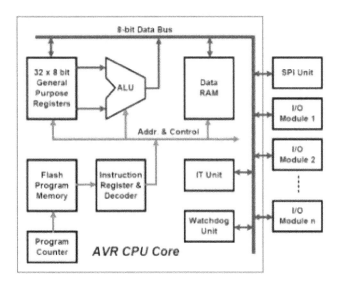

- **32 × 8-bit General Purpose Registers:** Used for fast data manipulation.
- **ALU (Arithmetic Logic Unit):** Performs arithmetic and logical operations.
- **Flash Program Memory:** Stores the program code.

- **Program Counter (PC):** Holds the address of the next instruction to execute.
- **Instruction Register & Decoder:** Decodes fetched instructions.
- **Data RAM (SRAM):** Stores temporary data during execution.
- **IT Unit (Interrupt Unit):** Handles interrupts for real-time applications.
- **Watchdog Timer (WDT):** Resets the microcontroller in case of a software failure.
- **SPI Unit, I/O Modules:** Handles communication and external interfacing.

Key Components of AVR Architecture

1. **Central Processing Unit (CPU)**
   a. Executes instructions stored in Flash memory.
   b. Operates with a 32-register file for efficient processing.
   c. Supports interrupts for real-time processing.

2. **Memory Organization**
   a. **Flash Memory:** Non-volatile memory for program storage.
   b. **SRAM (Static RAM):** Used for data storage and stack operations.
   c. **EEPROM (Electrically Erasable Programmable Read-Only Memory):** Stores non-volatile data, such as configuration settings.

3. **General-Purpose Registers**
   a. AVR microcontrollers feature 32 general-purpose registers.
   b. These registers provide fast access for arithmetic and logic operations.

4. **I/O Ports**
   a. Digital input/output pins for interfacing with external components.
   b. Configurable as input or output based on application requirements.

5. **Timers and Counters**
   a. Used for time-based operations, such as delays, PWM generation, and event counting.
   b. Supports multiple modes, including normal, CTC (Clear

Timer on Compare), and fast PWM.

6. **Interrupt System**
    a. Supports external and internal interrupts for event-driven applications.
    b. Provides interrupt vectors for handling different types of interrupts.

7. **Serial Communication Interfaces**
    a. **USART (Universal Synchronous/Asynchronous Receiver/Transmitter):** Used for serial data transmission.
    b. **SPI (Serial Peripheral Interface):** Enables communication with peripheral devices.
    c. **I2C (Inter-Integrated Circuit):** Supports multi-device communication.

8. **Analog-to-Digital Converter (ADC)**
    a. Converts analog signals to digital values for sensor interfacing.
    b. Supports multiple input channels with selectable reference voltages.

9. **Watchdog Timer (WDT)**
    a. A safety feature that resets the microcontroller in case of software failure.
    b. Helps prevent system crashes and ensures continuous operation.

10. **Power Management and Sleep Modes**
- Provides low-power operation for energy-efficient applications.
- Multiple sleep modes allow reduced power consumption during inactivity.

Advantages of AVR Architecture
- **Efficient Instruction Execution:** Most instructions execute in a single clock cycle.
- **Separate Memory for Program and Data:** Enables parallel data and instruction fetching.
- **Rich Peripheral Set:** Supports various communication protocols and interfacing options.
- **Low Power Consumption:** Ideal for battery-powered and energy-efficient applications.

- **Reliable and Scalable:** Used in various applications, from simple embedded systems to complex automation.

Conclusion The AVR microcontroller architecture provides a robust and efficient platform for embedded systems. Its combination of a high-speed CPU, separate program and data memory, and extensive peripheral support makes it a preferred choice for numerous applications.

This chapter detailed the AVR's internal components and their interactions, setting the foundation for understanding programming and interfacing with AVR microcontrollers.

Chapter 3: AVR Families

Introduction AVR microcontrollers come in different families, each designed for specific applications, ranging from simple embedded systems to high-performance automation. Atmel (now Microchip Technology) has classified AVR microcontrollers into three major families: **TinyAVR, MegaAVR, and XMEGA**. Each family varies in processing power, memory size, and peripheral features. This chapter explores these AVR families and their characteristics.

Diagram of AVR Families A hierarchical diagram can illustrate the classification of AVR families:

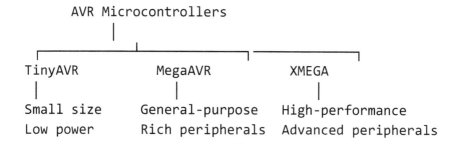

TinyAVR Series TinyAVR microcontrollers are small, cost-effective, and energy-efficient, designed for simple applications requiring minimal processing power and peripheral interfacing.

- **Features:**
    - Small size with low pin count (6-32 pins)
    - Low power consumption
    - Limited Flash, SRAM, and EEPROM memory
    - Basic peripherals such as timers, ADC, and I/O ports
    - Supports SPI and I2C communication
- **Applications:**
    - Simple automation systems
    - Battery-operated devices
    - LED control and basic sensor interfacing

- **Example Models:**
  - ATtiny13
  - ATtiny25
  - ATtiny85

MegaAVR Series MegaAVR microcontrollers are the most commonly used AVR family, offering a balance of processing power, memory, and peripheral support. They are widely used in Arduino boards and various embedded applications.

- **Features:**
  - Medium to high pin count (28-100 pins)
  - Large Flash memory (up to 256 KB)
  - More SRAM and EEPROM compared to TinyAVR
  - Rich set of peripherals including multiple timers, ADC, PWM, USART, SPI, and I2C
  - Enhanced processing speed and interrupt handling
- **Applications:**
  - Arduino-based projects
  - Robotics and motor control
  - Industrial automation
  - Communication systems
- **Example Models:**
  - ATmega8
  - ATmega16
  - ATmega32
  - ATmega328P (used in Arduino Uno)

XMEGA Series XMEGA microcontrollers are high-performance AVR devices designed for complex and high-speed applications requiring extensive peripherals and large memory.

- **Features:**
  - High-speed operation (up to 32 MHz)
  - Large Flash memory (up to 384 KB)
  - Higher SRAM and EEPROM compared to MegaAVR
  - Advanced peripherals including high-speed ADC, DAC, DMA, and multiple USART, SPI, I2C channels
  - Low power modes for energy-efficient applications
  - Enhanced security features

- **Applications:**
  - High-end automation
  - Advanced signal processing
  - Data acquisition systems
  - Wireless communication modules
- **Example Models:**
  - ATxmega128A1
  - ATxmega256A3

Recent Developments in AVR Families Microchip Technology has introduced new AVR series, including **AVR DA and AVR DB**, which bring enhanced features such as:

- **Core Independent Peripherals (CIPs)** for hardware-level control without CPU intervention.
- **Event System** allowing peripherals to communicate without CPU load.
- **Configurable Custom Logic (CCL)** for digital logic processing.
- **Improved low-power features**, making them ideal for IoT applications.

How to Choose the Right AVR Family? Choosing the right AVR microcontroller depends on the application requirements. Here's a quick guide:

- **For low-cost, power-sensitive applications:** TinyAVR
- **For general-purpose embedded projects (Arduino, robotics):** MegaAVR
- **For high-speed, real-time processing and complex tasks:** XMEGA
- **For modern IoT applications requiring advanced peripherals:** AVR DA/DB series

Comparison of AVR Families

Feature	TinyAVR	MegaAVR	XMEGA
Speed	Up to 20 MHz	Up to 20 MHz	Up to 32 MHz
Flash Memory	Up to 8 KB	Up to 256 KB	Up to 384 KB
SRAM	Up to 512 B	Up to 8 KB	Up to 32 KB
EEPROM	Up to 512 B	Up to 4 KB	Up to 8 KB

I/O Pins	Up to 32	Up to 86	Up to 100
Peripherals	Basic (Timers, ADC)	Rich (PWM, USART, SPI)	Advanced (DMA, DAC, High-speed ADC)
Power Consumption	Very Low	Moderate	Optimized for Performance
Applications	Simple embedded tasks	Robotics, Industrial use	High-end embedded applications

Comparison with Other Microcontroller Families

Feature	AVR (Mega/XMEGA)	PIC (Microchip)	8051 (Intel)	ARM (Cortex-M)
Architecture	RISC	RISC	CISC	RISC
Processing Speed	1 MIPS/MHz	0.5 MIPS/MHz	Slower	High (depends on core)
Power Consumption	Low	Medium	High	Very Low
Ease of Programming	Easy (Arduino, C, Assembly)	Moderate	Difficult	Moderate to Difficult
Peripherals	Rich (ADC, PWM, USART, SPI, I2C)	Moderate	Limited	Extensive (Ethernet, USB, DSP)
Applications	Embedded, Robotics, IoT	Industrial, Automotive	Legacy systems	IoT, AI, Mobile Devices

Conclusion AVR microcontrollers are classified into three main families: **TinyAVR for basic applications, MegaAVR for general-purpose projects, and XMEGA for high-performance tasks.** The latest **AVR DA and DB series** bring enhanced capabilities for modern embedded systems. AVR microcontrollers remain a strong choice in the industry due to their efficiency, ease of programming, and rich set of peripherals.

Chapter 4: Understanding Registers and Memory Structure

Introduction Registers and memory structure are fundamental components of AVR microcontrollers, playing a crucial role in data storage, processing, and execution. AVR microcontrollers follow the Harvard architecture, where program and data memory are separate, enabling fast execution. This chapter explores different types of registers and memory architecture in AVR microcontrollers.

Block Diagram of AVR Memory Architecture A visual representation of AVR's memory architecture can help in understanding how memory types are organized and accessed:

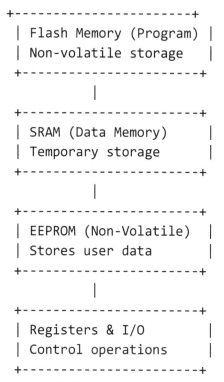

```
+-----------------------+
| Flash Memory (Program) |
| Non-volatile storage   |
+-----------------------+
            |
+-----------------------+
| SRAM (Data Memory)    |
| Temporary storage     |
+-----------------------+
            |
+-----------------------+
| EEPROM (Non-Volatile) |
| Stores user data      |
+-----------------------+
            |
+-----------------------+
| Registers & I/O       |
| Control operations    |
+-----------------------+
```

AVR Pinout Example (ATmega328P)

Pin Number	Pin Name	Function
1	PC6 (RESET)	Reset Pin
2	PD0 (RXD)	UART Receive

3	PD1 (TXD)	UART Transmit
4	PD2 (INT0)	External Interrupt 0
5	PD3 (INT1)	External Interrupt 1
6	PD4 (XCK/T0)	Timer/Counter 0 Clock Input
7	VCC	Power Supply
8	GND	Ground
9	PB6 (XTAL1)	External Oscillator Input
10	PB7 (XTAL2)	External Oscillator Output

Registers in AVR Microcontrollers Registers are small storage units inside the microcontroller that hold data temporarily during operations. AVR microcontrollers contain **General-Purpose Registers, Special Function Registers (SFRs), and I/O Registers.**

1. **General-Purpose Registers (GPRs)**
   a. AVR has **32 general-purpose registers (R0–R31).**
   b. These registers are directly connected to the Arithmetic Logic Unit (ALU), allowing most instructions to execute in a single clock cycle.
   c. Registers R0–R15 are used for general computation, while R16–R31 can also be used for immediate value assignments.
2. **Special Function Registers (SFRs)**
   a. SFRs are used to control peripherals and system functions.
   b. Examples:
      i. **Status Register (SREG):** Stores status flags such as Carry, Zero, and Overflow.
      ii. **Stack Pointer (SP):** Keeps track of the top of the stack.
      iii. **Timer Registers (TCCR, TCNT):** Control and count timing operations.
      iv. **General Purpose I/O Registers (GPIOR):** Used for temporary storage.
      v. **Interrupt Registers (GICR, MCUCR):** Control external and internal interrupts.

Status Register (SREG) in AVR The **Status Register (SREG)** in AVR is an 8-bit register that holds important flag bits used by the CPU to control and monitor program execution.

Bit	Name	Description	Example
7	I	Global Interrupt Enable	SEI (Set Global Interrupt) enables interrupts
6	T	Bit Copy Storage	Used in bit operations
5	H	Half Carry Flag	Used in BCD arithmetic
4	S	Sign Flag	S = N $\oplus$ V (Sign flag used for signed arithmetic)
3	V	Overflow Flag	Indicates signed overflow
2	N	Negative Flag	Set when result is negative
1	Z	Zero Flag	Set when result is zero
0	C	Carry Flag	Set when carry occurs

Example of Status Register (SREG) Usage in C

```c
#include <avr/io.h>

int main(void) {
    uint8_t result = 10 - 10; // This will result in 0

    // Check if the Zero Flag (Z) is set
    if (SREG & (1 << Z_FLAG)) {  // Z_FLAG is bit 1 in SREG
        PORTB |= (1 << PB0); // Turn ON LED at PB0
    } else {
        PORTB &= ~(1 << PB0); // Turn OFF LED at PB0
    }

    while(1); // Infinite loop
}
```

Memory Structure in AVR The AVR memory system consists of three primary types:

- **Flash Memory (Program Memory)**
- **SRAM (Data Memory)**
- **EEPROM (Non-Volatile Memory)**

1. **Flash Memory (Program Memory)**
    a. Used to store the program code (firmware).
    b. Non-volatile memory that retains data after power loss.
    c. AVR microcontrollers support **In-System Programming (ISP)** to update firmware without removing the chip.
    d. **Slowest access speed compared to SRAM.**
2. **SRAM (Static Random-Access Memory)**
    a. Used for temporary data storage during program execution.
    b. Includes **Register File, I/O Memory, Internal RAM, and Stack Memory**.
    c. The Stack Pointer (SP) manages function calls and interrupts.
    d. **Fastest access speed in AVR memory structure.**
3. **EEPROM (Electrically Erasable Programmable Read-Only Memory)**
    a. Non-volatile memory used for data storage.
    b. Used to store settings and calibration data.
    c. Can be written and erased multiple times during operation.
    d. **Slower than Flash and SRAM but retains data after power loss.**

Memory Addressing in AVR Memory addressing determines how data is accessed. AVR supports:

1. **Direct Addressing:** Uses specific addresses to access registers and memory locations.
2. **Indirect Addressing:** Uses pointers (registers X, Y, Z) to access memory locations dynamically.
3. **Immediate Addressing:** Uses immediate values in instructions (e.g., LDI R16, 0xFF).
4. **Stack Addressing:** Uses the Stack Pointer (SP) to store return addresses during function calls and interrupts.

Chapter 5: AVR Development Tools and Ecosystem

Introduction Developing applications for AVR microcontrollers requires a combination of hardware and software tools. The AVR ecosystem includes compilers, programming environments, debugging tools, and simulation platforms. This chapter explores the essential tools used for AVR development, from integrated development environments (IDEs) to hardware programmers.

1. Integrated Development Environments (IDEs) IDEs provide a complete environment for writing, compiling, and debugging AVR code. Some of the most commonly used IDEs include:

- **Atmel Studio (Microchip Studio)**
    - Official IDE for AVR development.
    - Supports C and Assembly programming.
    - Built-in debugging and simulation tools.
    - Direct support for Microchip hardware debuggers and programmers.
- **Arduino IDE**
    - User-friendly and widely used for ATmega-based microcontrollers (e.g., ATmega328P in Arduino Uno).
    - Simplifies programming with built-in libraries.
    - Open-source with extensive community support.
- **PlatformIO**
    - A modern alternative supporting multiple microcontroller platforms, including AVR.
    - Works with Visual Studio Code for an enhanced development experience.
- **AVR-GCC (GNU Compiler Collection)**
    - Open-source compiler for AVR development.
    - Used with command-line tools or integrated into other IDEs.

Comparison of AVR Development IDEs

IDE	Official Support	Programming Languages	Debugging	Ease of Use
Atmel Studio	Yes	C, Assembly	Yes	Moderate
Arduino IDE	No (for non-Arduino)	C++ (Arduino-based)	No	Very Easy
PlatformIO	No	C, C++	Yes	Easy
AVR-GCC + Makefile	No	C, Assembly	Limited	Advanced

2. AVR Programmers and Debuggers To load code onto an AVR microcontroller, a programmer is required. Debuggers help in troubleshooting issues.

- **USBasp**
    - A low-cost USB programmer for AVR microcontrollers.
    - Works with **AVRDUDE** software for flashing firmware.
- **AVRISP mkII**
    - An official in-system programmer from Atmel (Microchip).
    - Supports in-circuit programming via **ISP (In-System Programming)**.
- **Atmel ICE**
    - A powerful debugger and programmer.
    - Supports **JTAG, PDI, and DebugWIRE interfaces**.
    - Works with Atmel Studio for advanced debugging.
- **Arduino as ISP**
    - An Arduino board (e.g., Arduino Uno) can be used to program other AVR microcontrollers.
    - Requires a simple wiring setup and the "Arduino as ISP" sketch.

3. Simulation and Debugging Tools Simulation tools help test code before flashing it to hardware, reducing debugging time.

- **Proteus (ISIS)**
    - A popular simulation tool that supports AVR microcontroller simulation.
    - Allows users to design circuits and test firmware virtually.

- **AVR Simulator 2 (Atmel Studio)**
  - Built-in simulator in Atmel Studio.
  - Provides register and memory visualization for debugging.
- **SimulAVR**
  - Open-source command-line AVR simulator.
  - Useful for debugging AVR applications before hardware testing.
- **Online AVR Simulators:**
  - **Tinkercad Circuits** – Simulates Arduino-based AVR projects.
  - **Wokwi** – Simulates AVR (Arduino) projects online.
  - **EdSim51** – Useful for 8-bit microcontroller simulation.

4. AVR Libraries and Frameworks Libraries and frameworks simplify development by providing pre-written functions for common tasks.

- **AVR Libc**
  - Standard C library for AVR.
  - Includes functions for delay, EEPROM access, and I/O operations.
- **Arduino Core Libraries**
  - Provides an abstraction layer for programming AVR chips easily.
  - Includes functions for PWM, serial communication, and digital I/O.
- **LUFA (Lightweight USB Framework for AVRs)**
  - Used for developing USB applications on AVR.
  - Supports USB HID, Mass Storage, and CDC (serial over USB).

5. Common AVR Development Boards Many development boards simplify the use of AVR microcontrollers.

- **Arduino Uno** (ATmega328P-based)
  - Most popular AVR development board.
  - Supports Arduino IDE and various shields.

- **ATmega328P Xplained Mini**
  - Official Microchip board for ATmega328P.
  - Works seamlessly with Atmel Studio and Atmel ICE.
- **ATmega32 Development Board**
  - A general-purpose development board with LCD, keypad, and GPIO access.

6. Flashing Code to AVR Microcontrollers The process of uploading code to an AVR microcontroller involves:

- Writing code in an IDE (e.g., Atmel Studio, Arduino IDE).
- Compiling the code into a HEX file.
- Using a programmer (e.g., USBasp, AVRISP) to upload the HEX file to the microcontroller.
- Verifying the uploaded code using debugging tools.

Flashing Code Using Atmel Studio

1. Write your C or Assembly code in Atmel Studio.
2. Click **Build & Compile** to generate a .hex file.
3. Connect a programmer (e.g., **Atmel ICE**).
4. Click **Device Programming**, select the microcontroller, and choose **Flash**.

Flashing Code Using Arduino IDE

1. Select the board (e.g., **Arduino Uno**).
2. Write code and click **Upload**.
3. The built-in bootloader will program the microcontroller.

Example: Flashing a HEX File Using AVRDUDE (Command-Line Tool)

```
avrdude -c usbasp -p m328p -U flash:w:program.hex:i
```

This command:

- -c usbasp specifies the USBasp programmer.
- -p m328p defines the target microcontroller (ATmega328P).
- -U flash:w:program.hex:i writes the HEX file to Flash memory.

Chapter 6: Setting Up AVR Studio (Microchip Studio)

Introduction AVR Studio, now known as **Microchip Studio**, is the official development environment for AVR microcontrollers. It provides a full suite of tools, including an editor, compiler, debugger, and simulator. This chapter guides you through installing, configuring, and writing your first program in AVR Studio.

1. Installing Microchip Studio Microchip Studio is available for free from Microchip's website. Follow these steps to install it:

Step 1: Downloading the Software

- Visit the Microchip Studio Download Page.
- Select the latest version compatible with your system.
- Download the **.exe** installer.

Step 2: Installing the Software

- Run the downloaded installer.
- Follow the setup wizard, agreeing to the terms and selecting the installation directory.
- Choose to install optional **AVR Toolchain** (recommended).
- Click **Finish** after installation is complete.

2. Setting Up a New Project in Microchip Studio Once installed, follow these steps to create a new AVR project:

Step 1: Open Microchip Studio

- Launch the application.
- Click **File → New Project**.

Step 2: Select Project Type

- Choose **GCC C Executable Project** (for C programming).
- Choose **Assembler Project** (for Assembly programming).

Step 3: Select the Microcontroller

- In the device selection window, search for your microcontroller (e.g., **ATmega328P**).
- Click **OK** to create the project.

3. Writing and Compiling a Simple Program To test your setup, write a simple LED blinking program:

```c
#include <avr/io.h>
#include <util/delay.h>

int main(void) {
    DDRB |= (1 << PB0); // Set PB0 as an output
    while (1) {
        PORTB ^= (1 << PB0); // Toggle PB0
        _delay_ms(500); // Wait for 500 ms
    }
}
```

Step 1: Writing the Code

- write the code into the **main.c** file in Microchip Studio.

Step 2: Compiling the Code

- Click **Build → Build Solution (F7)**.
- Ensure there are no errors in the output window.

4. Uploading the Code to an AVR Microcontroller

To program an AVR microcontroller, you need a hardware programmer. Here's how to upload your compiled HEX file:

Step 1: Connect the Programmer

- Use a **USBasp, AVRISP mkII, or Atmel ICE**.
- Connect the programmer to your microcontroller's **ISP (In-System Programming) pins**.

Step 2: Open Device Programming

- In Microchip Studio, go to **Tools → Device Programming**.
- Select the connected programmer and microcontroller (e.g., **ATmega328P**).

Step 3: Flash the HEX File

- Click **Memories** on the left panel.
- Under **Flash**, select the compiled HEX file (.hex).
- Click **Program** to upload the code.

5. Debugging in Microchip Studio Microchip Studio includes debugging tools to analyze program execution.

Using Debugging Tools:

- Use **breakpoints** to pause execution at a specific line.
- View **register values and memory states**.

- Use the **Step Over (F10)** and **Step Into (F11)** commands for line-by-line debugging.

6. Using Microchip Studio with Arduino Boards If you are using an **Arduino Uno** or similar board, you can write and upload programs using Microchip Studio.

- Install the **Arduino Core Libraries** from the **Microchip Studio Extension Manager**.
- Select the **Arduino Bootloader Programmer** instead of an ISP programmer.
- Compile and upload the code directly from Microchip Studio.

7. AVR Programmer Compatibility Table Selecting the correct programmer is essential for flashing and debugging AVR microcontrollers.

Programmer	Supported Microcontrollers	Programming Interface	Usage
USBasp	ATmega, ATtiny	ISP (In-System Programming)	Low-cost, widely used
AVRISP mkII	ATmega, ATtiny	ISP	Official Atmel/Microchip tool
Atmel ICE	ATmega, ATtiny, SAM	JTAG, DebugWIRE, ISP	Advanced debugging support
Arduino as ISP	ATmega328P, ATtiny85	ISP	Uses an Arduino board as a programmer

8. Common Issues and Troubleshooting Tips Users may encounter issues while flashing AVR chips. Below are common errors and their solutions.

Issue	Possible Cause	Solution
Device Signature Mismatch	Incorrect microcontroller selection	Verify the selected microcontroller in Microchip Studio
Programmer Not Recognized	Missing drivers	Install USBasp/Atmel ICE drivers
Verification Error	Faulty wiring or corrupt HEX file	Check connections and rebuild the project

Clock Speed Issues	Wrong fuse bit settings	Adjust fuse bits correctly for internal/external clock
Low Voltage Warning	Insufficient power supply to the MCU	Ensure 5V (or 3.3V for some chips) is supplied

Conclusion Microchip Studio is a powerful IDE for developing AVR applications. By setting up a project, writing code, compiling, and debugging, developers can efficiently work with AVR microcontrollers. Whether using native AVR chips or Arduino boards, Microchip Studio provides a complete development environment. This chapter also covered essential tools, programmer compatibility, and troubleshooting common issues to help ensure a smooth development experience.

Chapter 7: First AVR Program

Introduction Writing and running your first AVR program is an essential step in learning embedded systems. This chapter will guide you through writing, compiling, and uploading your first AVR program using **Microchip Studio**. The example program will blink an LED, which is a simple and effective way to verify that your setup is working correctly.

1. Setting Up the Project

Before writing the code, follow these steps to create a new project:

Step 1: Open Microchip Studio

- Launch **Microchip Studio**.
- Click **File → New Project**.

Step 2: Select Project Type

- Choose **GCC C Executable Project** (for C programming).
- Click **Next**.

Step 3: Select the Microcontroller

- In the **device selection window**, search for your microcontroller (e.g., **ATmega328P**).
- Click **OK** to create the project.

2. Writing the LED Blinking Program

Once the project is set up, write the following code in **main.c**:

```
#include <avr/io.h>
#include <util/delay.h>

int main(void) {
    DDRB |= (1 << PB0); // Set PB0 as an output
    while (1) {
        PORTB ^= (1 << PB0); // Toggle PB0 (turn LED
on/off)
        _delay_ms(500); // Wait for 500 ms
    }
}
```

Code Line	Explanation	
`#include <avr/io.h>`	Includes AVR I/O header file to access ports and registers.	
`#include <util/delay .h>`	Includes delay functions for timing control.	
`` `DDRB ``	`= (1 << PB0);`	Sets PB0 as an output pin.
`PORTB ^= (1 << PB0);`	Toggles PB0 to turn LED on/off.	
`_delay_ms(5 00);`	Creates a delay of 500 milliseconds.	

3. Circuit Diagram for LED Connection To visualize the hardware setup, refer to the following table:

Component	Connection
Microcontroller Pin	PB0 (Digital Output)
LED (Anode +)	Connected to PB0 via 220Ω resistor
LED (Cathode -)	Connected to GND
Power Supply	5V (or 3.3V for low-power AVR models)

4. Compiling the Program After writing the code, compile it to generate the HEX file.

Step 1: Build the Code

- Click **Build → Build Solution (F7)**.
- Check for errors in the **Output Window**.

Step 2: Locate the HEX File

- After successful compilation, the **HEX file** will be located in:
  Project Folder → Debug → program.hex

5. Uploading the Code to the AVR Microcontroller

To upload the compiled HEX file, use an **ISP Programmer** (USBasp, Atmel ICE, or AVRISP mkII).

Step 1: Connect the Programmer

- Ensure your AVR microcontroller is powered.
- Connect the **ISP (In-System Programming) pins** to the programmer.

Step 2: Open Device Programming

- In Microchip Studio, go to **Tools → Device Programming**.
- Select your programmer and microcontroller (e.g., ATmega328P).

Step 3: Flash the HEX File

- Click **Memories** in the left panel.
- Under **Flash**, browse and select the compiled `.hex` file.
- Click **Program** to upload.

6. Comparing Different AVR Programming Methods

Programming Method	Interface Used	Pros	Cons
ISP (In-System Programming)	SPI (MOSI, MISO, SCK, RESET)	Direct access to Flash, works with most programmers	Requires external programmer
JTAG	JTAG Pins	Supports debugging	Not available in all AVR models
Bootloader (Arduino Method)	UART (TX, RX)	No external programmer needed	Slightly slower due to bootloader overhead

7. Troubleshooting Common Errors

Issue	Possible Cause	Solution
LED Not Blinking	Wrong pin selection	Check if LED is connected to the correct pin.
Compilation Error	Missing header files	Ensure `<avr/io.h>` and `<util/delay.h>` are included.
Upload Failure	Programmer not detected	Check connections and reinstall drivers.
No Power to AVR	Power supply issue	Ensure 5V (or 3.3V for some AVRs) is supplied.
Program Upload Fails Midway	Faulty USB cable or bad connection	Try a different USB cable, reconnect the programmer.
Fuse Bits Incorrectly Set	MCU bricked due to wrong fuse settings	Use an external clock source to recover.
LED Stays On /	Pin not set correctly	Double-check DDRx, PORTx,

Off Constantly	in code	and PINx settings.

8. Advanced LED Blinking Using Interrupts For a more advanced version, use **Timer Interrupts** instead of _delay_ms(), which makes the program more efficient.

```c
#include <avr/io.h>
#include <avr/interrupt.h>

ISR(TIMER1_COMPA_vect) {
    PORTB ^= (1 << PB0); // Toggle LED on PB0
}

void setupTimer() {
    TCCR1B |= (1 << WGM12) | (1 << CS12) | (1 << CS10);
// Set CTC mode, prescaler 1024
    OCR1A = 15624; // 1-second delay at 16MHz clock
    TIMSK1 |= (1 << OCIE1A); // Enable Timer1 compare
interrupt
}
int main(void) {
    DDRB |= (1 << PB0); // Set PB0 as output
    setupTimer(); // Configure timer
    sei(); // Enable global interrupts
    while (1); // Infinite loop
}
```

Explanation:

- Uses **Timer1 in CTC mode** to generate an interrupt every **1 second**.
- The **ISR (Interrupt Service Routine)** toggles the LED without using _delay_ms().

Conclusion This chapter covered writing and running your **first AVR program** using Microchip Studio. It introduced LED blinking using _delay_ms() and an **interrupt-based version** for better efficiency. A **circuit diagram table, comparison of AVR programming methods**, and **expanded troubleshooting** help users get started smoothly. Future chapters will build on this foundation with more advanced AVR programming concepts.

Chapter 8: Debugging Basics in AVR Studio

Introduction Debugging is an essential skill in embedded systems development. Microchip Studio (formerly AVR Studio) provides powerful debugging tools to help identify and fix issues in AVR microcontroller programs. This chapter covers the basics of debugging using **breakpoints, stepping through code, register inspection, and serial debugging**.

Debugging Methods Comparison

Debugging Method	Tools Required	Pros	Cons
Breakpoints & Stepping	Atmel ICE, JTAG, DebugWIRE	Step-by-step execution, variable inspection	Requires hardware debugger
Serial Debugging (UART)	USB-to-Serial adapter, USART	Works with all AVRs	Requires extra hardware
LED Debugging	Just an LED and a resistor	Simple and effective	Limited to binary states (ON/OFF)
Logic Analyzer	Logic analyzer hardware	Captures real-time signals	Expensive for beginners

Debugging Tools in Microchip Studio

Tool	Purpose
Breakpoints	Pause execution at a specific line of code.
Step Over (F10)	Execute the next line of code without entering functions.
Step Into (F11)	Execute line-by-line, stepping into functions.
Step Out (Shift+F11)	Exit the current function and return to the caller.
Watch Variables	Monitor variable values during execution.
Register Inspection	View and modify register values in real-time.
Serial Debugging	Print debug messages using UART (USART).

Setting Up Debugging in Microchip Studio
Step 1: Enable Debugging Mode
- Open **Microchip Studio** and load your AVR project.
- Click **Project → Properties**.
- Under **Tool**, select an appropriate debugger (e.g., Atmel ICE, JTAG, DebugWIRE).
- Set **Interface** to DebugWIRE or JTAG (depending on your microcontroller).

Step 2: Compile in Debug Mode
- Click **Build → Build Solution (F7)**.
- Ensure that there are no compilation errors.

Step 3: Start the Debugging Session
- Click **Debug → Start Debugging and Break (F5)**.
- Execution will start, and you can use the debugging tools.

Using Breakpoints to Pause Execution

Action	Description
Click in the left margin	Sets a **red dot** (breakpoint) next to the code line.
Press **F5**	Runs the program until it reaches a breakpoint.
Press **F10 (Step Over)**	Executes the next instruction without entering functions.
Press **F11 (Step Into)**	Steps into functions for detailed debugging.
Press **Shift+F11 (Step Out)**	Exits the current function and continues execution.

Watching Variables and Registers
Step 1: Open the Watch Window
- Click **Debug → Windows → Watch → Watch 1**.
- Right-click and select **Add Watch**.
- Enter the variable name to monitor.

Step 2: Inspect Registers
- Click **Debug → Windows → I/O View**.
- Select a register (e.g., **PORTB, DDRB**) to view or modify its value.

Serial Debugging with UART (USART)
Example: Print Debug Messages via Serial Communication

```c
#include <avr/io.h>
#include <util/delay.h>
#include <stdio.h>

void USART_init(unsigned int ubrr) {
    UBRR0H = (unsigned char)(ubrr >> 8);
    UBRR0L = (unsigned char)ubrr;
    UCSR0B = (1 << TXEN0); // Enable transmitter
    UCSR0C = (1 << UCSZ01) | (1 << UCSZ00); // 8-bit
data
}

void USART_send(char data) {
    while (!(UCSR0A & (1 << UDRE0))); // Wait for empty
transmit buffer
    UDR0 = data;
}

void USART_print(char* str) {
    while (*str) {
        USART_send(*str++);
    }
}

int main(void) {
    USART_init(9600);
    while (1) {
        USART_print("Debug: Loop running...\n");
        _delay_ms(1000);
    }
}
```

Common Debugging Issues and Solutions

Issue	Possible Cause	Solution
Breakpoints Not Working	Optimization removing code	Disable optimizations in **Project Properties →** **Optimization Level.**
DebugWIRE Not Working	Reset fuse bits incorrectly set	Disable DebugWIRE mode via **ISP Programmer.**
Serial Output Not Displaying	Wrong baud rate or missing driver	Ensure correct **baud rate** and check **USB-to-serial driver.**
Variables Not Updating in Watch Window	Compiler optimization skipping unused variables	Declare variables as **volatile.**

Debugging with LED Indicators

Example: Blink LED in Different Patterns for Debugging

```c
#include <avr/io.h>
#include <util/delay.h>
void error_signal() {
    for (int i = 0; i < 3; i++) { // Blink LED 3 times
        PORTB ^= (1 << PB0);
        _delay_ms(200);
    }
}
int main(void) {
    DDRB |= (1 << PB0); // Set PB0 as output
    if (1) { // Example error condition
        error_signal(); // Blink LED 3 times to
indicate an error
    }
    while (1) {
        PORTB ^= (1 << PB0);
        _delay_ms(500);
    }
}
```

Chapter 9: Introduction to Electrical Components for AVR

Introduction Understanding electrical components is crucial when working with AVR microcontrollers. Various components, such as resistors, capacitors, transistors, and sensors, play essential roles in circuits. This chapter provides an overview of fundamental electrical components used in AVR-based projects.

Active vs. Passive Components

Type	Components	Function
Active Components	Transistors, Diodes, Relays	Require power to operate
Passive Components	Resistors, Capacitors, Inductors	Do not require power to function

Common Electrical Components

Component	Symbol	Function
Resistor	R	Limits current flow, divides voltage
Capacitor	C	Stores and releases electrical charge
Diode	D	Allows current flow in one direction
LED (Light Emitting Diode)	LED	Emits light when current flows through
Transistor	Q	Acts as a switch or amplifier
Relay	-	Electrically operated switch
Inductor	L	Stores energy in a magnetic field
Potentiometer	VR	Variable resistor for adjusting voltage
Crystal Oscillator	XTAL	Provides clock signals for AVR timing

Resistors
- Used to **limit current**, divide voltage, and set pull-up/pull-down configurations.
- Common values: **1KΩ, 10KΩ, 100KΩ**.
- Formula: **V = IR** (Ohm's Law)

Capacitors
- Used for **filtering, noise reduction, and timing applications**.
- Types:
  - **Electrolytic Capacitors** (Higher capacitance, polarized)
  - **Ceramic Capacitors** (Lower capacitance, non-polarized)

Diodes and LEDs
- **Diodes** allow current to flow in one direction, preventing reverse voltage damage.
- **LEDs** (Light Emitting Diodes) require a **current-limiting resistor** (e.g., **220Ω** for 5V systems).

Transistors
- Used as **electronic switches** or amplifiers.
- Types:
  - **NPN (e.g., BC547)** – Common for switching applications.
  - **PNP (e.g., BC557)** – Used for current sourcing.
- Formula: **Ic = β * Ib** (Collector current = Gain * Base current)

Relays
- Electromechanical switches used to control **high-power devices** with low-power signals.
- Example: **5V relay module for controlling AC appliances**.

Inductors
- Stores **energy in a magnetic field**.
- Used in **power supplies, RF circuits, and noise suppression**.

Potentiometers
- Adjustable resistors for **controlling voltage or current**.
- Used in **volume controls, LCD contrast adjustment**.

Crystal Oscillators
- Provides **precise clock signals** for AVR microcontrollers.
- Connected to **XTAL1 and XTAL2** pins of AVR microcontrollers.
- Common frequencies: **4 MHz, 8 MHz, 16 MHz** (used in ATmega328P).
- Used when **higher accuracy** than the internal RC oscillator is required.
- Helps in **stable timing for UART, timers, and other clock-sensitive tasks**.
- Requires **two capacitors (typically 22pF) connected to ground** for stable operation.

Power Supply for AVR Circuits

Power Source	Voltage	Application
Battery	3.7V - 12V	Portable AVR projects
Regulated DC Adapter	5V, 9V, 12V	Powering AVR boards
USB Power	5V	Powering via PC or charger
Voltage Regulator (e.g., 7805)	5V	Provides stable 5V output

Connecting Components to AVR Microcontrollers
- **Pull-up resistors (10KΩ)** used on **input pins**.
- **Capacitors (0.1μF)** placed across power lines to reduce noise.
- **Transistors** used for **controlling high-current loads**.
- **Crystal oscillators** connected to **XTAL1 and XTAL2** for stable clock signals.

Example Circuit: Blinking LED with a Resistor

```
#include <avr/io.h>
#include <util/delay.h>
int main(void) {
    DDRB |= (1 << PB0); // Set PB0 as output
    while (1) {
        PORTB ^= (1 << PB0); // Toggle LED
        _delay_ms(500);
    }
}
```

Explanation:

- **PB0 is configured as an output.**
- **LED toggles ON/OFF every 500 ms.**
- **A 220Ω resistor** is used to limit current.

Conclusion Understanding **electrical components** is essential for designing AVR-based circuits. Each component serves a specific function, from **resistors limiting current** to **crystal oscillators providing clock signals**. Knowing how to interface these components correctly will improve the reliability and efficiency of AVR projects.

Chapter 10: Ohm's Law and Circuit Basics for AVR

Introduction Ohm's Law is a fundamental principle in electronics that describes the relationship between **voltage (V), current (I), and resistance (R)** in a circuit. This chapter covers Ohm's Law, basic circuit configurations, and how to apply these concepts when working with AVR microcontrollers.

Importance of Ohm's Law in AVR Circuits Ohm's Law is essential for designing AVR-based circuits as it helps in:

- **Protecting AVR GPIO Pins** – Ensures that current does not exceed safe levels, preventing damage to microcontroller pins.
- **Calculating Resistor Values for LEDs** – Prevents excessive current draw, ensuring the LED operates within safe limits.
- **Ensuring Proper Sensor Interfacing** – Helps in scaling voltage levels using voltage dividers for analog sensors.
- **Current Limiting in Power Circuits** – Prevents excessive power dissipation in voltage regulators and components.

Understanding Ohm's Law Ohm's Law states:

- **$V = I \times R$** (Voltage = Current × Resistance)
- **$I = V \div R$** (Current = Voltage ÷ Resistance)
- **$R = V \div I$** (Resistance = Voltage ÷ Current)

Parameter	Symbol	Unit
Voltage	V	Volts (V)
Current	I	Amperes (A)
Resistance	R	Ohms (Ω)

Example Calculation: If a **5V supply** is applied across a **1KΩ resistor**, the current flowing through it is:

Example Calculation

If a 5V supply is applied across a 1 kΩ resistor, the current flowing through it is:

$$I = \frac{V}{R}$$

5V · 1000Ω

0.005A

(5mA)

```
I = V ÷ R = 5V ÷ 1000Ω = 0.005A
(5mA)
```

Comparing Series vs. Parallel Resistors

Connection Type	Total Resistance Formula	Example Calculation
Series	R_total = R1 + R2 + R3 ...	If R1 = 1KΩ, R2 = 2KΩ, then R_total = 3KΩ
Parallel	1/R_total = 1/R1 + 1/R2 + ...	If R1 = 1KΩ, R2 = 2KΩ, then R_total ≈ 667Ω

Comparing Different Resistor Values in AVR Applications

Resistor Value	Application
220Ω - 330Ω	Current limiting for LEDs
1KΩ - 10KΩ	Pull-up/pull-down resistors for switches
10KΩ - 100KΩ	Voltage dividers for sensors
100KΩ+	High-impedance pull-downs and filtering applications

Voltage Dividers and Their Use in AVR Circuits A **voltage divider** is commonly used in AVR projects to reduce voltage levels for ADC (Analog-to-Digital Conversion) or sensor interfacing.

Voltage Divider Formula:

```
V_out = V_in × (R2 / (R1 + R2))
```

Use Case	Example
Scaling a 5V signal to 3.3V for ADC	Using R1 = 1KΩ, R2 = 2KΩ
Reading sensor output	Dividing a higher sensor output to match AVR input limits

Circuit Connection Table for AVR

Component	AVR Pin	Purpose
LED + Resistor	PB0 (Output)	Blinking an LED with current limiting
Push Button	PD2 (Input)	Detecting a button press
Temperature Sensor (LM35)	ADC0 (Analog Input)	Reading temperature data
Voltage Regulator (7805)	VCC, GND	Providing a stable 5V supply
Crystal Oscillator (16MHz)	XTAL1, XTAL2	Setting up an external clock

Example Application: Using a Resistor with an LED A 220Ω resistor is commonly used with an LED to limit current when connected to a **5V AVR output pin**.

Circuit Calculation:

```
I = V ÷ R = (5V - 2V) ÷ 220Ω = 0.0136A (13.6mA)
```

Example Code for Blinking LED with a Resistor

```
#include <avr/io.h>
#include <util/delay.h>

int main(void) {
    DDRB |= (1 << PB0); // Set PB0 as output
    while (1) {
        PORTB ^= (1 << PB0); // Toggle LED
        _delay_ms(500);
    }
}
```

Basic Fuse Calculation for AVR Power Management

Fuse Type	Current Rating	Application
Slow-Blow Fuse	500mA – 1A	Protects from prolonged overcurrent
Fast-Acting Fuse	100mA – 500mA	Protects sensitive ICs from sudden surges

Power Considerations in AVR Circuits
- **AVR operates at 5V or 3.3V, depending on the microcontroller.**
- **Maximum current per I/O pin is typically 20mA,** so resistors must be used to limit excessive current.
- **Voltage regulators (e.g., 7805) are used to provide a stable 5V supply.**

Conclusion Understanding **Ohm's Law and basic circuit concepts** is essential when designing circuits for AVR microcontrollers. Proper use of **resistors, capacitors, and voltage dividers** ensures stable operation and prevents damage to components. Additionally, using **fuse calculations** for power management helps protect circuits from excessive current. Applying these concepts correctly will lead to more reliable and efficient AVR-based projects.

Chapter 11: Resistors for AVR

Introduction Resistors are essential components in AVR circuits, used for current limiting, voltage division, and pull-up/pull-down applications. Understanding their role and selection is crucial for designing efficient and safe AVR-based circuits.

Types of Resistors

Resistor Type	Description	Common Usage in AVR
Fixed Resistor	Provides a constant resistance value	Current limiting for LEDs, pull-up resistors
Variable Resistor (Potentiometer)	Adjustable resistance	LCD contrast control, sensor calibration
Thermistor	Temperature-sensitive resistor	Temperature sensing and compensation
LDR (Light Dependent Resistor)	Resistance changes with light intensity	Light sensor applications
Pull-up/Pull-down Resistors	Used to keep input pins at a defined logic level	Button debounce, I2C pull-ups

Comparing Different Resistor Types by Power Rating

Power Rating	Usage in AVR Circuits
1/8W - 1/4W	General AVR applications (LEDs, pull-ups, sensors)
1/2W - 1W	Higher current applications (motor drivers, power circuits)
1W+	High-power applications (voltage regulators, amplifiers)

Resistor Color Code Chart

Color	Digit	Multiplier	Tolerance
Black	0	×1	N/A
Brown	1	×10	±1%
Red	2	×100	±2%
Orange	3	×1,000	N/A
Yellow	4	×10,000	N/A
Green	5	×100,000	±0.5%

Blue	6	×1,000,000	±0.25%
Violet	7	×10,000,000	±0.1%
Gray	8	×100,000,000	±0.05%
White	9	×1,000,000,000	N/A
Gold	N/A	×0.1	±5%
Silver	N/A	×0.01	±10%

Comparing Carbon vs. Metal Film Resistors

Resistor Type	Advantages	Disadvantages
Carbon Film	Low cost, widely available	Higher noise, lower accuracy
Metal Film	High precision, stable	Slightly more expensive

Common Resistor Values and Their Uses in AVR

Resistor Value	Application
220Ω - 330Ω	Current limiting for LEDs
1KΩ - 10KΩ	Pull-up/pull-down resistors for switches
10KΩ - 100KΩ	Voltage dividers for sensors
100KΩ+	High-impedance pull-downs and filtering applications

Using Resistors in AVR Circuits

Component	AVR Pin	Resistor Usage
LED + Resistor	PB0 (Output)	220Ω - 330Ω for current limiting
Push Button	PD2 (Input)	10KΩ pull-up resistor to avoid floating input
Temperature Sensor (LM35)	ADC0 (Analog Input)	10KΩ - 100KΩ voltage divider for proper ADC scaling
I2C Communication	SDA, SCL	4.7KΩ - 10KΩ pull-up resistors for signal integrity
Voltage Divider	ADC Input	Two resistors (e.g., 1KΩ and 2KΩ) for voltage scaling

Voltage Dividers and Their Use in AVR Circuits

A **voltage divider** is commonly used in AVR projects to scale voltages for ADC inputs or sensor interfacing.

Voltage Divider Formula:

$$V\_out = V\_in \times (R2 / (R1 + R2))$$

Example: Reading an LDR Sensor Value Using an ADC Pin

```c
#include <avr/io.h>
#include <util/delay.h
void ADC_init() {
    ADMUX |= (1 << REFS0); // AVCC as reference voltage
    ADCSRA |= (1 << ADEN) | (1 << ADPS2) | (1 <<
ADPS1); // Enable ADC, prescaler 64
}
uint16_t ADC_read(uint8_t channel) {
    ADMUX = (ADMUX & 0xF0) | (channel & 0x0F); //
Select channel
    ADCSRA |= (1 << ADSC); // Start conversion
    while (ADCSRA & (1 << ADSC)); // Wait for
completion
    return ADC;
}
int main() {
    ADC_init();
    while (1) {
        uint16_t light = ADC_read(0); // Read LDR value
        if (light < 512) {
            PORTB |= (1 << PB0); // Turn on LED in
darkness
        } else {
            PORTB &= ~(1 << PB0); // Turn off LED in
bright light
        }
        _delay_ms(500);
    }
}
```

Example: Blinking LED with Current Limiting Resistor

```c
#include <avr/io.h>
#include <util/delay.h>

int main(void) {
    DDRB |= (1 << PB0); // Set PB0 as output
    while (1) {
        PORTB ^= (1 << PB0); // Toggle LED
        _delay_ms(500);
    }
}
```

Example: Using a Pull-up Resistor with a Button

```c
#include <avr/io.h>
#include <util/delay.h>

int main(void) {
    DDRD &= ~(1 << PD2); // Set PD2 as input
    PORTD |= (1 << PD2); // Enable internal pull-up
resistor
    DDRB |= (1 << PB0); // Set PB0 as output
    while (1) {
        if (!(PIND & (1 << PD2))) { // If button is
pressed
            PORTB ^= (1 << PB0); // Toggle LED
            _delay_ms(200); // Debounce delay
        }
    }
}
```

Conclusion Resistors play a vital role in AVR circuits by ensuring proper current flow, signal integrity, and safe operation. Proper selection of resistors helps in designing **efficient, stable, and reliable** AVR-based systems.

Chapter 12: Capacitors for AVR

Introduction Capacitors are essential components in AVR circuits, used for filtering, energy storage, and signal conditioning. They play a critical role in ensuring stable voltage levels, noise reduction, and proper timing in microcontroller applications.

Types of Capacitors

Capacitor Type	Description	Common Usage in AVR
Ceramic Capacitor	Small, non-polarized, low ESR	Decoupling, noise filtering
Electrolytic Capacitor	High-capacity, polarized	Power supply smoothing
Tantalum Capacitor	Stable, low leakage, polarized	Precise voltage regulation
Polyester Film Capacitor	High stability, used in timing circuits	Oscillator circuits, precision applications
Super Capacitor	Very high capacity, used for energy storage	Backup power applications

Comparing Different Capacitor Types by Voltage Rating

Voltage Rating	Usage in AVR Circuits
6V - 16V	General AVR applications (decoupling, filtering)
25V - 50V	Power supply stabilization
100V+	High-voltage applications (specialized circuits)

Capacitor Marking Codes

Marking	Capacitance (pF)
100	10 pF
104	100 nF
220	22 pF
473	47 nF
105	1 µF

Comparing Ceramic vs. Electrolytic Capacitors

Capacitor Type	Advantages	Disadvantages
Ceramic	Low ESR, non-polarized, fast response	Lower capacitance values
Electrolytic	High capacitance, good for power filtering	Polarized, higher ESR

Common Capacitor Values and Their Uses in AVR

Capacitor Value	Application
0.1µF - 1µF	Decoupling capacitors for AVR power pins
10µF - 100µF	Power supply smoothing
22pF - 33pF	Used with crystal oscillators

Using Capacitors in AVR Circuits

Component	AVR Pin	Capacitor Usage
Decoupling Capacitor	VCC, GND	0.1µF to stabilize voltage
Power Supply Capacitor	VCC, GND	10µF to smooth power fluctuations
Crystal Oscillator Capacitor	XTAL1, XTAL2	22pF for stable clock operation

Example: Using Capacitors for Power Stabilization

```
#include <avr/io.h>
#include <util/delay.h>

int main(void) {
    DDRB |= (1 << PB0); // Set PB0 as output
    while (1) {
        PORTB ^= (1 << PB0); // Toggle LED
        _delay_ms(500);
    }
}
```

Example: Using a Capacitor for Button Debouncing

```
#include <avr/io.h>
#include <util/delay.h>

int main(void) {
```

```
    DDRD &= ~(1 << PD2); // Set PD2 as input
    PORTD |= (1 << PD2); // Enable internal pull-up
resistor
    DDRB |= (1 << PB0); // Set PB0 as output
    while (1) {
        if (!(PIND & (1 << PD2))) { // If button is
pressed
            PORTB ^= (1 << PB0); // Toggle LED
            _delay_ms(50); // Debounce delay
        }
    }
}
```

Conclusion Capacitors play a crucial role in AVR circuits by ensuring **stable voltage levels, noise filtering, and proper clock operation**. Selecting the right capacitor type and value improves **power efficiency and circuit reliability** in embedded system designs.

Chapter 13: Diodes for AVR

Introduction Diodes are essential components in AVR circuits, used for rectification, voltage regulation, and protection. They allow current to flow in one direction while blocking it in the opposite direction, making them useful for circuit protection, signal conditioning, and power applications.

Types of Diodes

Diode Type	Description	Common Usage in AVR
Rectifier Diode (1N4007)	General-purpose diode for AC-DC conversion	Power supply rectification
Schottky Diode (1N5819)	Low forward voltage drop, fast switching	Power efficiency, reverse protection
Zener Diode (5.1V, 3.3V)	Voltage regulation, allows reverse breakdown	Overvoltage protection, reference voltage
Light Emitting Diode (LED)	Emits light when current passes through	Status indication, displays
Photodiode	Converts light into current	Light sensing applications
TVS Diode	Protects against voltage spikes	Surge protection for microcontrollers

Comparing Diodes Based on Forward Voltage Drop

Diode Type	Forward Voltage Drop (Vf)	Importance for AVR
1N4007 (Rectifier)	~0.7V	Used in AVR power supply rectification, prevents reverse voltage damage
1N5819 (Schottky)	~0.3V - 0.4V	Provides efficient power delivery with minimal losses, ideal for low-power AVR circuits
LED (Red)	~1.8V - 2.2V	Used for status indicators and display circuits in AVR applications
Zener (5.1V)	Reverse breakdown	Ensures stable voltage for AVR, protects against overvoltage
TVS Diode	Varies (clamps	Protects AVR microcontrollers from

	surges)	voltage spikes and electrostatic discharge

Diode Marking Codes

Marking	Type
1N4007	General-purpose rectifier
1N5819	Schottky diode
5V1	5.1V Zener diode
LED	Light emitting diode

Comparing Schottky vs. Rectifier Diodes

Diode Type	Advantages	Disadvantages
Schottky	Low voltage drop, fast switching	Lower voltage rating
Rectifier	High voltage handling	Higher voltage drop

Common Diode Uses in AVR Circuits

Diode Application	AVR Circuit Usage
Flyback Diode	Protection in relay and motor circuits
Reverse Polarity Protection	Prevents damage due to incorrect power supply wiring
Zener Voltage Regulation	Provides a stable reference voltage
Rectification	Converts AC to DC in power circuits

Using Diodes in AVR Circuits

Component	AVR Pin	Diode Usage
Flyback Diode	Relay/Motor Control	Protects from back EMF (1N4007)
Reverse Protection	Power Input	Schottky diode prevents incorrect polarity
Zener Regulator	VCC	Limits voltage to 5.1V or 3.3V

Example: Using a Diode for Reverse Polarity Protection

```c
#include <avr/io.h>
#include <util/delay.h>

int main(void) {
    DDRB |= (1 << PB0); // Set PB0 as output
    while (1) {
        PORTB ^= (1 << PB0); // Toggle LED
        _delay_ms(500);
    }
}
```

Example: Using a Flyback Diode for a Relay

```c
#include <avr/io.h>
#include <util/delay.h>

int main(void) {
    DDRB |= (1 << PB0); // Set PB0 as output
    while (1) {
        PORTB |= (1 << PB0); // Activate relay
        _delay_ms(1000);
        PORTB &= ~(1 << PB0); // Deactivate relay
        _delay_ms(1000);
    }
}
```

Conclusion Diodes play a crucial role in AVR circuits by ensuring **current flow control, voltage regulation, and protection against electrical faults**. Proper diode selection improves **power efficiency and circuit reliability** in embedded system designs.

Chapter 14: LEDs for AVR

Introduction Light Emitting Diodes (LEDs) are commonly used in AVR circuits for **status indication, debugging, and display applications**. Understanding how to properly interface LEDs with AVR microcontrollers is essential for designing efficient and reliable circuits.

Types of LEDs

LED Type	Description	Common Usage in AVR
Standard LED	General-purpose LED (red, green, blue, yellow)	Status indicators, debugging
RGB LED	Combines red, green, and blue LEDs in one package	Multi-color display, lighting effects
Infrared LED (IR LED)	Emits infrared light (invisible to the human eye)	Remote control, object detection
Seven-Segment LED	Numeric display using multiple LEDs	Digital counters, numeric displays
Dot Matrix LED	Grid of LEDs used for text and graphics	Displaying scrolling text, visual output

Comparing LED Types Based on Brightness and Power Consumption

LED Type	Brightness (mcd)	Current Consumption (mA)	Application
Standard 5mm LED	1000 - 5000	10-20	Indicators, basic circuits
High-Brightness LED	5000 - 20000	20-50	Outdoor displays, warning lights
Infrared LED	N/A	10-50	Remote controls, sensors
RGB LED	2000 - 10000	20-60	Multi-color lighting effects

LED Electrical Characteristics

LED Color	Forward Voltage (Vf)	Current Requirement
Red	1.8V - 2.2V	10-20mA
Green	2.0V - 3.5V	10-20mA
Blue	3.0V - 3.5V	10-20mA
White	3.0V - 3.5V	10-20mA
IR LED	1.2V - 1.5V	10-50mA

Using LEDs in AVR Circuits

Component	AVR Pin	Usage
Single LED + Resistor	PB0 (Output)	Blinking, status indication
RGB LED	PB0, PB1, PB2 (PWM Output)	Multi-color indication
Seven-Segment LED	Multiple digital pins	Display numbers and characters
IR LED + Photodiode	PD2 (Input)	Remote control, proximity detection

Current Limiting Resistor Calculation To prevent excessive current from damaging an LED, a **current-limiting resistor** is required.

Formula:

R = (V_supply - V_LED) / I_LED

Example (for a red LED on a 5V system):

R = (5V - 2V) / 0.02A = 150Ω (use 220Ω for safety)

Current Limiting Resistor Calculation

To prevent excessive current from damaging an LED, a current-limiting resistor is required.

Formula:

$$R = \frac{(V_{supply} - V_{LED})}{I_{LED}}$$

$$= \frac{(5V - 2V)}{0.02A}$$

$$= 150\,\Omega$$

(use 220 Ω for safety)

Example: Blinking LED with AVR

```
#include <avr/io.h>
#include <util/delay.h>
int main(void) {
    DDRB |= (1 << PB0); // Set PB0 as output
    while (1) {
        PORTB ^= (1 << PB0); // Toggle LED state
        _delay_ms(500); // Wait 500ms
```

```
        }
}
```

Example: Controlling an RGB LED with PWM

```c
#include <avr/io.h>
#include <util/delay.h>

void setupPWM() {
    DDRB |= (1 << PB0) | (1 << PB1) | (1 << PB2); //
Set RGB LED pins as output
    TCCR0A |= (1 << COM0A1) | (1 << WGM00); // Fast PWM
mode
    TCCR0B |= (1 << CS01); // Prescaler 8
}

int main(void) {
    setupPWM();
    while (1) {
        OCR0A = 255; // Red on full brightness
        OCR0B = 128; // Green at half brightness
        OCR0C = 64;  // Blue at quarter brightness
        _delay_ms(1000);
    }
}
```

Example: Displaying Numbers on a Seven-Segment LED

```c
#include <avr/io.h>
#include <util/delay.h>

const uint8_t numbers[10] = {0x3F, 0x06, 0x5B, 0x4F,
0x66, 0x6D, 0x7D, 0x07, 0x7F, 0x6F};

void displayNumber(uint8_t num) {
    PORTD = numbers[num]; // Send corresponding pattern
to 7-segment LED
```

```
}

int main(void) {
    DDRD = 0xFF; // Set PORTD as output
    while (1) {
        for (uint8_t i = 0; i < 10; i++) {
            displayNumber(i);
            _delay_ms(1000);
        }
    }
}
```

Conclusion LEDs are essential components in AVR circuits, used for **visual indicators, displays, and communication**. Proper interfacing techniques, including **current limiting resistors and PWM control**, allow for safe and efficient LED operation in embedded systems.

Chapter 15: Transistors for AVR

Introduction Transistors are essential components in AVR circuits, used for **switching, amplification, and signal processing**. They enable microcontrollers to control **high-power devices like motors, relays, and LEDs** while consuming minimal current from the AVR's output pins.

Types of Transistors

Transistor Type	Description	Common Usage in AVR
NPN Bipolar Junction Transistor (BJT)	Conducts when base is HIGH	Switching low-power loads, amplifiers
PNP Bipolar Junction Transistor (BJT)	Conducts when base is LOW	High-side switching, current sinking
MOSFET (N-Channel)	Conducts with positive gate voltage	Controlling high-power loads efficiently
MOSFET (P-Channel)	Conducts with negative gate voltage	High-side switching of power supplies
Darlington Transistor	High current gain, combines two BJTs	Driving high-current loads

Comparing NPN vs. PNP Transistors

Feature	NPN Transistor	PNP Transistor
Switching Condition	Turns ON when **base is HIGH**	Turns ON when **base is LOW**
Current Flow	Collector to emitter	Emitter to collector
Common Example	**2N2222**	**BC557**
Application	Low-side switching	High-side switching

Comparing BJT vs. MOSFET for AVR Applications

Feature	BJT (NPN/PNP)	MOSFET (N-Channel/P-Channel)
Triggering Method	Requires base current	Requires gate voltage
Switching Speed	Moderate	Faster
Power Efficiency	Lower (wastes power in base current)	Higher (low gate power consumption)
Best Use Case	Small signal switching	High-power applications

Using Transistors in AVR Circuits

Component	AVR Pin	Usage
NPN BJT (2N2222)	Digital Output	Switching LEDs, small loads
PNP BJT (BC557)	Digital Output	High-side switching
N-Channel MOSFET (IRF540)	PWM Output	Controlling motors, high-power LEDs
P-Channel MOSFET (IRF9540)	Power Supply Control	Switching high-side power loads
Darlington Transistor (TIP120)	Digital Output	High-current relay and motor control

Common Transistor Applications

Application	Transistor Type	Example Component
LED Switching	NPN BJT	2N2222
Motor Control	N-Channel MOSFET	IRF540
Relay Control	Darlington Transistor	TIP120
Signal Amplification	BJT (NPN/PNP)	BC547

Example: Using an NPN Transistor to Control an LED

```
#include <avr/io.h>
#include <util/delay.h>

int main(void) {
    DDRB |= (1 << PB0); // Set PB0 as output
    while (1) {
        PORTB |= (1 << PB0); // Turn on transistor (LED
ON)
```

```
        _delay_ms(500);
        PORTB &= ~(1 << PB0); // Turn off transistor
(LED OFF)
        _delay_ms(500);
    }
}
```

Example: Controlling a Motor with an N-Channel MOSFET

```
#include <avr/io.h>
#include <util/delay.h>

int main(void) {
    DDRD |= (1 << PD6); // Set PD6 as output (PWM)
    TCCR0A |= (1 << COM0A1) | (1 << WGM00); // Fast PWM
mode
    TCCR0B |= (1 << CS01); // Set prescaler to 8

    while (1) {
        OCR0A = 128; // 50% Duty Cycle (Motor Half
Speed)
        _delay_ms(2000);
        OCR0A = 255; // 100% Duty Cycle (Motor Full
Speed)
        _delay_ms(2000);
    }
}
```

Example: Using a Darlington Transistor to Control a Relay

```
#include <avr/io.h>
#include <util/delay.h>

int main(void) {
    DDRB |= (1 << PB0); // Set PB0 as output
    while (1) {
```

```
        PORTB |= (1 << PB0); // Activate relay
        _delay_ms(1000);
        PORTB &= ~(1 << PB0); // Deactivate relay
        _delay_ms(1000);
    }
}
```

Conclusion Transistors are crucial for AVR applications, allowing **low-power microcontrollers to switch and control high-power devices**. Selecting the right type—**BJT for small loads, MOSFETs for power applications, and Darlington transistors for high-current needs**—ensures efficient and reliable circuit performance.

Chapter 16: Relays for AVR

Introduction Relays are electromechanical switches that allow AVR microcontrollers to control high-voltage or high-current loads using a low-power control signal. They are commonly used in **home automation, motor control, and industrial applications**.

Types of Relays

Relay Type	Description	Common Usage in AVR
Electromechanical Relay (EMR)	Uses a physical coil and mechanical switch	General switching applications
Solid-State Relay (SSR)	Uses semiconductor switching instead of a mechanical contact	Faster switching, no wear and tear
Latching Relay	Stays in position after activation	Power-saving applications
Reed Relay	Small, fast-switching relay using a magnetic field	Low-power circuits

Relay Contact Configurations

Configuration	Description
SPST (Single Pole Single Throw)	Basic ON/OFF switch
SPDT (Single Pole Double Throw)	One input, switches between two outputs
DPST (Double Pole Single Throw)	Two inputs, controlled by one switch
DPDT (Double Pole Double Throw)	Two inputs, switches between two outputs

Comparing Electromechanical vs. Solid-State Relays

Feature	Electromechanical Relay	Solid-State Relay (SSR)
Switching Speed	Slow (mechanical movement)	Fast (electronic switching)
Power Consumption	Higher due to coil	Low power consumption

Durability	Mechanical wear over time	No wear, longer lifespan
Best Use Case	General-purpose switching	High-speed, frequent switching

Comparing Mechanical vs. Semiconductor Switching

Feature	Electromechanical Relay	MOSFET Switching
Switching Speed	Slow (mechanical movement)	Fast (solid-state)
Wear & Tear	Yes (mechanical contacts)	No (solid-state)
Noise	Audible clicking	Silent operation
Use Case	High-voltage loads (AC, motors)	Low-power, fast switching (LEDs, PWM)

Using Relays in AVR Circuits

Component	AVR Pin	Usage
5V Relay Module	Digital Output (PB0)	Switching high-power AC/DC loads
Solid-State Relay (SSR)	Digital Output (PD6)	Fast switching of AC loads
Latching Relay	Digital Output (PD7)	Power-efficient state retention

Example: Controlling a Relay with an NPN Transistor

```
#include <avr/io.h>
#include <util/delay.h>

#define RELAY_PIN PB0
int main(void) {
    DDRB |= (1 << RELAY_PIN); // Set PB0 as output
    while (1) {
        PORTB |= (1 << RELAY_PIN); // Activate relay
        _delay_ms(1000);
        PORTB &= ~(1 << RELAY_PIN); // Deactivate relay
        _delay_ms(1000);
    }
}
```

Example: Using a Solid-State Relay to Control an AC Load

```c
#include <avr/io.h>
#include <util/delay.h>

#define SSR_PIN PD6

int main(void) {
    DDRD |= (1 << SSR_PIN); // Set PD6 as output
    while (1) {
        PORTD |= (1 << SSR_PIN); // Turn ON AC Load
        _delay_ms(2000);
        PORTD &= ~(1 << SSR_PIN); // Turn OFF AC Load
        _delay_ms(2000);
    }
}
```

Relay Driver Circuit To safely control a **5V relay**, a transistor (such as **2N2222**) is typically used to amplify the AVR's output signal.

Components Needed:

- **5V Relay** (SPDT or SPST)
- **NPN Transistor (2N2222)**
- **1N4007 Diode** (Flyback protection)
- **10KΩ Resistor** (Pull-down resistor)
- **AVR Digital Output Pin**

Working:

- When the AVR outputs HIGH, the transistor conducts, activating the relay.
- When the AVR outputs LOW, the transistor turns OFF, deactivating the relay.
- The **diode protects against voltage spikes** caused by the relay coil.

Applications of Relays in AVR Circuits

Application	Relay Type	Example Use Case
Home Automation	Electromechanical Relay	Controlling lights, appliances
Motor Control	Solid-State Relay	Switching high-power motors
Industrial Automation	DPDT Relay	Switching between power sources
Power Saving Circuits	Latching Relay	Maintaining ON state without constant power

Conclusion Relays are crucial components for AVR projects, enabling microcontrollers to control **high-power AC/DC loads safely**. Choosing between **electromechanical and solid-state relays** depends on the application, with **EMRs suited for general-purpose switching** and **SSRs for high-speed, high-frequency operations**. Proper interfacing with transistors and protection diodes ensures **safe and efficient relay operation** in embedded systems.

Chapter 17: Power Supply and Voltage Regulators for AVR

Introduction A stable and reliable power supply is essential for AVR microcontrollers to function correctly. AVR circuits typically require **5V or 3.3V**, and voltage regulators ensure a steady voltage despite fluctuations in the input power source.

Comparing Different AVR Power Sources

Power Source	Pros	Cons
USB Power (5V)	Easy to use, available everywhere	Limited current (~500mA)
Battery (Li-ion, 9V, AA)	Portable, independent operation	Limited lifespan, requires regulation
DC Adapter (Wall Adapter)	Reliable, stable voltage	Not portable
Solar Panel + Battery	Renewable, ideal for outdoor projects	Requires battery storage and regulator
Bench Power Supply	Adjustable voltage, ideal for testing	Bulky, not for permanent use

Types of Power Supplies for AVR

Power Source	Voltage Output	Common Usage in AVR
Battery (Li-ion, AA, 9V)	3.7V, 5V, 9V	Portable AVR projects
USB Power (from PC, charger)	5V	Development boards, debugging
DC Adapter (Wall Adapter)	5V, 9V, 12V	Long-term operation
Solar Panel + Battery	3.3V, 5V, 12V	Renewable energy projects
Regulated Power Supply (Bench Supply)	Adjustable (3.3V-12V)	Testing circuits with variable voltage

Voltage Regulators for AVR Voltage regulators provide a **stable 5V or 3.3V** supply to the AVR microcontroller, preventing fluctuations that can cause **malfunctions or resets**.

Regulator Type	Output Voltage	Efficiency	Common Use
Linear Regulator (7805, AMS1117)	Fixed 5V, 3.3V	Lower (wastes heat)	Simple AVR circuits, low power consumption
Switching Regulator (Buck Converter, LM2596)	Adjustable 3V-12V	Higher (efficient power conversion)	Battery-powered, high-efficiency circuits
LDO (Low Dropout Regulator)	3.3V, 5V	Higher	Works with lower input voltage, portable applications

Comparing Linear vs. Switching Regulators

Feature	Linear Regulator	Switching Regulator
Efficiency	Low (wastes power as heat)	High (efficient power conversion)
Complexity	Simple (few components)	More complex (requires inductor)
Heat Dissipation	High (needs heatsink)	Low (less heat)
Best Use Case	Small circuits, steady voltage	Battery-powered, high-current applications

Using Voltage Regulators in AVR Circuits

Component	Input Voltage	Output Voltage	Usage
7805 Linear Regulator	7V - 12V	5V	Provides a stable 5V for AVR boards
AMS1117-3.3V	4.5V - 12V	3.3V	Powers AVR projects using 3.3V sensors
LM2596 Buck Converter	7V - 40V	Adjustable 3.3V - 12V	Efficient power supply for high-current loads

Example: Using a 7805 Regulator to Power an AVR Circuit

```
// No AVR code required, but hardware setup:
// Connect 7V-12V input to 7805 VIN
// Connect GND to 7805 GND
// Connect VOUT (5V) to AVR power supply
```

Example: Using a Buck Converter to Power an AVR with a Battery

- **Input:** 12V Battery
- **Output:** 5V for AVR
- **Components:** LM2596 module

Steps:

1. Connect **battery positive** to the **VIN** of LM2596.
2. Connect **battery ground** to **GND** of LM2596.
3. Adjust the output **to 5V using a multimeter**.
4. Connect **5V output to AVR VCC**.

Example: Battery-Powered AVR with Power Optimization

```
#include <avr/sleep.h>
#include <avr/power.h>

void enterSleepMode() {
    set_sleep_mode(SLEEP_MODE_PWR_DOWN); // Lowest
power mode
    sleep_enable();
    sleep_cpu(); // AVR enters low-power mode
}

int main(void) {
    DDRB |= (1 << PB0); // Set PB0 as output (LED)
    while (1) {
        PORTB ^= (1 << PB0); // Toggle LED
        _delay_ms(500);
        enterSleepMode(); // Enter sleep mode to save
battery
    }
}
```

Choosing the Right Power Supply for AVR

Project Type	Recommended Power Source
Small sensor circuits	USB power, battery (3.7V Li-ion + boost converter)
Long-term automation	DC adapter (regulated 5V)
High-current applications	Switching regulator (buck converter)
Portable projects	Li-ion battery with boost converter
Renewable energy (solar)	Solar panel + battery management circuit

Conclusion A **stable power supply** is critical for AVR microcontrollers to work reliably. **Voltage regulators** ensure a **constant voltage**, preventing issues like **resets, brownouts, and incorrect sensor readings**. Choosing the right **power source and regulator type** ensures efficient power management in AVR-based projects.

Chapter 18: Understanding Data Types and Variables in C for AVR Microcontrollers

Understanding data types and variables is essential for programming AVR microcontrollers efficiently in C. Variables store data values, and data types define the kind of data a variable can hold. Choosing the correct data type is crucial for optimizing memory usage and ensuring proper execution of code on resource-constrained microcontrollers like AVR.

Key Concepts of Data Types and Variables

Different data types are used in AVR programming to store numbers, characters, and special data structures. Below is a summary of common data types and their characteristics.

Data Type	Size (Bytes)	Range	Example Usage
char	1	-128 to 127	Storing single characters
unsigned char	1	0 to 255	Holding small positive numbers
int	2	-32,768 to 32,767	General-purpose integers
unsigned int	2	0 to 65,535	Counting operations
long	4	-2,147,483,648 to 2,147,483,647	Large integer calculations
float	4	1.2E-38 to 3.4E+38	Decimal numbers
double	8	Higher precision floating point	Complex calculations

Basic Rules for Using Variables in AVR C

Rule	Correct Example	Incorrect Example
Declare variables before use.	`int count = 0;`	`count = 0;` (undeclared variable)
Use appropriate data types.	`float temperatur e = 25.5;`	`int temperature = 25.5;` (Loss of precision)
Use meaningful variable names.	`int sensorValu e;`	`int a;` (Unclear purpose)
Avoid unnecessary global variables.	`void function(i nt x) {}`	`int x; void function() {}` (Uses global variable unnecessarily)

Syntax Table

SL	Concept	Syntax/Example	Description
1	Declare a variable	`int x;`	Reserves memory for storing values.
2	Assign a value	`x = 10;`	Stores a value in a variable.
3	Declare and initialize	`int y = 5;`	Declares and assigns value simultaneously.
4	Use constants	`const float PI = 3.14;`	Defines a constant value.

Syntax Explanation

Declare a Variable
What does it do? Declaring a variable reserves memory space for storing data. This ensures that the compiler knows about the variable before its usage, preventing errors.
Syntax:
```
int x;
```

Example:
```
int counter;
```

Example Explanation: In this example, we declare an integer variable named `counter`. This tells the compiler to allocate memory for storing an integer. If we try to use `counter` without declaring it first, the program will fail to compile.

Assign a Value

What does it do? Assigning a value to a variable stores data in the memory allocated for that variable. The assigned value can be changed later in the program.
Syntax:
```
x = 10;
```

Example:
```
counter = 5;
```

Example Explanation: Here, the value 5 is assigned to `counter`. The assignment operator = is used to store values in variables. If `counter` was not declared beforehand, this statement would cause an error.

Declare and Initialize a Variable

What does it do? This combines variable declaration and assignment in one step, making the code cleaner and more efficient.
Syntax:
```
int y = 5;
```

Example:
```
float temperature = 25.5;
```

Example Explanation: Here, `temperature` is declared as a `float` variable and initialized with 25.5. Initializing variables at the time of declaration helps prevent undefined behavior due to uninitialized variables.

Using Constants

What does it do? A constant is a fixed value that cannot be changed once assigned. It ensures data integrity and prevents accidental modifications.

Syntax:
```
const float PI = 3.14;
```

Example:
```
const int MAX_LIMIT = 100;
```

Example Explanation: The MAX_LIMIT variable is declared as a constant integer with a value of 100. Any attempt to modify MAX_LIMIT later in the program will result in a compilation error, enforcing consistency.

Circuit Connection Table

Component	AVR Pin	Power Source	Purpose
LED	PWM Pin (OC0A - PB3)	5V	Controls brightness via PWM
Potentiometer	ADC Pin (PC0)	5V	Adjusts brightness level

Project Code

```
#include <avr/io.h>
#define F_CPU 16000000UL
#include <util/delay.h>

void PWM_init() {
    DDRB |= (1 << PB3);   // Set OC0A as output
    TCCR0A = (1 << COM0A1) | (1 << WGM00) | (1 <<
WGM01);   // Fast PWM mode
    TCCR0B = (1 << CS00);   // No prescaler
}


void set_brightness(uint8_t duty_cycle) {
    OCR0A = duty_cycle;   // Set duty cycle
```

```
}

int main() {
    PWM_init();
    while (1) {
        set_brightness(128);   // 50% brightness
        _delay_ms(1000);
        set_brightness(255);   // 100% brightness
        _delay_ms(1000);
    }
}
```

Expected Results

Once the code is uploaded, the LED brightness will toggle between
50% and 100% every second. The concept can be extended to
create dynamic lighting systems, fan speed control, and motor
speed regulation using PWM signals controlled by variables in AVR
microcontroller programming.

Chapter 19: Operators in C - Arithmetic for AVR Microcontrollers

Operators in C are fundamental components used to perform computations and manipulate data. Arithmetic operators allow mathematical operations on variables and constants, making them essential for AVR microcontroller programming. Understanding arithmetic operators is crucial for performing calculations in embedded systems, such as sensor data processing, timing operations, and control logic implementation.

Key Concepts of Arithmetic Operators in C

C provides several arithmetic operators to perform basic mathematical operations. These operators can work with different data types such as integers and floating-point numbers.

Operator	Symbol	Description	Example	Result
Addition	+	Adds two values	a + b	Sum of a and b
Subtraction	-	Subtracts second value from first	a - b	Difference of a and b
Multiplication	*	Multiplies two values	a * b	Product of a and b
Division	/	Divides first value by second	a / b	Quotient of a and b
Modulus	%	Returns the remainder of division	a % b	Remainder of a / b

Basic Rules for Using Arithmetic Operators in C

Rule	Correct Example	Incorrect Example
Use the correct operator precedence.	`int result = a + b * c;`	`int result = (a + b) * c;` (Fixes precedence issue)
Avoid division by zero.	`if (b != 0) a / b;`	`a / 0;` (Undefined behavior)
Use proper data types for precision.	`float result = a / 2.0;`	`int result = a / 2.0;` (Loss of precision)

Use modulus only with integers.	`int mod = a % b;`	`float mod = 5.5 % 2;` (Invalid for floats)

Syntax Table

SL	Operation	Syntax/Example	Description
1	Addition	`sum = a + b;`	Adds two numbers and stores the result.
2	Subtraction	`diff = a - b;`	Subtracts one number from another.
3	Multiplication	`prod = a * b;`	Multiplies two numbers.
4	Division	`quotient = a / b;`	Divides one number by another.
5	Modulus	`remainder = a % b;`	Returns the remainder of division.

Syntax Explanation

Addition
What does it do? Adds two values and returns the sum. Commonly used for incrementing counters, summing sensor data, or calculating totals.
Syntax:
`sum = a + b;`

Example:
```
int a = 5, b = 3;
int sum = a + b;
```

Example Explanation: Here, sum stores the result of 5 + 3, which is 8. Addition is useful for operations like increasing a counter in a loop or computing the total of multiple values.

Subtraction

What does it do? Finds the difference between two values. Often used for decrementing counters or calculating time differences.
Syntax:
`diff = a - b;`

Example:
```
int a = 10, b = 4;
int diff = a - b;
```

Example Explanation: The variable `diff` stores 10 - 4, which is 6. This is helpful for operations like measuring elapsed time or adjusting control parameters in embedded systems.

Multiplication

What does it do? Multiplies two numbers together, commonly used in scaling sensor readings and computing area or power calculations.
Syntax:
```
prod = a * b;
```

Example:
```
int a = 7, b = 2;
int prod = a * b;
```

Example Explanation: `prod` stores 7 * 2, which is 14. Multiplication is frequently used in control algorithms and sensor value adjustments.

Division

What does it do? Divides one value by another. Used in applications such as averaging sensor readings or calculating speed.
Syntax:
```
quotient = a / b;
```
Example:
```
int a = 8, b = 2;
int quotient = a / b;
```
Example Explanation: `quotient` stores 8 / 2, which results in 4. Integer division truncates decimal values, so for floating-point division, `float` or `double` should be used.

Modulus

What does it do? Finds the remainder after division. Commonly used for even/odd checks and cyclic operations.
Syntax:
```
remainder = a % b;
```

Example:
```
int a = 10, b = 3;
int remainder = a % b;
```

Example Explanation: `remainder` stores 10 % 3, which is 1. This is useful in time-based calculations and ensuring values remain within cyclic limits.

Circuit Connection Table

Component	AVR Pin	Power Source	Purpose
LCD Display	Digital Pins (PD0-PD7)	5V	Displays arithmetic results
Buttons	Digital Inputs (PB0-PB3)	5V	Inputs values for operations
Microcontroller (ATmega328P)	Multiple Pins	5V	Processes arithmetic operations

Project Code

```
#include <avr/io.h>
#include <util/delay.h>

int main() {
    int a = 10, b = 2;
    int sum, diff, prod, quotient, remainder;

    sum = a + b;
    diff = a - b;
    prod = a * b;
    quotient = a / b;
```

```
    remainder = a % b;

    while (1) {
        // Simulate displaying results on LCD
    }
}
```

Expected Results

Once the code is uploaded, the microcontroller will compute and store the results of arithmetic operations on predefined values. These results can be displayed on an LCD or sent to a serial monitor for verification. The program can be extended to take user input from buttons or sensors for dynamic calculations.

Chapter 21: Relational Operators in C for AVR Microcontrollers

Relational operators in C are used to compare values and make decisions in code. These operators return a boolean result (1 for true and 0 for false). In AVR microcontroller programming, relational operators are essential for handling sensor data, controlling devices, and making real-time decisions in embedded systems.

Key Concepts of Relational Operators in AVR C

Concept	Description	Example
Equal To (==)	Checks if two values are equal.	`if (a == b) {}`
Not Equal To (!=)	Checks if two values are different.	`if (a != b) {}`
Greater Than (>)	Checks if one value is greater than another.	`if (a > b) {}`
Less Than (<)	Checks if one value is less than another.	`if (a < b) {}`
Greater or Equal (>=)	Checks if one value is greater than or equal to another.	`if (a >= b) {}`
Less or Equal (<=)	Checks if one value is less than or equal to another.	`if (a <= b) {}`

Basic Rules for Using Relational Operators in AVR C

Rule	Correct Example	Incorrect Example
Use == for comparison, not =.	`if (a == b) {}`	`if (a = b) {}` (Assignment, not comparison)
Use parentheses for clarity.	`if ((a > b) && (b > c))`	`if (a > b && b > c)` (Less readable)
Relational operators return 1 or 0.	`int result = (a < b);`	`int result = a < b;` (Unclear behavior)
Avoid unnecessary comparisons.	`if (a > 0)`	`if (a > 0 == 1)` (Redundant)

Syntax Explanation

1. Equal To (==)

What does it do? The == operator checks if two values are equal. It is commonly used in decision-making statements like `if` conditions and loops.
Example:
```
int a = 5, b = 5;
if (a == b) {
    // Condition is true
}
```

Example Explanation: Since a and b both have the value 5, the condition evaluates to `true`, executing the code inside the `if` block.

2. Not Equal To (!=)

What does it do? Checks whether two values are different. If they are not equal, the condition returns 1 (true); otherwise, it returns 0 (false).
Example:
```
int a = 5, b = 3;
if (a != b) {
    // Condition is true
}
```

Example Explanation: Since a is 5 and b is 3, they are not equal, so the condition evaluates to `true`.

3. Greater Than (>)

What does it do? Compares two values and returns `true` if the left operand is greater than the right operand.
Example:
```
int a = 10, b = 5;
if (a > b) {
    // Condition is true
}
```

Example Explanation: Since 10 is greater than 5, the condition evaluates to true.

4. Less Than (<)

What does it do? Compares two values and returns true if the left operand is smaller than the right operand.
Example:
```
int a = 4, b = 8;
if (a < b) {
    // Condition is true
}
```

Example Explanation: Since 4 is less than 8, the condition is true, and the code inside the if block executes.

5. Greater Than or Equal To (>=)

What does it do? Checks whether the left operand is greater than or equal to the right operand.
Example:
```
int a = 10, b = 10;
if (a >= b) {
    // Condition is true
}
```

Example Explanation: Since a is equal to b, the condition evaluates to true.

6. Less Than or Equal To (<=)

What does it do? Checks whether the left operand is smaller than or equal to the right operand.
Example:
```
int a = 7, b = 9;
if (a <= b) {
    // Condition is true
}
```

Example Explanation: Since 7 is less than 9, the condition evaluates to `true`, and the code executes.

Real-life Applications Project: Sensor-Based Threshold Comparison

In this project, we will use relational operators to compare sensor readings and trigger an LED when a threshold is exceeded.

Required Components

Component	Description
AVR Microcontroller (ATmega328P)	Processes relational operations.
Temperature Sensor (LM35)	Measures temperature data.
LED	Turns on if temperature exceeds threshold.
Resistor (220Ω)	Limits current for LED.

Circuit Connection Table

Component	AVR Microcontroller Pin	Power Source	Purpose
LM35 Temperature Sensor	Analog Pin (e.g., RA0)	5V	Reads temperature.
LED	Digital Output (e.g., PB0)	5V	Turns on if temperature is high.

Project Code

```
#include <avr/io.h>
#include <util/delay.h>

#define TEMP_THRESHOLD 30  // Set threshold for comparison

int Read_Temperature();  // Function to simulate sensor reading
```

```
int main() {
    DDRB |= (1 << PB0);   // Set PB0 as output for LED

    while (1) {
        int temp = Read_Temperature();

        if (temp > TEMP_THRESHOLD) {
            PORTB |= (1 << PB0);   // Turn on LED
        } else {
            PORTB &= ~(1 << PB0);   // Turn off LED
        }

        _delay_ms(1000);
    }
}

int Read_Temperature() {
    return 32;   // Simulated sensor value
}
```

Expected Results

Once the code is uploaded, the microcontroller will continuously compare the temperature sensor value to the threshold. If the temperature exceeds 30°C, the LED will turn on; otherwise, it will remain off. This project demonstrates how relational operators help make real-time decisions in embedded applications.

Chapter 22: Control Structures in C for AVR Microcontrollers

Control structures in C dictate the flow of program execution. They allow programmers to implement decision-making, loops, and conditional execution, making them essential for AVR microcontroller programming. These structures help control external hardware, automate processes, and respond to sensor inputs in real-time.

Key Concepts of Control Structures in AVR C

Concept	Description	Example
If-Else Statement	Executes different blocks based on conditions.	`if (temp > 30) {}`
Switch Statement	Selects execution path based on variable values.	`switch (mode) {}`
For Loop	Repeats execution for a fixed number of times.	`for (i = 0; i < 10; i++) {}`
While Loop	Repeats execution while a condition is true.	`while (sensor == 1) {}`
Do-While Loop	Executes the loop at least once before checking the condition.	`do { ... } while (x > 0);`

Basic Rules for Using Control Structures in AVR C

Rule	Correct Example	Incorrect Example
Always use braces {} for clarity.	`if (x > 0) { y = 1; }`	`if (x > 0) y = 1;` (Less readable)
Avoid infinite loops.	`while (x > 0) {}`	`while (1) {}` (May hang system)
Use break inside switch.	`case 1: break;`	`case 1:` (No break, may cause fall-through)
Limit nested loops to avoid complexity.	`for (i=0; i<5; i++) {}`	`for (i=0; i<5; i++) { for(j=0; j<5; j++) {}}` (Hard to debug)

Syntax Explanation

1. If-Else Statement

What does it do? Allows conditional execution of code blocks based on whether a condition evaluates to true or false. It is commonly used for decision-making, such as turning a device on or off based on a sensor reading.
Example:
```
int temp = 35;
if (temp > 30) {
    // Activate fan
} else {
    // Keep fan off
}
```

Example Explanation: If temp is greater than 30, the fan is activated. Otherwise, it remains off. This structure is useful for real-time control in embedded systems.

2. Switch Statement

What does it do? Selects one execution path from multiple options based on a variable's value. It is useful for handling multiple predefined cases, such as selecting different operation modes in an embedded system.
Example:
```
int mode = 2;
switch (mode) {
    case 1:
        // Mode 1 operations
        break;
    case 2:
        // Mode 2 operations
        break;
    default:
        // Default operations
}
```

Example Explanation: If mode is 2, the second case executes. break prevents executing subsequent cases. This structure is ideal for menu-based applications.

3. For Loop

What does it do? Executes a block of code a fixed number of times. It is commonly used for repetitive tasks like blinking an LED or reading sensor values at set intervals.
Example:
```
for (int i = 0; i < 5; i++) {
    // Execute 5 times
}
```

Example Explanation: The loop runs 5 times with i increasing from 0 to 4. This is useful for tasks that require fixed iterations, such as displaying characters on an LCD screen.

4. While Loop

What does it do? Executes a block of code while a condition remains true. It is commonly used when the number of iterations is not known beforehand, such as waiting for a button press.
Example:
```
while (sensor == 1) {
    // Wait until sensor changes
}
```

Example Explanation: The loop runs continuously as long as sensor remains 1. This is useful for applications that require continuous monitoring.

5. Do-While Loop

What does it do? Executes the loop at least once, then continues execution while the condition is true. It ensures that the code inside the loop runs at least once, even if the condition is false initially.

Example:
```
do {
    // Execute at least once
} while (x > 0);
```

Example Explanation: The loop executes once, then checks if x > 0 before continuing. This is useful for applications that require an initial action, such as displaying a startup message on an LCD.

Real-life Applications Project: Automated Fan Control

Required Components

Component	Description
AVR Microcontroller (ATmega328P)	Controls fan operation.
Temperature Sensor (LM35)	Reads temperature values.
Relay Module	Turns fan on/off.
Resistor (1kΩ)	Limits current for sensor.

Circuit Connection Table

Component	AVR Microcontroller Pin	Power Source	Purpose
LM35 Temperature Sensor	Analog Pin (e.g., RA0)	5V	Reads temperature.
Relay Module	Digital Output (e.g., PB1)	5V	Controls fan.

Project Code

```c
#include <avr/io.h>
#include <util/delay.h>

#define TEMP_THRESHOLD 30  // Temperature threshold for fan control

int Read_Temperature();  // Function to simulate sensor reading

int main() {
    DDRB |= (1 << PB1);  // Set PB1 as output for relay
```

```c
while (1) {
    int temp = Read_Temperature();

    if (temp > TEMP_THRESHOLD) {
        PORTB |= (1 << PB1);   // Turn on fan
    } else {
        PORTB &= ~(1 << PB1);   // Turn off fan
    }

    _delay_ms(1000);
}
}

int Read_Temperature() {
    return 32;   // Simulated sensor value
}
```

Expected Results

Once the code is uploaded, the microcontroller continuously reads the temperature sensor value and decides whether to turn the fan on or off. If the temperature exceeds 30°C, the relay activates the fan; otherwise, it remains off. This project demonstrates how control structures automate decision-making in embedded systems.

Chapter 23: Arrays

Arrays in C provide an efficient way to store and manage multiple values of the same data type. They are essential for AVR microcontroller programming, as they allow the storage of sensor data, lookup tables, and configuration settings. Arrays simplify data handling and enable efficient iteration and processing in embedded applications.

Key Concepts of Arrays in AVR C

Concept	Description	Example
Array Declaration	Defines an array to store multiple values.	`int values[5];`
Array Initialization	Assigns values at declaration.	`int numbers[3] = {10, 20, 30};`
Accessing Elements	Retrieves a specific value using an index.	`x = values[2];`
Modifying Elements	Changes a specific array element.	`values[1] = 50;`
Looping Through Arrays	Iterates over array elements using loops.	`for (i = 0; i < 5; i++) {}`

Basic Rules for Using Arrays in AVR C

Rule	Correct Example	Incorrect Example
Declare array with a fixed size.	`int arr[5];`	`int arr[]; (Size must be defined)`
Indexing starts from 0.	`arr[0] = 10;`	`arr[5] = 20; (Index out of bounds)`
Use loops to access multiple elements.	`for(i=0; i<5; i++) {}`	`arr[0], arr[1], arr[2] (Redundant)`
Use `sizeof()` for array size.	`sizeof(arr)/sizeof(arr[0])`	Hardcoded size in loops (less flexible)

Syntax Table

SL	Operation	Syntax/Example	Description
1	Array Declaration	`int values[5];`	Declares an array of size 5.
2	Array Initialization	`int numbers[3] = {10, 20, 30};`	Declares and initializes an array.
3	Accessing Elements	`x = values[2];`	Retrieves value from index 2 of the array.
4	Modifying Elements	`values[1] = 50;`	Changes the value at index 1 to 50.
5	Looping Through Arrays	`for (i = 0; i < 5; i++) {}`	Iterates through the array using a loop.

Syntax Explanation

1. Array Declaration
What does it do? Declares an array, which reserves a fixed amount of memory to store multiple elements of the same data type. Each element is assigned an index starting from 0.
Example:
`int values[5];`

Example Explanation: This declares an integer array named values with space for five elements. The values in the array are uninitialized and contain garbage data until assigned specific values.

2. Array Initialization

What does it do? Allows assigning initial values to an array at the time of declaration.
Example:
`int numbers[3] = {10, 20, 30};`

Example Explanation: This initializes the array numbers with three values: 10, 20, and 30. The values are stored at indices 0, 1, and 2 respectively.

3. Accessing Elements

What does it do? Retrieves a value from an array using its index.
Example:
```
int x = numbers[1];
```

Example Explanation: Here, x will store the value 20, which is located at index 1 of the numbers array. Remember, array indexing starts from 0.

4. Modifying Elements

What does it do? Changes the value of an array element at a specific index.
Example:
```
values[2] = 50;
```

Example Explanation: The third element (index 2) of the values array is assigned the value 50. This updates the array dynamically during execution.

5. Looping Through Arrays

What does it do? Iterates through all elements using loops, allowing efficient processing of data stored in an array.
Example:
```
for (int i = 0; i < 5; i++) {
    values[i] = i * 10;
}
```

Example Explanation: This loop assigns each element of the values array a multiple of 10. The loop runs five times, setting:
- `values[0] = 0`
- `values[1] = 10`
- `values[2] = 20`
- `values[3] = 30`
- `values[4] = 40`

This approach is useful for initializing large arrays efficiently.

Real-life Applications Project: Storing Sensor Data in an Array
Required Components

Component	Description
AVR Microcontroller (ATmega328P)	Stores and processes sensor data.
Temperature Sensor (LM35)	Reads temperature values.
LCD Display	Displays stored values.
Resistor (1kΩ)	Limits current for sensor.

Circuit Connection Table

Component	AVR Microcontroller Pin	Power Source	Purpose
LM35 Temperature Sensor	Analog Pin (e.g., RA0)	5V	Reads temperature.
LCD Display	Digital Output (e.g., PB2)	5V	Displays sensor data.

Project Code

```c
#include <avr/io.h>
#include <util/delay.h>
#include <stdio.h>

#define NUM_SAMPLES 5

int Read_Temperature();

int main() {
    int temperature[NUM_SAMPLES];

    for (int i = 0; i < NUM_SAMPLES; i++) {
        temperature[i] = Read_Temperature();
        _delay_ms(500);
    }

    while (1) {
        // Display temperature readings on LCD
```

```
        }
}

int Read_Temperature() {
        return 25;   // Simulated temperature reading
}
```

Expected Results

Once the code is uploaded, the microcontroller continuously reads temperature values and stores them in an array. These values can be displayed on an LCD or used for further processing, demonstrating how arrays efficiently manage sensor data in embedded systems.

Chapter 24: Strings

Strings in C are arrays of characters terminated by a null character (\0). They are widely used in AVR microcontroller programming for displaying messages on LCDs, handling serial communication, and processing text-based data. Unlike standard integer arrays, strings require careful memory handling to avoid buffer overflows and ensure proper termination.

Key Concepts of Strings in AVR C

Concept	Description	Example
String Declaration	Defines a character array for storing a string.	char name[10];
String Initialization	Assigns a string to a character array.	char text[] = "Hello";
String Input	Reads user input into a string variable.	gets(string);
String Output	Displays a string on an output device.	puts(string);
String Functions	Performs operations like copying and comparison.	strcpy(dest, src);

Basic Rules for Using Strings in AVR C

Rule	Correct Example	Incorrect Example
Always use a null character (\0).	char str[] = "AVR\0";	char str[] = {'A', 'V', 'R'}; (No termination)
Use sizeof() or strlen() for length.	strlen(str);	sizeof(str); (Might include extra space)
Ensure the destination is large enough.	char dest[10]; strcpy(dest, src);	char dest[3]; strcpy(dest, src); (May overflow)
Use strcmp() for string comparison.	if(strcmp(a, b) == 0)	if(a == b) (Compares pointers, not values)

Syntax Table

SL	Operation	Syntax/Example	Description
1	**String Declaration**	`char name[20];`	Declares an array for storing a string.
2	**String Initialization**	`char text[] = "Hello";`	Assigns a string at declaration.
3	**String Input**	`fgets(string, sizeof(string), stdin);`	Reads input into a string safely.
4	**String Output**	`puts(string);`	Displays the string.
5	**String Copying**	`strcpy(dest, src);`	Copies src to dest.
6	**String Comparison**	`strcmp(str1, str2);`	Compares two strings.

Syntax Explanation

1. String Declaration

What does it do? Allocates memory for storing a string of characters. Declaring a string reserves a fixed-size array of characters, which must include space for the null terminator (\0).
Syntax:
`char string_name[size];`

Example:
`char name[20];`

Example Explanation: This declares a name array of 20 characters, allowing space to store a string. The string is uninitialized, meaning it will contain random memory values until explicitly assigned.

2. String Initialization

What does it do? Initializes a string during declaration, automatically appending the null terminator (\0).

Syntax:
```
char string_name[] = "text";
```

Example:
```
char text[] = "Hello";
```

Example Explanation: The string "Hello" is stored in `text[]`, and the compiler automatically appends \0 at the end. This ensures correct termination when used in functions like `printf()` or `strlen()`.

3. String Input

What does it do? Reads user input into a string variable. `fgets()` is preferred over `gets()` as it prevents buffer overflow.
Syntax:
```
fgets(string, sizeof(string), stdin);
```

Example:
```
char input[50];
fgets(input, sizeof(input), stdin);
```

Example Explanation: `fgets()` safely reads a string from user input into `input[]`, ensuring the input does not exceed the allocated size and always terminates with \0.

4. String Output

What does it do? Displays a string on an output device, such as an LCD or serial monitor.
Syntax:
```
puts(string);
```

Example:
```
char message[] = "AVR Programming";
puts(message);
```
Example Explanation: This prints "AVR Programming" to the output.

5. String Copying

What does it do? Copies the contents of one string to another. The destination string must be large enough to store the copied string.
Syntax:
```
strcpy(destination, source);
```

Example:
```
char dest[20];
char src[] = "Microcontroller";
strcpy(dest, src);
```

Example Explanation: The string "Microcontroller" is copied from src to dest. Ensure dest has enough space, or use strncpy() to prevent buffer overflow.

6. String Comparison

What does it do? Compares two strings and returns 0 if they are equal, a positive value if the first string is greater, or a negative value if it is smaller.
Syntax:
```
strcmp(string1, string2);
```

Example:
```
if (strcmp(str1, str2) == 0) {
    // Strings are equal
}
```

Example Explanation: If str1 and str2 contain the same characters, strcmp() returns 0. This is used for verifying passwords, user commands, or device configurations.

Real-life Applications Project: Displaying Sensor Status on an LCD

Required Components

Component	Description
AVR Microcontroller (ATmega328P)	Processes and displays strings.
16x2 LCD Display	Displays sensor status messages.
Temperature Sensor (LM35)	Reads temperature values.

Circuit Connection Table

Component	AVR Microcontroller Pin	Power Source	Purpose
LM35 Temperature Sensor	Analog Pin (e.g., RA0)	5V	Reads temperature values.
LCD Display	Digital Pins (e.g., PB0-PB7)	5V	Displays sensor messages.

Project Code

```c
#include <avr/io.h>
#include <util/delay.h>
#include <string.h>
#include <stdio.h>

void LCD_Init();
void LCD_Display(char *text);

int main() {
    char message[20];
    int temp = 28;  // Simulated temperature reading

    LCD_Init();

    if (temp > 30) {
        strcpy(message, "Temperature High!");
    } else {
```

```c
        strcpy(message, "Temperature Normal");
    }

    LCD_Display(message);

    while (1);
}
```

Expected Results

Once the code is uploaded, the LCD will display "Temperature High!" if the temperature exceeds 30°C, otherwise, it will show "Temperature Normal." This demonstrates how strings are used to display messages in embedded applications.

Chapter 25: Pointers

Pointers in C are variables that store memory addresses instead of actual values. They are essential in AVR microcontroller programming for efficient memory management, direct hardware access, and dynamic data manipulation. Pointers enable optimized handling of arrays, structures, and functions in embedded applications.

Key Concepts of Pointers in AVR C

Concept	Description	Example
Pointer Declaration	Defines a variable to store an address.	`int *ptr;`
Pointer Initialization	Assigns the address of a variable to a pointer.	`ptr = &var;`
Dereferencing	Accesses the value stored at a pointer's address.	`x = *ptr;`
Pointer Arithmetic	Performs operations like increment and decrement.	`ptr++;`
Pointer to Array	Points to the first element of an array.	`int *ptr = arr;`
Pointer to Function	Stores the address of a function.	`int (*funcPtr)();`

Basic Rules for Using Pointers in AVR C

Rule	Correct Example	Incorrect Example
Always initialize pointers before use.	`int *ptr = &x;`	`int *ptr;` (Undefined behavior)
Use & to get a variable's address.	`ptr = &var;`	`ptr = var;` (Wrong assignment)
Use * to access the value at an address.	`x = *ptr;`	`x = ptr;` (Wrong value usage)
Avoid dereferencing null pointers.	`if(ptr != NULL) *ptr;`	`*ptr;` (May cause crash)

Syntax Table

SL	Operation	Syntax/Example	Description
1	Pointer Declaration	`int *ptr;`	Declares a pointer to an integer variable.
2	Pointer Initialization	`ptr = &var;`	Stores the address of var in `ptr`.
3	Dereferencing	`value = *ptr;`	Accesses the value stored at `ptr`'s address.
4	Pointer Arithmetic	`ptr++;`	Moves pointer to the next memory location.
5	Pointer to Array	`ptr = arr;`	Points to the first element of an array.
6	Pointer to Function	`int (*funcPtr)();`	Declares a pointer to a function.

Syntax Explanation

1. Pointer Declaration

What does it do? Declares a pointer variable that can store the address of another variable. Pointers allow indirect access to variables stored in memory, making memory management efficient.
Syntax:
`int *ptr;`

Example:
`int *ptr;`

Example Explanation: This declares a pointer variable `ptr` that can store the memory address of an integer variable. However, it does not yet point to a valid address until it is initialized.

2. Pointer Initialization

What does it do? Assigns the address of a variable to a pointer, allowing it to reference the variable indirectly.

Syntax:
```
ptr = &variable;
```

Example:
```
int x = 10;
int *ptr = &x;
```

Example Explanation: The pointer `ptr` now stores the memory address of the variable x. Using `*ptr`, we can access or modify the value of x indirectly.

3. Dereferencing a Pointer

What does it do? Retrieves the value stored at the address pointed to by the pointer. This is how pointers are used to read and modify data.
Syntax:
```
variable = *ptr;
```

Example:
```
int x = 10;
int *ptr = &x;
int y = *ptr;
```

Example Explanation: Here, `*ptr` accesses the value stored at `ptr`, which is `10`. The value is assigned to y, making y equal to `10`.

4. Pointer Arithmetic

What does it do? Allows movement within an array by incrementing or decrementing the pointer. Adding 1 to a pointer moves it to the next element of an array.
Syntax:
```
ptr++;
```
Example:
```
int arr[] = {10, 20, 30};
int *ptr = arr;
ptr++;
```

Example Explanation: Initially, `ptr` points to `arr[0]`. After `ptr++`, it moves to `arr[1]`, effectively pointing to the next integer in memory.

5. Pointer to Array

What does it do? Points to the first element of an array, allowing efficient traversal using pointer arithmetic.
Syntax:
```
int *ptr = array;
```

Example:
```
int arr[3] = {1, 2, 3};
int *ptr = arr;
```

Example Explanation: `ptr` stores the address of `arr[0]`. Using `ptr++`, we can traverse the array efficiently without using indices.

6. Pointer to Function

What does it do? Stores the address of a function, allowing indirect function calls. This is useful in callback mechanisms and dynamic function execution.
Syntax:
```
int (*funcPtr)();
```

Example:
```
int add(int a, int b) { return a + b; }
int (*funcPtr)(int, int) = add;
```

Example Explanation: `funcPtr` stores the address of `add()`, enabling function execution using `funcPtr(a, b)`. This is used in interrupt handling and event-driven programming.

Real-life Applications Project: Using Pointers to Manipulate Sensor Data

Required Components

Component	Description
AVR Microcontroller (ATmega328P)	Processes sensor data using pointers.
Temperature Sensor (LM35)	Reads temperature values.
LCD Display	Displays processed sensor values.

Circuit Connection Table

Component	AVR Microcontroller Pin	Power Source	Purpose
LM35 Temperature Sensor	Analog Pin (e.g., RA0)	5V	Reads temperature.
LCD Display	Digital Output (e.g., PB2)	5V	Displays sensor data.

Project Code

```c
#include <avr/io.h>
#include <util/delay.h>
#include <stdio.h>

#define NUM_SAMPLES 5

int Read_Temperature();

int main() {
    int temperature[NUM_SAMPLES];
    int *ptr = temperature;

    for (int i = 0; i < NUM_SAMPLES; i++) {
        *(ptr + i) = Read_Temperature();
        _delay_ms(500);
    }

    while (1) {
```

```
        // Display temperature readings on LCD
    }
}
```

Expected Results

Once the code is uploaded, the microcontroller continuously reads temperature values and stores them using a pointer to an array. These values can be displayed on an LCD or processed further, demonstrating how pointers manage dynamic data in embedded systems.

Chapter 26: Memory Addresses

Memory addresses are fundamental to programming AVR microcontrollers, as they determine how data and instructions are stored and accessed. Understanding memory addresses is essential for efficient memory management, optimizing performance, and debugging embedded systems.

AVR microcontrollers feature multiple memory types, including Flash, SRAM, and EEPROM, each serving distinct purposes. Memory addressing enables direct interaction with registers, variables, and peripheral devices.

Key Concepts of Memory Addresses in AVR C

Concept	Description	Example	
Memory Address	The unique identifier for a memory location.	`&var`	
Flash Memory	Stores program code (non-volatile).	`const char msg[] PROGMEM = "Hello";`	
SRAM (Static RAM)	Stores runtime variables (volatile).	`int x = 10;`	
EEPROM (Electrically Erasable Programmable ROM)	Stores non-volatile data.	`EEPROM.write(address, value);`	
Pointer to Memory Address	Stores and accesses a memory location dynamically.	`int *ptr = &x;`	
Registers and I/O Memory	Control peripherals like timers and ports.	`` `PORTB ``	`= (1 << PB0 );` ``

Basic Rules for Working with Memory Addresses in AVR C

Rule	Correct Example	Incorrect Example
Always initialize memory before use.	`int x = 10;`	`int x;` (Contains garbage value)
Use & to obtain the address of a variable.	`int *ptr = &x;`	`int *ptr = x;` (Incorrect assignment)
Use pointers to access memory dynamically.	`int y = *ptr;`	`ptr = 1000;` (Invalid memory access)
Avoid accessing unallocated memory.	`int arr[5]; ptr = arr;`	`int *ptr; *ptr = 10;` (Undefined behavior)

Syntax Table

SL	Operation	Syntax/Example	Description
1	Obtain Address of Variable	`ptr = &var;`	Retrieves memory address of var.
2	Dereferencing Pointer	`value = *ptr;`	Accesses value stored at memory address.
3	Reading Flash Memory	`pgm_read_byte(&msg);`	Reads stored constant from Flash memory.
4	Writing to EEPROM	`EEPROM.write(address, value);`	Stores non-volatile data in EEPROM.
5	Reading from EEPROM	`EEPROM.read(address);`	Retrieves stored data from EEPROM.

Syntax Explanation

1. Obtaining the Address of a Variable

What does it do? Retrieves the memory address of a variable and stores it in a pointer. This allows indirect access to the variable's value using the pointer.
Syntax:
`ptr = &variable;`

Example:
```
int x = 10;
int *ptr = &x;
```

Example Explanation: Here, `ptr` now contains the memory address of x. This enables `ptr` to reference x, allowing indirect access to its value.

2. Dereferencing a Pointer

What does it do? Accesses or modifies the value stored at a given memory address by using the pointer.
Syntax:
```
value = *ptr;
```

Example:
```
int x = 10;
int *ptr = &x;
int y = *ptr;
```

Example Explanation: The pointer `ptr` holds the address of x. By dereferencing it (*ptr), we retrieve 10 and store it in y. This is useful in scenarios where variables need to be accessed indirectly.

3. Reading Data from Flash Memory

What does it do? Retrieves a stored constant from Flash memory, where program code is stored in AVR microcontrollers.
Syntax:
```
pgm_read_byte(&variable);
```

Example:
```
#include <avr/pgmspace.h>
const char msg[] PROGMEM = "Hello";
char read_data = pgm_read_byte(&msg[0]);
```

Example Explanation: `msg[]` is stored in Flash memory instead of SRAM. `pgm_read_byte()` reads the first character ('H') from the Flash memory, ensuring efficient program execution and memory usage.

4. Writing Data to EEPROM

What does it do? Writes non-volatile data to EEPROM memory, allowing data retention even after power loss.
Syntax:
```
EEPROM.write(address, value);
```

Example:
```
#include <EEPROM.h>
EEPROM.write(0x10, 55);
```

Example Explanation: Stores the value 55 at EEPROM memory address 0x10. This stored data can be retrieved even after the microcontroller is restarted.

5. Reading Data from EEPROM

What does it do? Retrieves stored non-volatile data from EEPROM memory.
Syntax:
```
value = EEPROM.read(address);
```

Example:
```
int value = EEPROM.read(0x10);
```

Example Explanation: Reads the stored value from EEPROM memory address 0x10 into value. This method ensures data persistence across power cycles.

6. Accessing Hardware Registers

What does it do? Modifies hardware registers to control I/O operations such as setting a pin high or low.
Syntax:
```
PORTx |= (1 << PINx);
```

Example:
```
PORTB |= (1 << PB0);
```

Example Explanation: Sets the PB0 pin of PORTB to HIGH, turning on an LED or activating another connected device.

Real-life Applications Project: Storing and Retrieving Sensor Data in EEPROM

Project Overview This project demonstrates how to use memory addresses in an AVR microcontroller to store and retrieve sensor data in EEPROM. The system reads temperature values from a sensor, stores them in EEPROM, and retrieves them for display on an LCD.

Required Components

Component	Description
AVR Microcontroller (ATmega328P)	Stores and retrieves memory data.
Temperature Sensor (LM35)	Reads temperature values.
LCD Display	Displays stored sensor readings.
Resistors (1kΩ, 10kΩ)	Required for sensor interfacing.

Circuit Connection Table

Component	AVR Microcontroller Pin	Power Source	Purpose
LM35 Temperature Sensor	Analog Pin (e.g., RA0)	5V	Reads temperature.
LCD Display	Digital Output (e.g., PB2)	5V	Displays sensor data.
Pull-up Resistor	Connected to I2C lines	5V	Stabilizes communication.

Project Code

```
#include <avr/io.h>
#include <util/delay.h>
#include <EEPROM.h>
#include <stdio.h>

#define TEMP_ADDRESS 0x10

int Read_Temperature();
void Display_Data(int temp);
```

```c
int main() {
    int temp = Read_Temperature();
    EEPROM.write(TEMP_ADDRESS, temp); // Store
temperature in EEPROM

    while (1) {
        int stored_temp = EEPROM.read(TEMP_ADDRESS); //
Retrieve stored value
        Display_Data(stored_temp); // Display on LCD
        _delay_ms(1000);
    }
}

int Read_Temperature() {
    return 25;   // Simulated temperature reading
}

void Display_Data(int temp) {
    char buffer[10];
    sprintf(buffer, "Temp: %dC", temp);
    // Code to display buffer on LCD
}
```

Expected Results

Once the code is uploaded, the microcontroller reads temperature values and stores them in EEPROM. Even after a reset, the stored data can be retrieved and displayed on an LCD. This demonstrates how AVR memory addresses are used for efficient data storage and retrieval in embedded systems. The LCD will continuously update to display the stored temperature reading, ensuring persistent data handling.

Chapter 27: Functions and Macros

Functions and macros are essential components of Embedded C programming for AVR microcontrollers. Functions allow modular programming, reducing redundancy and enhancing code reusability, while macros provide efficient ways to define reusable code blocks at compile time. Understanding functions and macros helps optimize performance and improve maintainability in embedded applications.

Key Concepts of Functions and Macros in AVR C

Concept	Description	Example
Function Declaration	Defines a reusable block of code.	`int add(int a, int b);`
Function Definition	Implements the function logic.	`int add(int a, int b) { return a + b; }`
Function Call	Executes a function in the program.	`result = add(5, 3);`
Return Statement	Sends a value back to the caller.	`return sum;`
Macros	Preprocessor directives for defining constants or expressions.	`#define LED_PIN PB0`
Inline Functions	Optimized functions that avoid function call overhead.	`inline int square(int x) { return x*x; }`

Basic Rules for Using Functions and Macros in AVR C

Rule	Correct Example	Incorrect Example
Always declare functions before calling them.	`int add(int, int); int main() {}`	`int main() { add(5,3); }` (May cause compiler error)
Functions must return a value if declared as non-void.	`int getValue() { return 10; }`	`int getValue() { }` (Undefined behavior)

Use macros for constants and simple expressions.	`#define PI 3.14`	`const float PI = 3.14;` (Not optimized at compile time)
Use inline functions when possible to reduce overhead.	`inline int multiply(int a) { return a*2; }`	Using complex logic in macros (Less readable)

Syntax Table

SL	Operation	Syntax/Example	Description
1	Function Declaration	`int add(int a, int b);`	Declares a function before its definition.
2	Function Definition	`int add(int a, int b) { return a + b; }`	Implements a function.
3	Function Call	`sum = add(5, 10);`	Calls a function in the main program.
4	Macro Definition	`#define LED_PIN PB0`	Defines a constant value.
5	Inline Function	`inline int square(int x) { return x*x; }`	Optimized function for fast execution.

Syntax Explanation

1. Function Declaration

What does it do? A function declaration tells the compiler that a function exists and specifies its return type and parameters before it is defined. This is necessary when the function definition appears after the `main()` function.
Syntax:
`return_type function_name(parameters);`

Example:
`int add(int a, int b);`

Example Explanation: This declaration informs the compiler that a function named add will take two integer parameters and return an integer value. The function body (implementation) must be defined elsewhere in the code.

2. Function Definition

What does it do? Provides the implementation of a function, specifying what operations it performs.
Syntax:
```
return_type function_name(parameters) {
    // Function logic
    return value;
}
```

Example:
```
int add(int a, int b) {
    return a + b;
}
```

Example Explanation: The function add takes two integers as input, calculates their sum, and returns the result. When called, it executes this logic and provides the output.

3. Function Call

What does it do? Executes a function's logic by passing arguments and receiving the return value.
Syntax:
```
variable = function_name(arguments);
```

Example:
```
int sum = add(5, 10);
```

Example Explanation: Here, the function add(5, 10) is called, and the returned value (15) is assigned to the variable sum. This allows modular execution of code blocks.

4. Macro Definition

What does it do? Defines a preprocessor directive that replaces occurrences of a name with a specified value during compilation. Macros improve code readability and efficiency.
Syntax:
```
#define MACRO_NAME value
```

Example:
```
#define LED_PIN PB0
```

Example Explanation: This macro assigns PB0 to LED_PIN. Any occurrence of LED_PIN in the code will be replaced with PB0 before compilation, making the code more readable and easier to modify.

5. Inline Function

What does it do? Defines a function that is expanded directly at the call site, avoiding function call overhead and improving performance.
Syntax:
```
inline return_type function_name(parameters) {
    return expression;
}
```

Example:
```
inline int square(int x) {
    return x * x;
}
```

Example Explanation: When square(5) is called, it directly substitutes 5 * 5, avoiding a function call. This makes execution faster for simple operations.
Real-life Applications Project: LED Blinking using Functions and Macros
Project Overview This project demonstrates the use of functions and macros to control an LED connected to an AVR microcontroller. The LED will blink at predefined intervals using a function call, with macros defining pin configurations.

Required Components

Component	Description
AVR Microcontroller (ATmega328P)	Controls the LED.
LED	Indicates output status.
Resistor (330Ω)	Limits current to the LED.
Push Button	Allows manual LED control.
Pull-down Resistor (10kΩ)	Ensures stable button input.

Circuit Connection Table

Component	AVR Microcontroller Pin	Power Source	Purpose
LED	Digital Output (e.g., PB0)	5V	Blinks to indicate function execution.
Resistor	In series with LED	5V	Prevents excess current flow.
Push Button	Digital Input (e.g., PD2)	5V	Provides manual LED control.
Pull-down Resistor	Connected to button pin	5V	Ensures a stable input signal.

Project Code

```
#include <avr/io.h>
#include <util/delay.h>

#define LED_PIN PB0
#define BUTTON_PIN PD2
#define LED_PORT PORTB
#define LED_DDR DDRB
#define BUTTON_PORT PORTD
#define BUTTON_PINR PIND

void initializeLED();
void toggleLED();
int isButtonPressed();

int main() {
```

```
    initializeLED();
    while (1) {
        if (isButtonPressed()) {
            toggleLED();
            _delay_ms(500); // Wait 500ms
        }
    }
}

void initializeLED() {
    LED_DDR |= (1 << LED_PIN); // Set LED pin as output
    BUTTON_PORT |= (1 << BUTTON_PIN); // Enable pull-up
resistor on button pin
}

void toggleLED() {
    LED_PORT ^= (1 << LED_PIN); // Toggle LED state
}

int isButtonPressed() {
    return !(BUTTON_PINR & (1 << BUTTON_PIN)); //
Return true if button is pressed
}
```

Expected Results

Once the code is uploaded, the LED connected to PB0 will blink
when the button connected to PD2 is pressed. The initializeLED
function sets up the LED and button, toggleLED toggles the LED
state, and isButtonPressed checks if the button is pressed. The
use of macros simplifies pin definitions, making the code more
readable and maintainable.

Chapter 28: Enumerations (enum) and typedef

Enumerations (enum) and `typedef` are two important features in Embedded C for AVR microcontrollers. Enumerations provide a way to define a set of named integer constants, making code more readable and manageable. The `typedef` keyword allows the creation of new type names, simplifying complex data structures and improving code clarity.

These features are commonly used in embedded systems for defining states, error codes, configuration settings, and structured data.

Key Concepts of Enumerations and typedef in AVR C

Concept	Description	Example
Enumeration (enum)	Defines named integer constants.	`enum Color {RED, GREEN, BLUE};`
Assigning Values	Assigns specific values to enumeration members.	`enum Level {LOW=1, MEDIUM=5};`
Using enum Variables	Declares variables of an enumeration type.	`enum State mode;`
typedef Definition	Creates an alias for a type.	`typedef unsigned char BYTE;`
typedef with struct	Defines a custom data structure.	`typedef struct { int x; } Point;`

Basic Rules for Using Enumerations and typedef in AVR C

Rule	Correct Example	Incorrect Example
Use enum for defining named constants.	`enum Days {SUN, MON, TUE};`	`#define SUN 0` (Less readable)
Assign specific values when needed.	`enum Status {OK=1, ERROR=2};`	`enum Status {OK, ERROR=1};` (Incorrect sequence)

Use typedef for simplifying complex types.	typedef unsigned int uint;	#define uint unsigned int (Not type-safe)
Combine typedef and struct for clarity.	typedef struct {int x;} Point;	struct {int x;} point; (Less flexible)

Syntax Table

SL	Operation	Syntax/Example	Description
1	**Enumeration Definition**	enum State {ON, OFF};	Declares an enumeration with values.
2	**Assigning Values to Enum**	enum Level {LOW=1, MEDIUM=5};	Assigns specific integer values.
3	**Using Enum Variables**	enum State mode = ON;	Declares a variable of an enum type.
4	**typedef for Simplicity**	typedef unsigned char BYTE;	Defines a custom type alias.
5	**typedef with Struct**	typedef struct {int x;} Point;	Creates a named structure type.

Syntax Explanation

1. Enumeration Definition

What does it do? Defines a list of named integer constants, improving code readability and maintainability.
Syntax:
```
enum EnumName { VALUE1, VALUE2, VALUE3 };
```

Example:
```
enum State { ON, OFF };
```

Example Explanation: This defines an enumeration State with two possible values: ON (0) and OFF (1). These values can be used in control structures to enhance code clarity.

2. Assigning Values to Enum

What does it do? Allows specific values to be assigned to enumeration members instead of using the default sequential numbering.
Syntax:
```
enum EnumName { VALUE1 = x, VALUE2 = y };
```

Example:
```
enum Level { LOW=1, MEDIUM=5, HIGH=10 };
```

Example Explanation: The enumeration Level explicitly sets integer values: LOW is 1, MEDIUM is 5, and HIGH is 10. This helps when specific values are needed for calculations or settings.

3. Using Enum Variables

What does it do? Declares a variable of an enumeration type and assigns it a value.
Syntax:
```
enum EnumName variable;
```

Example:
```
enum State mode;
mode = ON;
```

Example Explanation: A variable mode of type enum State is declared and assigned the ON value. This improves code readability by using meaningful names instead of raw numbers.

4. typedef for Simplicity

What does it do? Creates an alias for a data type, making the code easier to read and maintain.
Syntax:
```
typedef existing_type new_type_name;
```

Example:
```
typedef unsigned char BYTE;
```

Example Explanation: BYTE now represents unsigned char, making it more intuitive when dealing with byte-sized data.

5. typedef with Struct

What does it do? Simplifies structure declarations by defining a named type for them.
Syntax:
```
typedef struct {
    type member;
} StructName;
```

Example:
```
typedef struct {
    int x;
    int y;
} Point;
```

Example Explanation: Point is now a type that represents a structure containing two integers, x and y. This simplifies variable declarations: Point p1, p2; instead of struct Point p1, p2;.

Real-life Applications Project: Controlling LED States Using Enums and Typedefs

Project Overview This project demonstrates how to use enum and typedef to manage LED states in an AVR microcontroller system. The LED will be controlled using an enumeration, making the code more readable and maintainable.

Required Components

Component	Description
AVR Microcontroller (ATmega328P)	Controls the LED state.
LED	Indicates state visually.
Resistor (330Ω)	Limits current to the LED.

Circuit Connection Table

Compon ent	AVR Microcontroller Pin	Power Source	Purpose
LED	Digital Output (e.g., PB0)	5V	Indicates LED state.
Resistor	In series with LED	5V	Prevents excess current.

Project Code

```c
#include <avr/io.h>
#include <util/delay.h>

typedef enum {
    LED_OFF,
    LED_ON
} LED_State;

#define LED_PIN PB0
#define LED_PORT PORTB
#define LED_DDR DDRB

void setLEDState(LED_State state);

int main() {
    LED_DDR |= (1 << LED_PIN); // Set LED pin as output
    while (1) {
        setLEDState(LED_ON);
        _delay_ms(1000);
        setLEDState(LED_OFF);
        _delay_ms(1000);
    }
}

void setLEDState(LED_State state) {
    if (state == LED_ON) {
        LED_PORT |= (1 << LED_PIN);
```

```
    } else {
        LED_PORT &= ~(1 << LED_PIN);
    }
}
```

Expected Results

The LED will turn ON and OFF at 1-second intervals, controlled by an enum representing LED states. Using typedef makes the function calls more intuitive and the code more readable.

Chapter 29: Memory Management

Memory management in AVR microcontrollers is crucial for optimizing resource usage, improving performance, and preventing memory-related errors. Unlike general-purpose computers, AVR microcontrollers have limited memory resources, including Flash, SRAM, and EEPROM. Efficient use of these memory types ensures stable and efficient embedded applications.

This chapter explores different memory types in AVR microcontrollers, their allocation, usage, and techniques for memory optimization.

Key Concepts of Memory Management in AVR C

Concept	Description	Example	
Flash Memory	Stores program code (non-volatile).	`const char msg[] PROGMEM = "AVR";`	
SRAM	Stores runtime variables (volatile).	`int x = 10;`	
EEPROM	Stores non-volatile data.	`EEPROM.write(address, value);`	
Stack Memory	Temporary storage for function calls and local variables.	`void func() { int x; }`	
Heap Memory	Dynamically allocated memory.	`ptr = (int*) malloc(10 * sizeof(int));`	
Registers	Special memory locations for direct hardware access.	`` `PORTB ``	`= (1 << PB0);` `

Basic Rules for Memory Management in AVR C

Rule	Correct Example	Incorrect Example
Use Flash for constant data.	`const char str[] PROGMEM = "Data";`	`char str[] = "Data";` (Uses SRAM)
Use EEPROM for persistent storage.	`EEPROM.write(0x10, 55);`	Storing persistent data in RAM

| Avoid excessive stack usage. | ```
void
function() {
int array[10];
}
``` | Large local arrays may cause stack overflow |
| Free dynamically allocated memory. | `free(ptr);` | Forgetting to release memory |
| Use global variables cautiously. | ```
static int
counter;
``` | Overuse of global variables leads to high RAM usage |

Syntax Table

SL	Operation	Syntax/Example	Description
| 1 | **Storing Data in Flash** | ```
const char text[]
PROGMEM =
"Hello";
``` | Stores constant data in Flash memory. |
2	**Reading from Flash**	`pgm_read_byte(&text[0]);`	Retrieves data from Flash.
3	**Writing to EEPROM**	`EEPROM.write(0x10, 100);`	Saves a value in EEPROM.
4	**Reading from EEPROM**	`EEPROM.read(0x10);`	Reads a value from EEPROM.
| 5 | **Allocating Heap Memory** | ```
ptr = (int*)
malloc(10 *
sizeof(int));
``` | Allocates memory dynamically. |
| 6 | **Freeing Heap Memory** | `free(ptr);` | Releases allocated memory. |

Syntax Explanation

1. Storing Data in Flash

What does it do? Stores constant data in Flash memory instead of SRAM, reducing RAM usage and ensuring constant data is not altered during execution.
Syntax:
```
const char text[] PROGMEM = "Hello";
```

Example:
```
#include <avr/pgmspace.h>
const char message[] PROGMEM = "AVR Programming";
```

Example Explanation: The string message is stored in Flash memory, which preserves valuable SRAM space for other runtime operations.

2. Reading from Flash

What does it do? Retrieves stored constant data from Flash memory at runtime.
Syntax:
```
pgm_read_byte(&variable);
```

Example:
```
char ch = pgm_read_byte(&message[0]);
```

Example Explanation: Reads the first character of message stored in Flash memory, ensuring minimal SRAM usage.

3. Writing to EEPROM

What does it do? Saves data in EEPROM, ensuring persistence across power cycles, which is useful for storing user preferences and sensor calibrations.
Syntax:
```
EEPROM.write(address, value);
```

Example:
```
EEPROM.write(0x10, 100);
```

Example Explanation: Writes the value 100 to EEPROM address 0x10, ensuring that it remains available even after a reset.

4. Reading from EEPROM

What does it do? Retrieves stored non-volatile data from EEPROM memory at runtime.

Syntax:
```
EEPROM.read(address);
```

Example:
```
int value = EEPROM.read(0x10);
```

Example Explanation: Reads the stored value from EEPROM address 0x10 into value, allowing the system to retrieve persistent data.

5. Allocating Heap Memory

What does it do? Dynamically allocates memory on the heap, allowing runtime flexibility in memory usage.
Syntax:
```
ptr = (type*) malloc(size);
```

Example:
```
int *ptr = (int*) malloc(10 * sizeof(int));
```

Example Explanation: Allocates memory for an array of 10 integers at runtime. This is useful when the required memory size is unknown at compile time.

6. Freeing Heap Memory

What does it do? Releases previously allocated heap memory, preventing memory leaks.
Syntax:
```
free(pointer);
```

Example:
```
free(ptr);
```

Example Explanation: Releases dynamically allocated memory, ensuring that it is available for other processes in the system.

Real-life Applications Project: Logging Sensor Data to EEPROM

Project Overview This project demonstrates how to log sensor data in EEPROM for later retrieval, ensuring data persistence even after a power loss. A temperature sensor (LM35) is used to collect temperature readings, which are periodically stored in EEPROM and displayed on an LCD.

Required Components

Component	Description
AVR Microcontroller (ATmega328P)	Stores and retrieves memory data.
Temperature Sensor (LM35)	Reads temperature values.
LCD Display	Displays stored sensor readings.
Resistors (10kΩ, 330Ω)	Required for sensor interfacing and LED connection.

Circuit Connection Table

Component	AVR Microcontroller Pin	Power Source	Purpose
LM35 Temperature Sensor	Analog Pin (e.g., RA0)	5V	Reads temperature.
LCD Display	Digital Output (e.g., PB2)	5V	Displays sensor data.
LED Indicator	Digital Output (e.g., PB5)	5V	Indicates data logging operation.

Project Code

```
#include <avr/io.h>
#include <util/delay.h>
#include <EEPROM.h>
#include <stdio.h>

#define TEMP_ADDRESS 0x10
#define LED_PIN PB5
```

```c
int Read_Temperature();
void Store_Temperature(int temp);
int Retrieve_Temperature();
void Display_Data(int temp);

void initializeLED() {
    DDRB |= (1 << LED_PIN); // Set LED pin as output
}

void blinkLED() {
    PORTB |= (1 << LED_PIN);
    _delay_ms(200);
    PORTB &= ~(1 << LED_PIN);
}

int main() {
    initializeLED();
    int temp = Read_Temperature();
    Store_Temperature(temp);
    blinkLED();

    while (1) {
        int stored_temp = Retrieve_Temperature();
        Display_Data(stored_temp);
        _delay_ms(1000);
    }
}

int Read_Temperature() {
    return 25;  // Simulated temperature reading
}

void Store_Temperature(int temp) {
    EEPROM.write(TEMP_ADDRESS, temp);
}

int Retrieve_Temperature() {
```

```
    return EEPROM.read(TEMP_ADDRESS);
}

void Display_Data(int temp) {
    char buffer[10];
    sprintf(buffer, "Temp: %dC", temp);
    // Code to display buffer on LCD
}
```

Expected Results

Once the code is uploaded, the microcontroller will read temperature data, store it in EEPROM, and blink an LED to indicate successful logging. The stored data will be retrieved and displayed on an LCD, demonstrating efficient memory management and persistent data handling in an AVR microcontroller.

Chapter 30: Timers and Counters

Timers and counters are essential peripherals in AVR microcontrollers that enable time-based operations such as event scheduling, frequency measurement, PWM generation, and real-time clock functions. Timers in AVR microcontrollers operate based on internal clock sources, while counters count external pulses. Understanding their working principles is crucial for precise timing and control in embedded applications.

Key Concepts of Timers and Counters in AVR C

Concept	Description	Example
Timer Registers	Special registers controlling timer behavior.	TCCR0, TCNT0, TIMSK
Prescaler	Controls timer speed by dividing clock frequency.	`TCCR0
Overflow Mode	Increments timer until it overflows.	ISR(TIMER0_OVF_vect);
Compare Match Mode	Triggers an interrupt when timer matches a value.	OCR0 = 200;
PWM Mode	Generates Pulse Width Modulation signals.	`TCCR0
External Clock Source	Uses an external signal to count pulses.	`TCCR0

Basic Rules for Using Timers and Counters in AVR C

Rule	Correct Example	Incorrect Example
Always configure the timer mode.	`TCCR0	= (1 << WGM01);`
Set a proper prescaler for timing accuracy.	`TCCR0	= (1 << CS01);`
Enable timer interrupts if required.	`TIMSK	= (1 << TOIE0);`
Use the correct ISR for the timer.	ISR(TIMER0_OVF_vect) {}	Using a wrong ISR name may cause compilation errors.

Clear flags before re-enabling timers.	`TIFR	= (1 << TOV0);`

Syntax Table

SL	Operation	Syntax/Example	Description
1	Configuring Timer Mode	`TCCR0	= (1 << WGM01);`
2	Setting Prescaler	`TCCR0	= (1 << CS01);`
3	Timer Overflow Interrupt	ISR(TIMER0_OVF_vect) {}	Handles overflow interrupts.
4	Compare Match Interrupt	ISR(TIMER0_COMPA_vect) {}	Handles compare match event.
5	Generating PWM	`TCCR0	= (1 << WGM00)
6	Using External Clock	`TCCR0	= (1 << CS02);`

Syntax Explanation

1. Configuring Timer Mode

What does it do? Sets the timer operation mode, such as normal, CTC, or PWM mode.
Syntax:
```
TCCR0 |= (1 << WGM01);
```

Example:
```
TCCR0 |= (1 << WGM01); // Configure Timer0 in CTC mode
```

Example Explanation: This configures Timer0 to operate in Clear Timer on Compare Match (CTC) mode, where it resets upon reaching the compare match value.

2. Setting Prescaler

What does it do? Divides the system clock frequency to control the timer speed.
Syntax:
```
TCCR0 |= (1 << CS01);
```

Example:

```
TCCR0 |= (1 << CS01); // Sets prescaler to divide clock
by 8
```

Example Explanation: This sets the timer to run at the system clock divided by 8, slowing down the timer increments.

3. Timer Overflow Interrupt

What does it do? Executes an interrupt service routine (ISR) when the timer overflows.
Syntax:

```
ISR(TIMER0_OVF_vect) {
    // Code to execute on overflow
}
```

Example:

```
ISR(TIMER0_OVF_vect) {
    PORTB ^= (1 << PB0); // Toggle LED on Timer0
overflow
}
```

Example Explanation: This ISR is triggered when Timer0 overflows, toggling an LED connected to PB0.

4. Compare Match Interrupt

What does it do? Triggers an ISR when the timer value matches the compare register value.
Syntax:

```
ISR(TIMER0_COMPA_vect) {
    // Code to execute on compare match
}
```

Example:

```
OCR0 = 200; // Set compare match value
ISR(TIMER0_COMPA_vect) {
    PORTB ^= (1 << PB0); // Toggle LED on compare match
}
```

Example Explanation: The ISR runs when the timer count reaches 200, toggling an LED on PB0.

5. Generating PWM

What does it do? Configures the timer in PWM mode to generate a pulse-width modulated signal.
Syntax:
```
TCCR0 |= (1 << WGM00) | (1 << COM01);
```

Example:
```
TCCR0 |= (1 << WGM00) | (1 << COM01); // Set Fast PWM
mode
OCR0 = 128; // Set 50% duty cycle
```

Example Explanation: Configures Timer0 to generate a PWM signal with a 50% duty cycle.

Real-life Applications Project: LED Blinking using Timer Interrupts

Project Overview This project demonstrates how to use timers to blink an LED at a precise interval using Timer0 overflow interrupts.

Required Components

Component	Description
AVR Microcontroller (ATmega328P)	Controls the LED timing.
LED	Indicates timer execution.
Resistor (330Ω)	Limits current to the LED.

Circuit Connection Table

Component	AVR Microcontroller Pin	Power Source	Purpose
LED	Digital Output (e.g., PB0)	5V	Blinks based on timer interrupts.
Resistor	In series with LED	5V	Prevents excess current flow.

Project Code

```c
#include <avr/io.h>
#include <avr/interrupt.h>

#define LED_PIN PB0

void Timer0_Init();

int main() {
    DDRB |= (1 << LED_PIN); // Set LED pin as output
    Timer0_Init();
    sei(); // Enable global interrupts
    while (1);
}

void Timer0_Init() {
    TCCR0 |= (1 << CS02) | (1 << CS00); // Set
prescaler to 1024
    TIMSK |= (1 << TOIE0); // Enable Timer0 overflow
interrupt
}

ISR(TIMER0_OVF_vect) {
    PORTB ^= (1 << LED_PIN); // Toggle LED on overflow
}
```

Expected Results

The LED connected to PB0 will blink at a precise interval, controlled by Timer0 overflow interrupts. The use of timers ensures accurate time-based operations in AVR microcontrollers.

Chapter 31: Analog to Digital Conversion (ADC)

Analog to Digital Conversion (ADC) is a crucial feature in AVR microcontrollers, allowing them to process real-world analog signals by converting them into digital values. ADCs are commonly used in applications like sensor interfacing, voltage measurement, and signal processing. AVR microcontrollers, such as the ATmega328P, include a 10-bit ADC capable of converting analog inputs into digital values ranging from 0 to 1023.

Key Concepts of ADC in AVR C

Concept	Description	Example
ADC Resolution	Determines the number of digital steps.	`10-bit = 1024 steps (0-1023)`
ADC Reference Voltage	Defines the voltage range for conversion.	`AREF, AVCC, Internal 1.1V`
ADC Channels	Specifies which analog pin is used for input.	`ADC0, ADC1, ... ADC7`
Prescaler	Adjusts the ADC clock speed.	`ADCSRA= (1 << ADPS2);`
ADC Interrupt	Triggers an ISR when conversion is complete.	`ISR(ADC_vect) {}`
Free Running Mode	Enables continuous ADC conversion.	`ADCSRA= (1 << ADATE);`

Basic Rules for Using ADC in AVR C

Rule	Correct Example	Incorrect Example
Choose the correct ADC channel.	`ADMUX = (1 << MUX0);`	ADMUX = (1 << MUX3); (Wrong channel)
Set a proper prescaler for accuracy.	`ADCSRA = (1 << ADPS2);`	Using too high a clock speed reduces accuracy.
Enable ADC before starting conversion.	`ADCSRA = (1 << ADEN);`	ADCSRA &= ~(1 << ADEN); (Disables ADC)

Use polling or interrupts for data retrieval.	while (!(ADCSRA & (1 << ADIF)));	Reading ADC without checking completion.

Syntax Explanation

1. Enable ADC

What does it do? Activates the ADC module, allowing it to perform conversions.
Syntax:
```
ADCSRA |= (1 << ADEN);
```

Example:
```
ADCSRA |= (1 << ADEN); // Enable ADC
```

Example Explanation: This line enables the ADC in the microcontroller, allowing it to process analog signals. Without enabling the ADC, no conversions can take place.

2. Select Reference Voltage

What does it do? Configures the reference voltage used for ADC conversions. The reference voltage defines the highest voltage the ADC can measure.
Syntax:
```
ADMUX |= (1 << REFS0);
```

Example:
```
ADMUX |= (1 << REFS0); // Set AVCC as reference voltage
```

Example Explanation: This sets AVCC (5V) as the reference voltage, meaning the ADC will interpret 0V as 0 and 5V as 1023. The reference voltage must be selected correctly to match the sensor's voltage range.

3. Select ADC Channel

What does it do? Chooses the input channel from which the ADC reads data. The ADC module has multiple input channels corresponding to different analog pins.
Syntax:
```
ADMUX |= (1 << MUX0);
```

Example:
```
ADMUX |= (1 << MUX0); // Select ADC1 (Analog pin 1) as
input
```

Example Explanation: This selects ADC1 as the input channel, enabling the ADC to read voltage from pin A1. The correct channel must be chosen based on sensor wiring.

4. Start Conversion

What does it do? Begins an ADC conversion process, where the analog input is converted to a digital value.
Syntax:
```
ADCSRA |= (1 << ADSC);
```

Example:
```
ADCSRA |= (1 << ADSC); // Start ADC conversion
```

Example Explanation: This starts an ADC conversion; the result will be stored in the ADC register once completed. The conversion process must be completed before reading the value.

5. Wait for Conversion

What does it do? Ensures that the ADC conversion has finished before reading the result. If the conversion is not complete, reading the ADC value may result in incorrect data.
Syntax:
```
while (!(ADCSRA & (1 << ADIF))); // Wait until ADC
conversion is complete
```

Example Explanation: This loop waits until the ADC conversion is complete before proceeding to read the result, ensuring accurate data is retrieved.

6. Read ADC Value

What does it do? Retrieves the converted digital value from the ADC register.
Syntax:
```
int value = ADC;
```

Example:
```
int sensor_value = ADC; // Read converted ADC value
```

Example Explanation: This reads the ADC register and stores the converted digital value in the variable sensor_value. This value represents the voltage applied to the selected ADC channel, scaled according to the reference voltage.

Real-life Applications Project: Temperature Measurement Using ADC

Project Overview This project demonstrates how to use ADC in an AVR microcontroller to read temperature values from an LM35 sensor and display the results on an LCD. The LM35 sensor outputs an analog voltage proportional to the temperature, which the ADC converts into a digital value for processing.

Required Components

Component	Description
AVR Microcontroller (ATmega328P)	Processes ADC conversion.
LM35 Temperature Sensor	Outputs temperature as an analog voltage.
LCD Display	Displays the measured temperature.
Resistors (10kΩ, 330Ω)	Used for pull-down and limiting current.

Circuit Connection Table

Component	AVR Microcontroller Pin	Power Source	Purpose
LM35 Temperature Sensor	Analog Pin (e.g., ADC0)	5V	Reads temperature voltage.
LCD Display	Digital Output (e.g., PB2)	5V	Displays temperature.

Project Code

```c
#include <avr/io.h>
#include <util/delay.h>
#include <stdio.h>
#include <lcd.h> // Include LCD library

#define TEMP_SENSOR_PIN 0  // Using ADC0

void ADC_Init() {
    ADMUX = (1 << REFS0); // AVCC as reference voltage
    ADCSRA = (1 << ADEN) | (1 << ADPS2) | (1 << ADPS1);
// Enable ADC, set prescaler to 64
}

uint16_t Read_ADC(uint8_t channel) {
    ADMUX = (ADMUX & 0xF8) | channel; // Select ADC
channel
    ADCSRA |= (1 << ADSC); // Start conversion
    while (!(ADCSRA & (1 << ADIF))); // Wait for
conversion
    ADCSRA |= (1 << ADIF); // Clear interrupt flag
    return ADC;
}

int main() {
    ADC_Init();
```

```
    LCD_Init();
    char buffer[16];

    while (1) {
        uint16_t adc_value = Read_ADC(TEMP_SENSOR_PIN);
        float temperature = adc_value * 5.0 / 1024.0 *
100.0; // Convert ADC to temperature
        snprintf(buffer, 16, "Temp: %.2f C",
temperature);
        LCD_Clear();
        LCD_String(buffer);
        _delay_ms(1000);
    }
}
```

Expected Results

Once the code is uploaded, the microcontroller will continuously read the analog voltage from the LM35 sensor, convert it into a digital value using the ADC, and calculate the corresponding temperature in Celsius. The temperature readings will be displayed on the LCD and updated every second.

Chapter 32: Serial Communication

Serial communication is essential in embedded systems for data exchange between microcontrollers, sensors, and external devices. AVR microcontrollers support multiple serial communication protocols, including UART, SPI, and I2C. Each protocol has its unique advantages and use cases:

- **UART (Universal Asynchronous Receiver-Transmitter)**: Used for asynchronous communication over serial ports.
- **SPI (Serial Peripheral Interface)**: A fast, synchronous, full-duplex communication protocol used for high-speed data transfer.
- **I2C (Inter-Integrated Circuit)**: A synchronous, multi-master, multi-slave protocol that uses only two wires for communication.

Key Concepts of Serial Communication in AVR C

Concept	Description	Example
Baud Rate	Determines the speed of UART communication.	`9600, 115200 bps`
Full-Duplex (UART, SPI)	Allows simultaneous sending and receiving of data.	`USART_TxRx(data);`
Master-Slave (SPI, I2C)	Defines the role of devices in communication.	`SPI_MasterInit();`
Synchronous (SPI, I2C)	Data transfer occurs with a shared clock signal.	`TWI_Start();`
Asynchronous (UART)	Communication without a shared clock.	`USART_Init(9600);`

Basic Rules for Using Serial Communication in AVR C

Rule	Correct Example	Incorrect Example
Set the correct baud rate for UART.	UBRR0L = 103; (9600 baud @ 16MHz)	Setting an incorrect baud rate causes garbled data.
Configure SPI mode before communication.	`SPCR = (1 << MSTR);` (Master Mode)	Not setting master/slave mode leads to undefined behavior.
Use pull-up resistors for I2C communication.	SDA, SCL require 4.7kΩ pull-ups.	Missing pull-ups results in communication failure.
Enable interrupts for efficient data handling.	USART_RX_vect for UART reception.	Polling continuously wastes CPU cycles.
Properly handle start/stop conditions in I2C.	TWI_Start(); and TWI_Stop();	Incorrect sequence can hang the bus.

Syntax Explanation

UART Initialization

What does it do? Configures UART for serial communication by setting baud rate, frame format, and enabling TX/RX.
Syntax:
```
void USART_Init(unsigned int ubrr) {
    UBRR0L = (unsigned char)ubrr;
    UBRR0H = (unsigned char)(ubrr >> 8);
    UCSR0B = (1 << RXEN0) | (1 << TXEN0);
    UCSR0C = (1 << UCSZ01) | (1 << UCSZ00);
}
```

Example:
```
USART_Init(103); // Initialize UART at 9600 baud rate
(16MHz clock)
```
Example Explanation: This function sets up the UART communication at a baud rate of 9600, enabling both transmission and reception.

Sending Data via UART

What does it do? Transmits a single character over UART.
Syntax:
```
void USART_Transmit(char data) {
    while (!(UCSR0A & (1 << UDRE0))); // Wait for
buffer to be empty
    UDR0 = data;
}
```

Example:
```
USART_Transmit('A'); // Send character 'A'
```

Example Explanation: The function waits until the transmit buffer is empty before sending the character over UART.

Receiving Data via UART

What does it do? Receives a character from UART.
Syntax:
```
char USART_Receive() {
    while (!(UCSR0A & (1 << RXC0))); // Wait for data
reception
    return UDR0;
}
```

Example:
```
char receivedData = USART_Receive();
```

Example Explanation: This function waits until data is received and then returns the received character.

SPI Initialization (Master Mode)

What does it do? Configures the SPI interface in master mode.
Syntax:
```
void SPI_MasterInit() {
    SPCR = (1 << SPE) | (1 << MSTR) | (1 << SPR0);
}
```

Example:
```
SPI_MasterInit();
```

Example Explanation: This function enables SPI in master mode and sets the clock rate for communication.

SPI Data Transfer

What does it do? Transfers a byte of data over SPI.
Syntax:
```
char SPI_Transmit(char data) {
    SPDR = data;
    while (!(SPSR & (1 << SPIF)));
    return SPDR;
}
```

Example:
```
char receivedData = SPI_Transmit(0x55);
```

Example Explanation: The function sends a byte of data over SPI and returns the received byte from the slave device.

I2C Start Condition

What does it do? Generates a start condition for I2C communication.
Syntax:
```
void TWI_Start() {
    TWCR = (1 << TWSTA) | (1 << TWEN) | (1 << TWINT);
    while (!(TWCR & (1 << TWINT)));
}
```

Example:
```
TWI_Start();
```

Example Explanation: This function initiates I2C communication by generating a start condition.

Real-life Applications Project: Serial Communication Between Two Microcontrollers

Project Overview This project demonstrates serial communication between two AVR microcontrollers using UART. One microcontroller will act as a transmitter, while the other will act as a receiver. The transmitter will send a string message to the receiver, which will display it on an LCD.

Required Components

Component	Description
ATmega328P (Transmitter)	Sends data over UART.
ATmega328P (Receiver)	Receives and processes data.
USB-to-Serial Adapter	Connects the transmitter to a PC.
LCD Display	Displays the received message.
Resistors (10kΩ)	Used for pull-up where necessary.

Circuit Connection Table

Component	Transmitter Pin	Receiver Pin	Purpose
TX (Data Out)	PD1 (TX)	PD0 (RX)	Sends data from TX to RX
RX (Data In)	PD0 (RX)	PD1 (TX)	Receives data from TX
LCD Display	PB0-PB7	-	Displays received data

Project Code

Transmitter Code:

```c
#include <avr/io.h>
#include <util/delay.h>

void USART_Init(unsigned int ubrr) {
    UBRR0L = (unsigned char)ubrr;
    UBRR0H = (unsigned char)(ubrr >> 8);
    UCSR0B = (1 << TXEN0);  // Enable transmitter
    UCSR0C = (1 << UCSZ01) | (1 << UCSZ00);  // 8-bit data
}
```

```
void USART_Transmit(char data) {
    while (!(UCSR0A & (1 << UDRE0)));   // Wait for
buffer to be empty
    UDR0 = data;
}

void USART_SendString(char *str) {
    while (*str) {
        USART_Transmit(*str++);
    }
}

int main() {
    USART_Init(103);   // 9600 baud rate @16MHz
    while (1) {
        USART_SendString("Hello, AVR!");
        _delay_ms(1000);
    }
}
```

Receiver Code:

```
#include <avr/io.h>
#include <util/delay.h>
#include <lcd.h>   // Include LCD library

void USART_Init(unsigned int ubrr) {
    UBRR0L = (unsigned char)ubrr;
    UBRR0H = (unsigned char)(ubrr >> 8);
    UCSR0B = (1 << RXEN0);   // Enable receiver
    UCSR0C = (1 << UCSZ01) | (1 << UCSZ00);   // 8-bit
data
}

char USART_Receive() {
    while (!(UCSR0A & (1 << RXC0)));   // Wait for data
reception
```

```
        return UDR0;
}

void USART_ReceiveString(char *buffer) {
    char ch;
    int i = 0;
    while ((ch = USART_Receive()) != '�') {
        buffer[i++] = ch;
    }
    buffer[i] = '�';
}

int main() {
    char receivedData[20];
    USART_Init(103);   // 9600 baud rate @16MHz
    LCD_Init();
    while (1) {
        USART_ReceiveString(receivedData);
        LCD_Clear();
        LCD_String(receivedData);
        _delay_ms(1000);
    }
}
```

Expected Results

Once the code is uploaded, the transmitter microcontroller will continuously send the message **"Hello, AVR!"** over UART every second. The receiver microcontroller will capture this message and display it on an LCD screen. This demonstrates real-time serial communication using AVR microcontrollers.

Chapter 33: Watchdog Timer (WDT)

The Watchdog Timer (WDT) in AVR microcontrollers is a safety mechanism designed to reset the system in case of a software failure. It helps recover from crashes, infinite loops, or unexpected behavior by automatically resetting the microcontroller if it does not receive a reset signal within a predefined time interval.

This chapter explains how the WDT functions, its configuration, and its implementation in AVR-based applications.

Key Concepts of Watchdog Timer in AVR C

Concept	Description	Example
WDT Timeout	The time before the watchdog resets the MCU.	16ms to 8s (Varies by model)
WDT Enable	Activates the watchdog timer.	`WDTCSR = (1 << WDE);`
WDT Disable	Turns off the watchdog timer.	`WDTCSR = (1 << WDTOE)`
WDT Prescaler	Controls timeout duration.	`WDTCSR = (1 << WDP2);`
Reset Condition	Occurs when WDT times out.	System restarts automatically.

Basic Rules for Using WDT in AVR C

Rule	Correct Example	Incorrect Example
Enable WDT before setting prescaler.	`WDTCSR = (1 << WDE);`	Configuring prescaler before enabling WDT.
Always reset WDT in main loop.	`wdt_reset();` in the main loop.	Missing `wdt_reset();` leads to unwanted resets.
Use proper timeout settings.	`WDTCSR = (1 << WDP2);`	Using too short timeout may cause unnecessary resets.
Disable WDT if not needed.	`WDTCSR = (1 << WDTOE)`	Keeping WDT on unnecessarily consumes power.

Syntax Table

SL	Operation	Syntax/Example	Description
1	**Enable Watchdog Timer**	`` `WDTCSR = (1 << WDE);` ``	Activates the watchdog timer.
2	**Set Watchdog Timeout**	`= (1 << WDP2);`	Configures timeout duration.
3	**Reset Watchdog Timer**	`wdt_reset();`	Prevents an unwanted system reset.
4	**Disable Watchdog Timer**	`` `WDTCSR = (1 << WDTOE) ``	Turns off the watchdog timer.

Syntax Explanation

1. Enabling Watchdog Timer

What does it do? Activates the watchdog timer to monitor program execution. Once enabled, the WDT starts counting towards the preset timeout, and if the microcontroller fails to reset it within this time, the system automatically resets.
Syntax:
```
WDTCSR |= (1 << WDE);
```

Example:
```
void Enable_WDT() {
    WDTCSR |= (1 << WDE);  // Enable Watchdog Timer
}
```

Example Explanation: This function enables the watchdog timer, initiating its countdown. If `wdt_reset();` is not called within the configured timeout period, the microcontroller will reset.

2. Setting Watchdog Timeout

What does it do? Configures the watchdog timer prescaler to determine how long before it resets the system.
Syntax:
```
WDTCSR |= (1 << WDP2);
```

Example:
```
void Set_WDT_Timeout() {
    WDTCSR |= (1 << WDP2);   // Set timeout to
approximately 250ms
}
```

Example Explanation: This function sets the watchdog timer timeout to around 250ms. If `wdt_reset();` is not called within this duration, the system will reset automatically.

3. Resetting the Watchdog Timer

What does it do? Resets the watchdog timer to prevent an unnecessary system reset.
Syntax:
```
wdt_reset();
```

Example:
```
void main() {
    while (1) {
        wdt_reset();   // Prevent watchdog reset
        // Other tasks
    }
}
```

Example Explanation: Calling `wdt_reset();` in the main loop ensures that the watchdog timer does not expire while the system is running correctly. If this function is omitted, the system will eventually reset once the timeout occurs.

4. Disabling Watchdog Timer

What does it do? Turns off the watchdog timer to prevent automatic system resets.
Syntax:
```
WDTCSR = (1 << WDTOE) | (1 << WDE);
```

Example:
```
void Disable_WDT() {
    WDTCSR = (1 << WDTOE) | (1 << WDE);   // Disable
Watchdog Timer
}
```

Example Explanation: This function disables the watchdog timer to stop it from resetting the system. This is useful when debugging or when the watchdog is no longer needed in the program execution.

Real-life Applications Project: Automatic System Recovery with WDT

Project Overview This project demonstrates how the watchdog timer can help recover an AVR microcontroller from a system crash. If the main program fails to execute properly, the WDT will reset the system, ensuring continuous operation.

Required Components

Component	Description
AVR Microcontroller	Main processing unit.
LED	Indicates normal operation.
Push Button	Simulates a system crash.
Resistor (330Ω)	Limits current for LED operation.

Circuit Connection Table

Component	AVR Microcontroller Pin	Power Source	Purpose
LED	Digital Output (e.g., PB0)	5V	Indicates normal operation.
Button	Digital Input (e.g., PD2)	5V	Simulates software crash.

Project Code

```
#include <avr/io.h>
#include <avr/wdt.h>
#include <util/delay.h>

void WDT_Init() {
```

```
    WDTCSR |= (1 << WDE) | (1 << WDP2);   // Enable WDT
with 250ms timeout
}

void WDT_Reset() {
    wdt_reset();  // Reset watchdog timer
}

int main() {
    DDRB |= (1 << PB0);   // Set PB0 as output (LED)
    WDT_Init();   // Enable watchdog timer
    while (1) {
        if (PIND & (1 << PD2)) {   // If button is
pressed (simulate crash)
            while (1);   // Infinite loop (system crash)
        }
        PORTB ^= (1 << PB0);   // Toggle LED
        _delay_ms(100);
        WDT_Reset();   // Prevent reset if working
normally
    }
}
```

Expected Results

When the system operates normally, the LED blinks continuously, and the watchdog timer is reset in each loop. If the push button is pressed, the system enters an infinite loop (crash). The watchdog timer detects this and automatically resets the microcontroller, restoring normal operation.

Chapter 34: Configuring GPIO Pins

General-Purpose Input/Output (GPIO) pins in AVR microcontrollers allow interaction with external devices such as LEDs, switches, sensors, and motors. Configuring GPIO pins correctly is crucial for proper digital communication and system functionality.

This chapter covers the configuration and usage of GPIO pins, including input/output modes, pull-up resistors, and bitwise operations for efficient control.

Key Concepts of GPIO in AVR C

Concept	Description	Example	
DDR Register	Configures the pin as input or output.	`DDRB	= (1 << PB0);`
PORT Register	Controls output states (HIGH/LOW).	`PORTB	= (1 << PB0);`
PIN Register	Reads the current state of an input pin.	if (PINB & (1 << PB0))	
Pull-up Resistors	Enables internal pull-ups for input pins.	`PORTB	= (1 << PB0);`
Bitwise Operations	Allows direct register manipulation.	PORTB ^= (1 << PB0);	

Basic Rules for Using GPIO in AVR C

Rule	Correct Example	Incorrect Example
Always configure DDR before using GPIO.	`DDRB = (1 << PB0);`	Using PORT without setting DDR.
Use pull-ups for input buttons.	`PORTB = (1 << PB0);`	Floating inputs cause unpredictable behavior.
Toggle bits using XOR for efficiency.	PORTB ^= (1 << PB0);	Using if-else for toggling is inefficient.
Use PIN register for reading input.	if (PINB & (1 << PB0)) {}	Reading PORT instead of PIN.

Syntax Explanation

1. Configuring a Pin as Output

What does it do? This operation sets a specific pin as an output so
that the microcontroller can send signals to external devices like
LEDs, buzzers, or motors.
Syntax:
```
DDRB |= (1 << PB0);
```

Example:
```
void Configure_Output() {
    DDRB |= (1 << PB0);   // Set PB0 as an output pin
}
```

Example Explanation: Setting the DDRB register with a bitwise OR
operation ensures that the PB0 pin is configured as an output. This
enables the microcontroller to drive connected devices by sending
HIGH (5V) or LOW (0V) signals.

2. Setting an Output HIGH or LOW

What does it do? Controls the state of an output pin. Setting the pin
HIGH means applying a voltage (5V), while setting it LOW means
grounding it (0V).
Syntax:
```
PORTB |= (1 << PB0);   // Set PB0 HIGH
PORTB &= ~(1 << PB0);   // Set PB0 LOW
```

Example:
```
void Set_Output_High() {
    PORTB |= (1 << PB0);   // Turn PB0 HIGH
}

void Set_Output_Low() {
    PORTB &= ~(1 << PB0);   // Turn PB0 LOW
}
```

Example Explanation: By manipulating the PORTB register using bitwise operations, we can turn an output pin ON or OFF. The bitwise OR (|=) sets the pin, while bitwise AND with negation (&= ~) clears it.

3. Configuring a Pin as Input

What does it do? Sets a pin as an input so that it can receive signals from buttons, sensors, or other devices.
Syntax:
```
DDRB &= ~(1 << PB0);
```

Example:
```
void Configure_Input() {
    DDRB &= ~(1 << PB0);   // Set PB0 as input
}
```

Example Explanation: Clearing the corresponding bit in the DDRB register ensures that the PB0 pin operates in input mode. This allows external signals to be read by the microcontroller.

4. Enabling an Internal Pull-up Resistor

What does it do? Activates the internal pull-up resistor on an input pin to ensure a defined logic level when no external signal is applied.
Syntax:
```
PORTB |= (1 << PB0);
```

Example:
```
void Enable_Pullup() {
    PORTB |= (1 << PB0);   // Enable internal pull-up
resistor
}
```

Example Explanation: When an input pin is left floating, it may produce unpredictable results. Enabling the internal pull-up resistor ensures the pin reads HIGH when no signal is applied.

5. Reading an Input Pin

What does it do? Reads the current logic level of an input pin to determine if it is HIGH or LOW.

Syntax:
```
if (PINB & (1 << PB0)) {}
```

Example:
```
int Read_Input() {
    return (PINB & (1 << PB0)) ? 1 : 0;   // Return HIGH
or LOW
}
```

Example Explanation: Using the `PINB` register, we can check whether an input pin is receiving a HIGH (1) or LOW (0) signal.

6. Toggling an Output Pin

What does it do? Flips the state of an output pin, switching between HIGH and LOW.

Syntax:
```
PORTB ^= (1 << PB0);
```

Example:
```
void Toggle_Output() {
    PORTB ^= (1 << PB0);   // Toggle PB0 state
}
```

Example Explanation: The XOR (^=) operation inverts the pin state efficiently without needing conditional statements.

Real-life Applications Project: LED Blinking with Button Control

Project Overview This project demonstrates how to control an LED using a button press. The button input is read using GPIO, and the LED toggles its state whenever the button is pressed.

Required Components

Component	Description
AVR Microcontroller	The main processing unit.
LED	Indicates button press.
Push Button	Used as an input control.
Resistor (10kΩ, 330Ω)	Required for pull-up and LED operation.

Circuit Connection Table

Component	AVR Microcontroller Pin	Power Source	Purpose
LED	PB0	5V	Lights up on press.
Button	PD2	5V	Reads user input.

Project Code

```c
#include <avr/io.h>
#include <util/delay.h>
#define LED_PIN PB0
#define BUTTON_PIN PD2
void GPIO_Init() {
    DDRB |= (1 << LED_PIN);  // Set LED pin as output
    DDRD &= ~(1 << BUTTON_PIN);  // Set button pin as input
    PORTD |= (1 << BUTTON_PIN);  // Enable pull-up resistor for button
}
int main() {
    GPIO_Init();
    while (1) {
        if (!(PIND & (1 << BUTTON_PIN))) {  // Check if button is pressed
            PORTB ^= (1 << LED_PIN);  // Toggle LED
            _delay_ms(300);  // Debounce delay
        }
    }
}
```

Chapter 35: Using Internal and External Pull-up Resistors

Pull-up resistors are essential components in digital circuits that ensure a default HIGH state for input pins. AVR microcontrollers support both **internal pull-up resistors** (activated via software) and **external pull-up resistors** (physically connected). These resistors prevent floating input states, reduce noise, and improve signal stability.

This chapter covers the configuration, use cases, and practical implementation of pull-up resistors in AVR microcontrollers.

Key Concepts of Pull-up Resistors in AVR C

Concept	Description	Example	
Internal Pull-up	Enabled in software, avoids floating inputs.	`PORTB	= (1 << PB0);`
External Pull-up	Physically connected resistor to VCC.	10kΩ between VCC & PB0	
Floating Input	Undefined state when no signal is applied.	PINB fluctuating values	
Pull-down Resistor	Opposite of pull-up, holds pin LOW by default.	10kΩ between GND & PB0	

Basic Rules for Using Pull-up Resistors in AVR C

Rule	Correct Example	Incorrect Example
Always enable pull-ups for open switches.	`PORTB = (1 << PB0);`	Leaving input pin floating.
Use a 10kΩ resistor for external pull-ups.	Connecting 10kΩ between VCC & PB0.	Using a very low resistance like 100Ω.
Disable internal pull-ups if using external.	PORTB &= ~(1 << PB0);	Enabling both internal and external.
Read the PIN register, not PORT, for input.	if (PINB & (1 << PB0)) {}	if (PORTB & (1 << PB0)) {}

Syntax Table

SL	Operation	Syntax/Example	Description
1	**Enable Internal Pull-up**	`` `PORTB = (1 << PB0);` ``	Sets internal pull-up to keep input HIGH.
2	**Disable Internal Pull-up**	`PORTB &= ~(1 << PB0);`	Disables internal pull-up resistor.
3	**Configure External Pull-up**	`10kΩ resistor between VCC & PB0`	Uses an external resistor to pull HIGH.
4	**Read Input with Pull-up**	`if (PINB & (1 << PB0)) {}`	Checks if input is HIGH or LOW.

Syntax Explanation

1. Enabling Internal Pull-up Resistor

What does it do? Activates the internal pull-up resistor on an input pin to maintain a HIGH state when no external signal is applied. This ensures the pin does not remain in a floating state, which could cause unpredictable behavior.

Syntax:
```
PORTB |= (1 << PB0);
```

Example:
```
void Enable_Internal_Pullup() {
    DDRB &= ~(1 << PB0);   // Set PB0 as input
    PORTB |= (1 << PB0);   // Enable internal pull-up
resistor
}
```

Example Explanation: This function ensures that PB0 is set as an input and enables the internal pull-up resistor to keep the pin in a stable HIGH state when no external signal is applied.

2. Disabling Internal Pull-up Resistor

What does it do? Turns off the internal pull-up resistor when using external pull-ups or when an open-drain configuration is needed.

Disabling the pull-up allows external hardware to control the state of the pin.

Syntax:
```
PORTB &= ~(1 << PB0);
```

Example:
```
void Disable_Internal_Pullup() {
    PORTB &= ~(1 << PB0);   // Disable internal pull-up
}
```

Example Explanation: This function clears the pull-up resistor on PB0, allowing an external circuit to determine the pin state.

3. Using an External Pull-up Resistor

What does it do? Connects an external pull-up resistor between the input pin and VCC to maintain a HIGH default state. This is commonly used in I2C communication or when driving switches.

Circuit Example:
```
VCC (5V)
 |
10kΩ Resistor
 |
PB0 (Input pin)
 |
Switch (to Ground)
 |
GND
```

Example:
```
void Configure_External_Pullup() {
    DDRB &= ~(1 << PB0);   // Set PB0 as input
    PORTB &= ~(1 << PB0); // Ensure internal pull-up is
disabled
}
```
Example Explanation: This function configures PB0 as an input and ensures the internal pull-up is disabled so that an external pull-up resistor can be used instead.

4. Reading an Input with Pull-up Resistor

What does it do? Reads the state of an input pin configured with a pull-up resistor. This allows detecting button presses or other signals.

Syntax:
```
if (PINB & (1 << PB0)) {}
```

Example:
```
int Read_Input() {
    return (PINB & (1 << PB0)) ? 1 : 0;  // Return HIGH
or LOW
}
```

Example Explanation: This function reads the state of PB0 and returns either HIGH (1) if the pin is not pulled LOW, or LOW (0) if the pin is grounded (e.g., by a button press).

Real-life Applications Project: Button Press Detection with Pull-up Resistor

Project Overview This project demonstrates how to read button input using a pull-up resistor. The button is normally HIGH due to the pull-up and goes LOW when pressed. This method ensures stable input readings without unpredictable fluctuations.

Required Components

Component	Description
AVR Microcontroller	The main processing unit.
Push Button	Provides user input.
Resistor (10kΩ)	Ensures a stable HIGH signal.
LED (Optional)	Indicator for button press.

Circuit Connection Table

Component	AVR Microcontroller Pin	Power Source	Purpose
Button	PD2	5V via 10kΩ	Detects button press.

LED (Optional)	PB0	5V	Turns ON when button is pressed.

Project Code

```c
#include <avr/io.h>
#include <util/delay.h>
#define BUTTON_PIN PD2
#define LED_PIN PB0
void GPIO_Init() {
    DDRD &= ~(1 << BUTTON_PIN);  // Set button pin as input
    PORTD |= (1 << BUTTON_PIN);  // Enable internal pull-up resistor
    DDRB |= (1 << LED_PIN);  // Set LED pin as output
}
int main() {
    GPIO_Init();
    while (1) {
        if (!(PIND & (1 << BUTTON_PIN))) {  // Check if button is pressed
            PORTB |= (1 << LED_PIN);  // Turn ON LED
            _delay_ms(300);  // Debounce delay
        } else {
            PORTB &= ~(1 << LED_PIN);  // Turn OFF LED when button is released
        }
    }
}
```

Expected Results

- When the button is not pressed, the input pin remains HIGH due to the pull-up resistor.
- When the button is pressed, the pin is pulled LOW, and the microcontroller detects the change.
- If an LED is connected, it turns ON when the button is pressed and OFF when released.
- The pull-up resistor prevents floating input values, ensuring reliable button detection.

Chapter 36: Generating PWM Signals

Pulse Width Modulation (PWM) is a technique used to generate analog-like signals using digital outputs. In AVR microcontrollers, PWM is commonly used for motor control, LED brightness control, and signal generation. The AVR's built-in timers support PWM generation with different modes, including **Fast PWM** and **Phase Correct PWM**.

This chapter covers the configuration and usage of PWM signals in AVR microcontrollers using registers and timer modules.

Key Concepts of PWM in AVR C

Concept	Description	Example
Duty Cycle	Percentage of time the signal is HIGH in a cycle.	`50% duty cycle = 128/255`
PWM Frequency	The speed at which PWM pulses are generated.	`1kHz, 10kHz, etc.`
Fast PWM Mode	Provides higher frequency with faster transitions.	`TCCR0A = (1 << WGM00);`
Phase Correct PWM	Produces symmetric signals around the center.	`TCCR0A = (1 << WGM01);`
OCR (Output Compare Register)	Determines the duty cycle.	`OCR0A = 128;`

Basic Rules for Using PWM in AVR C

Rule	Correct Example	Incorrect Example
Select the correct PWM mode.	`TCCR0A = (1 << WGM00);`	Using the wrong mode for application.
Set the prescaler for accurate timing.	`TCCR0B = (1 << CS01);`	Using an incorrect prescaler value.
Use OCR register to adjust duty cycle.	`OCR0A = 128;`	Modifying TCCR register instead.
Ensure output pin is set as output.	`DDRB = (1 << PB1);`	Leaving pin as input.

Syntax Explanation

1. Configuring Fast PWM Mode

What does it do? Enables Fast PWM mode on Timer0, which generates a high-frequency PWM signal suitable for motor control and LED dimming. Fast PWM mode rapidly switches the output signal, allowing smooth transitions in brightness or speed.
Syntax:
```
TCCR0A |= (1 << WGM00) | (1 << WGM01);
```

Example:
```
void Configure_PWM() {
    TCCR0A |= (1 << WGM00) | (1 << WGM01);   // Enable
Fast PWM Mode
}
```

Example Explanation: Fast PWM mode is ideal for applications requiring a high-speed signal with quick ON/OFF transitions, such as motor control and LED dimming. The combination of WGM00 and WGM01 configures the timer to generate the PWM waveform.

2. Setting PWM Duty Cycle

What does it do? Defines how long the PWM signal stays HIGH in one cycle, adjusting brightness or speed. The duty cycle controls the effective voltage delivered to the connected component.
Syntax:
```
OCR0A = 128;
```
Example:
```
void Set_Duty_Cycle(uint8_t duty) {
    OCR0A = duty;   // Set duty cycle (0-255)
}
```
Example Explanation: The OCR0A register determines the duty cycle percentage of the PWM signal. A value of 128 (out of 255) results in a 50% duty cycle, meaning the signal stays HIGH for half the time and LOW for the other half. Adjusting this value changes the intensity of an LED or the speed of a motor.

3. Setting the Prescaler

What does it do? Defines the speed of the PWM signal by setting a timer prescaler value, which scales the system clock frequency to produce the desired PWM frequency.

Syntax:
```
TCCR0B |= (1 << CS01);
```

Example:
```
void Set_Prescaler() {
    TCCR0B |= (1 << CS01);   // Set prescaler to 8
}
```

Example Explanation: The prescaler determines how quickly the PWM cycle repeats. A lower prescaler results in a faster PWM frequency, while a higher prescaler slows it down. In this example, the prescaler is set to 8, meaning the timer increments every 8 clock cycles.

4. Configuring PWM Output Pin

What does it do? Sets the correct pin as an output for the PWM signal to ensure the generated waveform is properly transmitted to connected devices.

Syntax:
```
DDRB |= (1 << PB1);
```

Example:
```
void Set_PWM_Output() {
    DDRB |= (1 << PB1);   // Configure PB1 as PWM output
}
```

Example Explanation: PWM requires a designated output pin to generate the signal. Setting PB1 as an output ensures that the waveform is delivered to external components such as LEDs or motors.

Real-life Applications Project: LED Brightness Control Using PWM

Project Overview This project demonstrates how to use PWM to control LED brightness. By varying the duty cycle, the LED appears dimmer or brighter.

Required Components

Component	Description
AVR Microcontroller	The main processing unit.
LED	Visual indicator of PWM effect.
Resistor (330Ω)	Limits LED current.

Circuit Connection Table

Component	AVR Microcontroller Pin	Power Source	Purpose
LED	PB1 (OC0A)	5V	Adjusts brightness.
Resistor	In series with LED	5V	Protects LED.

Project Code

```c
#include <avr/io.h>
#include <util/delay.h>

#define LED_PIN PB1

void PWM_Init() {
    DDRB |= (1 << LED_PIN);   // Set LED pin as output
    TCCR0A |= (1 << WGM00) | (1 << WGM01);   // Fast PWM Mode
    TCCR0A |= (1 << COM0A1);   // Non-inverting mode
    TCCR0B |= (1 << CS01);   // Prescaler set to 8
}

void Set_Brightness(uint8_t brightness) {
    OCR0A = brightness;   // Adjust duty cycle
}
```

```
int main() {
    PWM_Init();
    while (1) {
        for (uint8_t i = 0; i < 255; i++) {
            Set_Brightness(i);   // Increase brightness
            _delay_ms(10);
        }
        for (uint8_t i = 255; i > 0; i--) {
            Set_Brightness(i);   // Decrease brightness
            _delay_ms(10);
        }
    }
}
```

Expected Results

- The LED brightness gradually increases and decreases in a smooth cycle.
- The duty cycle variation directly controls the LED's brightness level.
- This technique can be expanded to control motors, fans, and audio signals.

Chapter 37: Working with Interrupts

Interrupts in AVR microcontrollers allow efficient handling of external and internal events without constant polling. An interrupt temporarily halts the main program execution to execute an Interrupt Service Routine (ISR), improving system responsiveness and power efficiency.

This chapter explores how to configure and use external and timer-based interrupts in AVR microcontrollers.

Key Concepts of Interrupts in AVR C

Concept	Description	Example
ISR (Interrupt Service Routine)	A special function executed when an interrupt occurs.	`ISR(INT0_vect) {}`
External Interrupts	Triggered by external events (e.g., button press).	`EIMSK
Timer Interrupts	Generated by internal timers for periodic tasks.	`TIMSK0
Global Interrupt Enable	Enables all configured interrupts.	`sei();`
Global Interrupt Disable	Disables all interrupts.	`cli();`

Basic Rules for Using Interrupts in AVR C

Rule	Correct Example	Incorrect Example
Enable global interrupts before use.	`sei();`	Not enabling interrupts before use.
Define ISR correctly with vector name.	`ISR(INT0_vect) {}`	Using a regular function instead.
Use volatile variables for shared data.	`volatile int count;`	Not declaring shared variables as volatile.
Avoid long execution times in ISR.	Keep ISR short and efficient.	Performing time-consuming tasks in ISR.

Syntax Table

SL	Operation	Syntax/Example	Description
1	Enable Global Interrupts	`sei();`	Allows all configured interrupts.
2	Disable Global Interrupts	`cli();`	Stops all interrupts.
3	Enable External Interrupt	`EIMSK	= (1 << INT0);`
4	Configure Interrupt Mode	`EICRA	= (1 << ISC01);`
5	Define ISR Function	`ISR(INT0_vect) {}`	Defines the routine for INT0.
6	Enable Timer Overflow Int.	`TIMSK0	= (1 << TOIE0);`

Syntax Explanation

1. Enabling Global Interrupts

What does it do? Activates all enabled interrupts in the microcontroller. This allows any configured interrupt to trigger its corresponding ISR.
Syntax:
```
sei();
```

Example:
```
void Enable_Interrupts() {
    sei();  // Enable global interrupts
}
```

Example Explanation: The `sei();` function enables global interrupts so that any pre-configured external or timer interrupt can function properly. Without calling `sei();`, no interrupts will execute.

2. Configuring External Interrupts

What does it do? Enables an external interrupt (e.g., button press detection) on INT0. This allows a button press or other external signal to trigger an ISR without constant polling.
Syntax:
```
EIMSK |= (1 << INT0);
EICRA |= (1 << ISC01);   // Falling edge trigger
```

Example:
```
void Configure_External_Interrupt() {
    EICRA |= (1 << ISC01);   // Falling edge trigger
    EIMSK |= (1 << INT0);    // Enable INT0 interrupt
}
```

Example Explanation: This function configures INT0 to trigger on a falling edge, which happens when a button is pressed. The interrupt will execute the associated ISR when INT0 detects this event.

3. Defining an ISR

What does it do? Executes a function automatically when the associated interrupt occurs, handling real-time events such as button presses or sensor triggers.
Syntax:
```
ISR(INT0_vect) {
    // Code to execute when INT0 occurs
}
```

Example:
```
ISR(INT0_vect) {
    PORTB ^= (1 << PB0);   // Toggle LED state
}
```

Example Explanation: When the external interrupt INT0 is triggered, the ISR toggles an LED connected to PB0. The ISR should be kept short and efficient to avoid delaying other tasks.

4. Configuring Timer Interrupts

What does it do? Enables a timer overflow interrupt for periodic execution, which can be used for time-based tasks like LED blinking or event scheduling.

Syntax:
```
TIMSK0 |= (1 << TOIE0);
```

Example:
```
void Configure_Timer_Interrupt() {
    TCCR0B |= (1 << CS01);  // Prescaler set to 8
    TIMSK0 |= (1 << TOIE0); // Enable Timer0 overflow
interrupt
}


ISR(TIMER0_OVF_vect) {
    PORTB ^= (1 << PB0);  // Toggle LED every timer
overflow
}
```

Example Explanation: This function sets up Timer0 to trigger an interrupt whenever it overflows, which happens at a fixed interval. The ISR toggles an LED each time this event occurs, demonstrating a simple timer-based periodic task.

Real-life Applications Project: Button-Triggered LED Toggle Using Interrupts

Project Overview This project demonstrates the use of an external interrupt to toggle an LED state when a button is pressed.

Required Components

Component	Description
AVR Microcontroller	The main processing unit.
Push Button	Used to trigger an interrupt.
LED	Toggles ON/OFF upon interrupt.
Resistor (10kΩ)	Pull-up resistor for the button.

Circuit Connection Table

Component	AVR Microcontroller Pin	Power Source	Purpose
LED	PB0	5V	Indicator for interrupt.
Button	INT0 (PD2)	5V	External interrupt trigger.

Project Code

```c
#include <avr/io.h>
#include <avr/interrupt.h>

#define LED_PIN PB0

void Configure_External_Interrupt() {
    DDRB |= (1 << LED_PIN);   // Set LED pin as output
    EICRA |= (1 << ISC01);    // Falling edge trigger
    EIMSK |= (1 << INT0);     // Enable INT0 interrupt
    sei();  // Enable global interrupts
}

ISR(INT0_vect) {
    PORTB ^= (1 << LED_PIN);  // Toggle LED state
}

int main() {
    Configure_External_Interrupt();
    while (1) {
        // Main loop remains idle, ISR handles the
event
    }
}
```

Expected Results

- Pressing the button triggers an external interrupt that toggles an LED.
- The LED state remains unchanged until another button press occurs.
- Interrupts provide a more efficient way to handle input without constant polling.

Chapter 38: External Interrupts and Pin Change Interrupts

External and pin change interrupts in AVR microcontrollers provide a way to respond to real-world events without constantly polling input pins. **External interrupts** occur on dedicated INTx pins, while **pin change interrupts** can trigger on any GPIO pin.

This chapter covers configuring and handling both types of interrupts, along with practical applications.

Key Concepts of External and Pin Change Interrupts in AVR C

Concept	Description	Example
External Interrupts (INTx)	Dedicated interrupt pins triggered by events.	ISR(INT0_vect) {}
Pin Change Interrupts (PCINTx)	Detects state changes on any GPIO pin.	ISR(PCINT0_vect) {}
Interrupt Sense Control	Defines trigger conditions (falling, rising, etc.).	`EICRA = (1 << ISC01);`
Global Interrupt Enable	Allows interrupts to be processed.	sei();
Interrupt Mask Register	Enables specific interrupts.	`PCMSK0 = (1 << PCINT0);`

Basic Rules for Using External and Pin Change Interrupts in AVR C

Rule	Correct Example	Incorrect Example
Enable global interrupts before use.	`sei();`	Not enabling interrupts before use.
Define ISR correctly with the vector name.	`ISR(INT0_vect) {}`	Using a regular function instead.
Select the correct trigger mode.	`` `EICRA = (1 << ISC01);` ``	Using the wrong sense control.
Avoid long execution times in ISR.	Keep ISR short and efficient.	Performing time-consuming tasks in ISR.

Syntax Table

SL	Operation	Syntax/Example	Description
1	Enable Global Interrupts	`sei();`	Allows all configured interrupts.
2	Enable External Interrupt (INT0)	`` `EIMSK = (1 << INT0);` ``	Enables external interrupt INT0.
3	Configure Interrupt Trigger Mode	`` `EICRA = (1 << ISC01);` ``	Sets INT0 for falling edge trigger.
4	Define ISR Function	`ISR(INT0_vect) {}`	Defines the routine for INT0.
5	Enable Pin Change Interrupt	`` `PCMSK0 = (1 << PCINT0);` ``	Enables pin change interrupt on PCINT0.
6	Define Pin Change ISR	`ISR(PCINT0_vect) {}`	Defines the ISR for pin change.

Syntax Explanation

1. Enabling Global Interrupts

What does it do? Activates all configured interrupts, allowing them to trigger their corresponding ISR functions.
Syntax:
```
sei();
```

Example:
```
void Enable_Interrupts() {
    sei();  // Enable global interrupts
}
```

Example Explanation: The `sei();` function ensures the microcontroller can process interrupts when triggered. Without enabling global interrupts, no ISR will execute.

2. Configuring External Interrupts (INT0)

What does it do? Configures an external interrupt on INT0 to trigger when a falling edge occurs (e.g., button press). This eliminates the need for constant polling.
Syntax:
```
EIMSK |= (1 << INT0);
EICRA |= (1 << ISC01);
```

Example:
```
void Configure_External_Interrupt() {
    EICRA |= (1 << ISC01);  // Falling edge trigger
    EIMSK |= (1 << INT0);   // Enable INT0 interrupt
}
```

Example Explanation: This function sets up an external interrupt on INT0 that triggers when a signal transitions from HIGH to LOW. It is useful for handling input events like button presses.

3. Defining an ISR for INT0

What does it do? Executes when INT0 is triggered by an external event, such as a button press.
Syntax:
```
ISR(INT0_vect) {
    // Code to execute when INT0 occurs
}
```

Example:
```
ISR(INT0_vect) {
    PORTB ^= (1 << PB0);   // Toggle LED state
}
```

Example Explanation: When INT0 is triggered, this ISR toggles an LED connected to PB0, showing the response to an external event.

4. Configuring Pin Change Interrupts (PCINTx)

What does it do? Enables pin change interrupts on PCINT0, allowing any change in the pin state to trigger an ISR. This is useful for detecting button presses or sensor changes on general-purpose input pins.
Syntax:
```
PCICR |= (1 << PCIE0);
PCMSK0 |= (1 << PCINT0);
```

Example:
```
void Configure_Pin_Change_Interrupt() {
    PCICR |= (1 << PCIE0);   // Enable Pin Change
Interrupt
    PCMSK0 |= (1 << PCINT0); // Enable interrupt for
PCINT0
}
```
Example Explanation: This function configures PCINT0 so that any state change on the corresponding pin triggers an ISR. Unlike external interrupts, pin change interrupts can monitor multiple pins at once.

5. Defining an ISR for Pin Change Interrupt

What does it do? Executes when the state of the PCINT0 pin changes, allowing real-time response to input events.
Syntax:
```
ISR(PCINT0_vect) {
    // Code to execute on pin change
}
```

Example:
```
ISR(PCINT0_vect) {
    PORTB ^= (1 << PB0);   // Toggle LED on pin change
}
```

Example Explanation: Any state change on PCINT0 triggers this ISR, toggling an LED as a visual indication of the event.
Real-life Applications Project: Button-Triggered LED Toggle Using External and Pin Change Interrupts
Project Overview This project demonstrates how to use both external and pin change interrupts to toggle an LED when a button is pressed. The project uses an external interrupt for a dedicated interrupt pin and a pin change interrupt for a general GPIO pin.
Required Components

Component	Description
AVR Microcontroller	The main processing unit.
Push Button	Used to trigger an interrupt.
LED	Toggles ON/OFF upon interrupt.
Resistor (10kΩ)	Pull-up resistor for the button.

Circuit Connection Table

Component	AVR Microcontroller Pin	Power Source	Purpose
LED	PB0	5V	Indicator for interrupt.
Button	INT0 (PD2)	5V	External interrupt trigger.
Button	PCINT0 (PB0)	5V	Pin change interrupt trigger.

Project Code

```c
#include <avr/io.h>
#include <avr/interrupt.h>

#define LED_PIN PB0

void Configure_External_Interrupt() {
    DDRB |= (1 << LED_PIN);  // Set LED pin as output
    EICRA |= (1 << ISC01);   // Falling edge trigger
    EIMSK |= (1 << INT0);    // Enable INT0 interrupt
}

void Configure_Pin_Change_Interrupt() {
    PCICR |= (1 << PCIE0);   // Enable Pin Change
Interrupt
    PCMSK0 |= (1 << PCINT0); // Enable PCINT0
}

ISR(INT0_vect) {
    PORTB ^= (1 << LED_PIN);  // Toggle LED state via
external interrupt
}

ISR(PCINT0_vect) {
    PORTB ^= (1 << LED_PIN);  // Toggle LED state via
pin change interrupt
}
int main() {
    Configure_External_Interrupt();
    Configure_Pin_Change_Interrupt();
    sei();   // Enable global interrupts
    while (1) {
        // Main loop remains idle, interrupts handle
events
    }
}
```

Chapter 39: Interfacing Temperature Sensors

Temperature sensors are essential for monitoring environmental conditions, industrial applications, and home automation. AVR microcontrollers can interface with analog and digital temperature sensors like **LM35**, **DHT11**, and **DS18B20** to measure temperature accurately.

This chapter covers how to connect, configure, and read temperature values from different types of sensors using AVR microcontrollers.

Key Concepts of Temperature Sensor Interfacing in AVR C

Concept	Description	Example
Analog Temperature Sensor	Outputs voltage proportional to temperature.	LM35
Digital Temperature Sensor	Communicates via serial protocols like I2C, SPI, or 1-Wire.	DHT11, DS18B20
ADC (Analog-to-Digital Conversion)	Converts sensor's analog output to a digital value.	ADC_Read();
Sensor Calibration	Adjusts raw sensor data for accuracy.	calibrated_temp = raw_temp + offset;
Resolution	Determines the smallest temperature change detectable.	DS18B20 (9-bit to 12-bit)

Basic Rules for Using Temperature Sensors in AVR C

Rule	Correct Example	Incorrect Example
Select the correct ADC reference voltage.	`ADMUX = (1 << REFS0);`	Using an unstable reference voltage.
Use appropriate delay for digital sensors.	_delay_ms(1000);	Reading data too frequently.

Convert raw ADC value to temperature.	temp = (adc_value * 5.0) / 1024.0;	Using incorrect conversion formula.
Check data integrity for digital sensors.	if (checksum_corre ct)	Using invalid data without verification.

Syntax Table

S L	Operation	Syntax/Example	Description
1	Initialize ADC for LM35	`ADMUX = (1 << REFS0);`	Selects AVCC as reference voltage.
2	Read ADC Value	adc_value = ADC_Read();	Reads the analog output from LM35.
3	Convert ADC to Temperature	temp = (adc_value * 5.0) / 1024.0 * 100;	Converts ADC reading to Celsius.
4	Read Data from DHT11	DHT11_Read();	Reads temperature and humidity.
5	Read Temperature from DS18B20	DS18B20_Read();	Reads digital temperature data over 1-Wire.

Syntax Explanation

1. Initializing ADC for LM35

What does it do? Configures the ADC (Analog-to-Digital Converter) to read analog values from the LM35 temperature sensor. The ADC converts the sensor's voltage output into a digital value that can be processed by the microcontroller.

Syntax:

ADMUX |= (1 << REFS0);

Example:

```
void ADC_Init() {
    ADMUX |= (1 << REFS0);  // Set AVCC as reference
voltage
    ADCSRA |= (1 << ADEN) | (1 << ADPS2);  // Enable
ADC with prescaler
}
```

Example Explanation: The ADC is initialized with AVCC as the reference voltage to ensure consistent readings. The prescaler is set to control the conversion speed, balancing accuracy and processing time.

2. Reading ADC Value

What does it do? Reads the raw analog value from the LM35 temperature sensor and converts it into a digital format.
Syntax:
```
adc_value = ADC_Read();
```

Example:
```
uint16_t ADC_Read() {
    ADCSRA |= (1 << ADSC);   // Start conversion
    while (ADCSRA & (1 << ADSC));   // Wait for
conversion to complete
    return ADC;
}
```

Example Explanation: The function starts an ADC conversion, waits for it to complete, and then retrieves the converted digital value. This value represents the sensor's output voltage, which can later be converted into a temperature reading.

3. Converting ADC Value to Temperature

What does it do? Converts the raw ADC reading from the LM35 sensor into a Celsius temperature value. The LM35 outputs 10mV per degree Celsius, so a proper conversion formula is required.
Syntax:
```
temp = (adc_value * 5.0) / 1024.0 * 100;
```

Example:
```
float Convert_Temperature(uint16_t adc_value) {
    return (adc_value * 5.0) / 1024.0 * 100;   //
Convert ADC to Celsius
}
```

Example Explanation: The formula scales the ADC value to a temperature reading. The multiplication by 100 accounts for the LM35's 10mV/°C sensitivity.

4. Reading Temperature from DHT11

What does it do? Reads temperature and humidity data from the DHT11 sensor using digital communication. Unlike the LM35, the DHT11 sends temperature data digitally via a single-wire communication protocol.
Syntax:
```
DHT11_Read();
```

Example:
```
uint8_t DHT11_Read() {
    // Communication with DHT11 sensor and reading data
    return temperature;
}
```

Example Explanation: This function establishes communication with the DHT11 sensor, retrieves the temperature value, and returns it. Proper delay handling is essential to prevent errors in data transmission.

5. Reading Temperature from DS18B20
What does it do? Retrieves temperature data from the DS18B20 sensor over a 1-Wire interface. The DS18B20 provides high-precision temperature readings with configurable resolution (9-bit to 12-bit).
Syntax:
```
DS18B20_Read();
```
Example:
```
float DS18B20_Read() {
    // Read temperature from DS18B20 sensor using 1-
Wire protocol
    return temperature;
}
```

Example Explanation: The function reads temperature data from the DS18B20 using the 1-Wire protocol and returns the value in Celsius. This sensor allows multiple devices to communicate over a single data line.

Real-life Applications Project: Digital Temperature Display Using LM35 and AVR

Project Overview This project demonstrates how to interface an LM35 temperature sensor with an AVR microcontroller to measure and display temperature readings on an LCD. The system continuously reads temperature values, converts them, and updates the display in real-time.

Required Components

Component	Description
AVR Microcontroller	The main processing unit.
LM35 Temperature Sensor	Provides analog temperature output.
16x2 LCD Display	Displays the temperature readings.
Resistor (10kΩ)	Used as a pull-up resistor for stability.

Circuit Connection Table

Component	AVR Microcontroller Pin	Power Source	Purpose
LM35 Sensor	ADC0 (PC0)	5V	Outputs analog voltage proportional to temperature.
LCD Display	PD4-PD7, RS=PB0, EN=PB1	5V	Displays temperature values.

Project Code

```
#include <avr/io.h>
#include <util/delay.h>
#include "lcd.h"
#define LM35_PIN 0  // ADC0
void ADC_Init() {
    ADMUX |= (1 << REFS0);  // Select AVCC as reference
```

```c
voltage
    ADCSRA |= (1 << ADEN) | (1 << ADPS2);   // Enable
ADC with prescaler
}


uint16_t ADC_Read(uint8_t channel) {
    ADMUX = (ADMUX & 0xF0) | (channel & 0x0F);   //
Select ADC channel
    ADCSRA |= (1 << ADSC);   // Start conversion
    while (ADCSRA & (1 << ADSC));   // Wait for
conversion
    return ADC;
}
float Convert_Temperature(uint16_t adc_value) {
    return (adc_value * 5.0) / 1024.0 * 100;   //
Convert ADC to Celsius
}


int main() {
    LCD_Init();   // Initialize LCD
    ADC_Init();   // Initialize ADC
    char buffer[16];

    while (1) {
        uint16_t adc_value = ADC_Read(LM35_PIN);
        float temperature =
Convert_Temperature(adc_value);

        LCD_Clear();
        LCD_Set_Cursor(1, 1);
        snprintf(buffer, sizeof(buffer), "Temp: %.2f
C", temperature);
        LCD_Write_String(buffer);

        _delay_ms(1000);
    }
}
```

Chapter 40: LDR Sensors

Light-dependent resistors (LDRs) are sensors that change resistance based on light intensity. AVR microcontrollers can use **LDRs** with **analog-to-digital converters (ADC)** to measure and react to ambient light conditions. Common applications include automatic lighting systems, solar trackers, and security systems. This chapter covers the configuration and implementation of LDR sensors in AVR microcontrollers.

Key Concepts of LDR Sensor Interfacing in AVR C

Concept	Description	Example
LDR Resistance Variation	Changes resistance based on light intensity.	`Bright Light → Low Ω`
Voltage Divider	Converts LDR resistance into a measurable voltage.	`Vout = (R2 / (R1 + R2)) * VCC`
ADC (Analog-to-Digital Conversion)	Reads voltage to determine light level.	`ADC_Read();`
Thresholding	Sets limits for light/dark detection.	`if (adc_value > threshold)`
PWM-Based Dimming	Adjusts brightness of an LED based on light levels.	`OCR0A = adc_value / 4;`

Basic Rules for Using LDR Sensors in AVR C

Rule	Correct Example	Incorrect Example
Use a stable reference voltage for ADC.	`` `ADMUX ``	`= (1 << REFS0);` `
Place LDR in a voltage divider circuit.	`Vout = (R2 / (R1 + R2)) * VCC;`	Directly connecting LDR to ADC.
Read ADC value periodically.	`_delay_ms(500);`	Reading ADC too frequently.
Implement filtering for stability.	`adc_avg = (adc1 + adc2) / 2;`	Using raw ADC values without smoothing.

Syntax Table

SL	Operation	Syntax/Example	Description
1	Initialize ADC for LDR	`ADMUX	= (1 << REFS0);`
2	Read ADC Value	adc_value = ADC_Read();	Reads the analog voltage from the LDR.
3	Check Light Level	if (adc_value > threshold) {}	Determines if light level is high or low.
4	Control LED Based on LDR	`PORTB	= (1 << PB0);`
5	Adjust Brightness Using PWM	OCR0A = adc_value / 4;	Changes LED brightness based on light.

Syntax Explanation

1. Initializing ADC for LDR

What does it do? Configures the ADC to read analog values from the LDR sensor. The ADC converts the voltage from the voltage divider circuit into a digital value that the microcontroller can process.
Syntax:
```
ADMUX |= (1 << REFS0);
```

Example:
```
void ADC_Init() {
    ADMUX |= (1 << REFS0);   // Select AVCC as reference
voltage
    ADCSRA |= (1 << ADEN) | (1 << ADPS2);   // Enable
ADC with prescaler
}
```
Example Explanation: The ADC is configured with AVCC as the reference voltage, ensuring consistent readings from the LDR. The prescaler is set to balance speed and accuracy.

2. Reading ADC Value

What does it do? Retrieves the analog voltage level corresponding to light intensity and converts it into a digital value.
Syntax:
```
adc_value = ADC_Read();
```

Example:
```
uint16_t ADC_Read() {
    ADCSRA |= (1 << ADSC);   // Start conversion
    while (ADCSRA & (1 << ADSC));   // Wait for
conversion
    return ADC;
}
```

Example Explanation: This function initiates an ADC conversion and waits for completion before returning the result. The ADC value represents the voltage level, which correlates with light intensity.

3. Checking Light Level

What does it do? Determines if the light level is above or below a predefined threshold to trigger an action, such as turning on an LED.
Syntax:
```
if (adc_value > threshold) {}
```

Example:
```
if (adc_value > 512) {
    PORTB |= (1 << PB0);   // Turn ON LED
} else {
    PORTB &= ~(1 << PB0);   // Turn OFF LED
}
```

Example Explanation: When the ADC reading surpasses a threshold, indicating a dark environment, the LED is turned ON. Otherwise, the LED remains OFF.

4. Adjusting LED Brightness Using PWM

What does it do? Controls LED brightness dynamically based on ambient light conditions using PWM.

Syntax:
```
OCR0A = adc_value / 4;
```

Example:
```
void Adjust_Brightness(uint16_t adc_value) {
    OCR0A = adc_value / 4;  // Scale ADC value to PWM
range
}
```

Example Explanation: Since the ADC value ranges from 0-1023, dividing it by 4 scales it to the 0-255 range suitable for PWM control. This allows smooth LED brightness transitions based on ambient light.

Real-life Applications Project: Automatic Night Lamp Using LDR and AVR

Project Overview This project demonstrates how to build an automatic night lamp system using an LDR sensor and an AVR microcontroller. The system detects ambient light levels and turns the LED ON in darkness while adjusting brightness gradually using PWM.

Required Components

Component	Description
AVR Microcontroller	The main processing unit.
LDR Sensor	Detects ambient light levels.
Resistor (10kΩ)	Forms a voltage divider with the LDR.
LED	Light source controlled based on LDR input.

Circuit Connection Table

Component	AVR Microcontroll er Pin	Power Source	Purpose
LDR Sensor	ADC0 (PC0)	5V	Detects light intensity.

LED	PB0 (PWM Output)	5V	Adjusts brightness based on light level.

Project Code

```c
#include <avr/io.h>
#include <util/delay.h>
#define LDR_PIN 0  // ADC0
void ADC_Init() {
    ADMUX |= (1 << REFS0);  // Select AVCC as reference
voltage
    ADCSRA |= (1 << ADEN) | (1 << ADPS2);  // Enable
ADC with prescaler
}
uint16_t ADC_Read(uint8_t channel) {
    ADMUX = (ADMUX & 0xF0) | (channel & 0x0F);  //
Select ADC channel
    ADCSRA |= (1 << ADSC);  // Start conversion
    while (ADCSRA & (1 << ADSC));  // Wait for
conversion
    return ADC;
}
int main() {
    ADC_Init();  // Initialize ADC
    while (1) {
        uint16_t adc_value = ADC_Read(LDR_PIN);
        Adjust_Brightness(adc_value);
        _delay_ms(500);
    }
}
```

Expected Results

- The system detects ambient light levels and adjusts LED brightness accordingly.
- The LED turns ON in low light and gradually dims as light levels increase.

Chapter 41: IR Sensors

Infrared (IR) sensors are commonly used for proximity detection, obstacle avoidance, and remote control applications. AVR microcontrollers can interface with both **analog and digital IR sensors** to detect objects or receive IR signals.

This chapter covers the configuration and implementation of IR sensors in AVR microcontrollers.

Key Concepts of IR Sensor Interfacing in AVR C

Concept	Description	Example
Analog IR Sensor	Outputs varying voltage based on object distance.	`Sharp IR Sensor`
Digital IR Sensor	Provides HIGH or LOW signal based on detection.	`IR Proximity Sensor`
TSOP IR Receiver	Detects IR signals from remote controls.	`TSOP1738`
ADC (Analog-to-Digital Conversion)	Reads analog IR sensor values.	`ADC_Read();`
Interrupt-based Detection	Uses external interrupts for real-time IR signal processing.	`ISR(INT0_vect){}`

Basic Rules for Using IR Sensors in AVR C

Rule	Correct Example	Incorrect Example
Select the correct ADC reference voltage.	`ADMUX`	`= (1 << REFS0);`
Use an appropriate pull-up resistor for TSOP sensors.	`PORTD`	`= (1 << PD2);`
Read ADC values periodically.	`_delay_ms(100);`	Continuously reading the sensor in a tight loop.
Use interrupts for TSOP receivers.	`EIMSK`	`= (1 << INT0);`

Syntax Table

SL	Operation	Syntax/Example	Description
1	Initialize ADC for IR Sensor	`` `ADMUX = (1 << REFS0);` ``	
2	Read ADC Value	`adc_value = ADC_Read();`	Reads the analog output from the IR sensor.
3	Detect Object Using Digital IR Sensor	`if (PIND & (1 << PD2)) {}`	Checks if the sensor detects an object.
4	Enable External Interrupt for TSOP	`` `EIMSK = (1 << INT0);` ``	
5	Read IR Remote Data	`TSOP_Read();`	Reads the decoded IR signal from the TSOP module.

Syntax Explanation

1. Initializing ADC for Analog IR Sensor

What does it do? Configures the ADC to read analog values from an IR distance sensor. This setup allows the microcontroller to process object proximity based on sensor voltage output.

Syntax:
```
ADMUX |= (1 << REFS0);
```
Example:
```
void ADC_Init() {
    ADMUX |= (1 << REFS0);  // Select AVCC as reference
voltage
    ADCSRA |= (1 << ADEN) | (1 << ADPS2);  // Enable
ADC with prescaler
}
```
Example Explanation: Setting AVCC as the ADC reference ensures accurate analog-to-digital conversion, while enabling the ADC and configuring the prescaler optimizes performance.

2. Reading ADC Value

What does it do? Retrieves the analog voltage level corresponding to object distance from the IR sensor and converts it into a usable digital value.
Syntax:
```
adc_value = ADC_Read();
```

Example:
```
uint16_t ADC_Read() {
    ADCSRA |= (1 << ADSC);  // Start conversion
    while (ADCSRA & (1 << ADSC));  // Wait for
conversion
    return ADC;
}
```

Example Explanation: The function starts ADC conversion, waits for completion, and then returns the corresponding digital value representing the detected object's proximity.

3. Detecting Objects Using a Digital IR Sensor

What does it do? Reads the digital IR sensor output to determine if an object is detected (HIGH or LOW signal) and triggers an action.
Syntax:
```
if (PIND & (1 << PD2)) {}
```

Example:
```
if (PIND & (1 << PD2)) {
    PORTB |= (1 << PB0);  // Turn ON LED when object
detected
} else {
    PORTB &= ~(1 << PB0);  // Turn OFF LED
}
```

Example Explanation: When the digital IR sensor detects an object, it outputs a HIGH signal, which activates the LED connected to PB0. If no object is detected, the LED remains OFF.

4. Enabling External Interrupt for TSOP IR Receiver

What does it do? Configures an external interrupt to detect IR signals from a TSOP1738 receiver. The interrupt allows immediate response when an IR signal is received.

Syntax:
```
EIMSK |= (1 << INT0);
```

Example:
```
void Configure_TSOP_Interrupt() {
    EICRA |= (1 << ISC01);   // Falling edge trigger
    EIMSK |= (1 << INT0);    // Enable INT0 interrupt
}
```

Example Explanation: The TSOP1738 IR receiver outputs a LOW pulse when it detects an IR signal. The interrupt is triggered on the falling edge, ensuring real-time response to incoming signals.

Real-life Applications Project: IR-Based Obstacle Detection System

Project Overview This project demonstrates how to use an IR proximity sensor to detect obstacles and trigger a response.

Required Components

Component	Description
AVR Microcontroller	The main processing unit.
IR Sensor (Digital)	Detects object presence.
LED	Indicates object detection.

Circuit Connection Table

Component	AVR Microcontroller Pin	Power Source	Purpose
IR Sensor	PD2	5V	Detects obstacles.
LED	PB0	5V	Turns ON when object detected.

Project Code

```c
#include <avr/io.h>
#include <util/delay.h>

#define IR_PIN PD2
#define LED_PIN PB0

void IR_Sensor_Init() {
    DDRD &= ~(1 << IR_PIN);   // Set PD2 as input for IR
sensor
    DDRB |= (1 << LED_PIN);   // Set PB0 as output for
LED
}

int main() {
    IR_Sensor_Init();
    while (1) {
        if (PIND & (1 << IR_PIN)) {
            PORTB |= (1 << LED_PIN);   // Turn ON LED if
obstacle detected
        } else {
            PORTB &= ~(1 << LED_PIN);   // Turn OFF LED
if no obstacle
        }
        _delay_ms(100);
    }
}
```

Expected Results

- The system detects IR signals and activates an LED when an obstacle is present.
- The microcontroller processes sensor data in real-time using digital inputs or ADC readings.
- The setup can be expanded to include remote control functionality using a TSOP IR receiver.

Chapter 42: Motion Sensors

Motion sensors are widely used in security systems, automation, and human presence detection. AVR microcontrollers can interface with **Passive Infrared (PIR) sensors**, **Ultrasonic sensors**, and **Accelerometers** to detect motion, measure distance, and track movement.

This chapter covers how to configure and use different motion sensors with AVR microcontrollers.

Key Concepts of Motion Sensor Interfacing in AVR C

Concept	Description	Example
PIR Sensor	Detects infrared radiation from moving objects.	HC-SR501
Ultrasonic Sensor	Measures distance using sound waves.	HC-SR04
Accelerometer (MEMS)	Measures acceleration and tilt angles.	ADXL345
External Interrupts	Used for real-time detection of motion.	ISR(INT0_vect){}
Pulse Measurement	Used to measure echo time for ultrasonic sensors.	pulse_width = Timer_Read();

Basic Rules for Using Motion Sensors in AVR C

Rule	Correct Example	Incorrect Example
Use pull-up resistors for digital sensors.	`PORTD = (1 << PD2);`	Leaving the pin floating.
Debounce PIR sensor signals.	_delay_ms(500);	Reacting to false triggers instantly.
Use precise timing for ultrasonic sensors.	TCNT1 = 0; before sending a trigger.	Measuring pulse width without reset.
Read accelerometer data using I2C/SPI.	TWI_Read_Accel();	Attempting to read without protocol setup.

Syntax Table

SL	Operation	Syntax/Example	Description
1	Initialize PIR Sensor	`DDRD &= ~(1 << PD2);`	Configures PIR sensor input pin.
2	Detect Motion with PIR	`if (PIND & (1 << PD2)) {}`	Checks if motion is detected.
3	Trigger Ultrasonic Sensor	`` `PORTB = (1 << PB1);` ``	Sends a pulse to start distance measurement.
4	Measure Echo Pulse	`pulse_width = Timer_Read();`	Reads time taken for sound waves to return.
5	Read Accelerometer Data	`accel_x = I2C_Read();`	Reads acceleration data over I2C.

Syntax Explanation

1. Initializing PIR Sensor

What does it do? This initializes the PIR sensor by configuring the designated pin as an input to detect motion and enables a pull-up resistor to stabilize the signal.
Syntax:
```
DDRD &= ~(1 << PD2);
PORTD |= (1 << PD2);
```

Example:
```
void PIR_Init() {
    DDRD &= ~(1 << PD2);   // Set PD2 as input for PIR sensor
    PORTD |= (1 << PD2);   // Enable pull-up resistor
}
```

Example Explanation: This function ensures that the PIR sensor is correctly set up and ready to detect motion.

2. Detecting Motion with PIR Sensor

What does it do? Reads the PIR sensor's signal to check if motion has been detected and triggers an appropriate response.
Syntax:
```
if (PIND & (1 << PD2)) {}
```

Example:
```
if (PIND & (1 << PD2)) {
    PORTB |= (1 << PB0);  // Turn ON LED if motion detected
} else {
    PORTB &= ~(1 << PB0);  // Turn OFF LED
}
```

Example Explanation: If motion is detected, the LED connected to PB0 turns ON; otherwise, it remains OFF.

3. Triggering an Ultrasonic Sensor

What does it do? Sends a trigger pulse to an ultrasonic sensor to initiate a distance measurement.
Syntax:
```
PORTB |= (1 << PB1);
```

Example:
```
void Trigger_Ultrasonic() {
    PORTB |= (1 << PB1);  // Send trigger pulse
    _delay_us(10);
    PORTB &= ~(1 << PB1);  // Stop trigger pulse
}
```

Example Explanation: This function sends a 10-microsecond pulse to the ultrasonic sensor to start the distance measurement process.

4. Measuring Echo Pulse

What does it do? Captures the time taken for an ultrasonic signal to reflect back, which can be used to calculate distance.
Syntax:
```
pulse_width = Timer_Read();
```

Example:
```
uint16_t Measure_Distance() {
    while (!(PIND & (1 << PD3)));   // Wait for echo
start
    TCNT1 = 0;   // Reset timer
    while (PIND & (1 << PD3));   // Wait for echo end
    return TCNT1;   // Return pulse duration
}
```

Example Explanation: The function monitors the echo pulse, resets the timer, and calculates the total time taken for the signal to travel.

5. Reading Accelerometer Data

What does it do? Reads acceleration data from a MEMS accelerometer via I2C communication.
Syntax:
```
accel_x = I2C_Read();
```

Example:
```
uint8_t Read_Accel_X() {
    TWI_Start();
    TWI_Write(ACCEL_ADDRESS);
    TWI_Write(ACCEL_X_REG);
    return TWI_Read();
}
```

Example Explanation: This function sends a request to the accelerometer over I2C, retrieves the X-axis acceleration data, and returns it for further processing.

Real-life Applications Project: Motion-Activated Security System

Project Overview This project demonstrates a motion-activated security system using a PIR sensor, an ultrasonic sensor for distance measurement, and an LED alarm indicator.

Required Components

Component	Description
AVR Microcontroller	The main processing unit.
PIR Sensor	Detects motion using infrared radiation.
Ultrasonic Sensor	Measures distance using sound waves.
Buzzer/LED	Provides an alert when motion is detected.
Resistors (10kΩ)	Used for pull-up connections.

Circuit Connection Table

Component	AVR Microcontroller Pin	Power Source	Purpose
PIR Sensor	PD2	5V	Detects motion presence.
Ultrasonic Sensor Trigger	PB1	5V	Sends trigger pulse.
Ultrasonic Sensor Echo	PD3	5V	Reads reflected pulse.
Buzzer/LED	PB0	5V	Alarm indicator.

Project Code

```
#include <avr/io.h>
#include <util/delay.h>
#define PIR_PIN PD2
#define LED_PIN PB0
#define TRIGGER_PIN PB1
#define ECHO_PIN PD3
void PIR_Init() {
    DDRD &= ~(1 << PIR_PIN);  // Set PIR pin as input
    PORTD |= (1 << PIR_PIN);  // Enable pull-up
    DDRB |= (1 << LED_PIN);   // Set LED pin as output
}
void Trigger_Ultrasonic() {
    PORTB |= (1 << TRIGGER_PIN);  // Send trigger pulse
```

```c
    _delay_us(10);
    PORTB &= ~(1 << TRIGGER_PIN);   // Stop trigger
pulse
}
uint16_t Measure_Distance() {
    while (!(PIND & (1 << ECHO_PIN)));   // Wait for
echo start
    TCNT1 = 0;   // Reset timer
    while (PIND & (1 << ECHO_PIN));   // Wait for echo
end
    return TCNT1;   // Return pulse duration
}
int main() {
    PIR_Init();
    DDRB |= (1 << TRIGGER_PIN);   // Set trigger pin as
output
    DDRD &= ~(1 << ECHO_PIN);   // Set echo pin as input
    while (1) {
        if (PIND & (1 << PIR_PIN)) {
            PORTB |= (1 << LED_PIN);   // Turn on alarm
if motion detected
            _delay_ms(500);
        } else {
            PORTB &= ~(1 << LED_PIN);   // Turn off
alarm
        }
        Trigger_Ultrasonic();
        uint16_t distance = Measure_Distance();
    }
}
```

Expected Results

- The system detects motion using a PIR sensor and turns on an LED indicator.
- The ultrasonic sensor continuously measures distance.
- The LED or buzzer alerts whenever motion is detected.
- The system can be expanded to trigger an alarm or send alerts via wireless communication.

Chapter 43: Ultrasonic Sensors

Ultrasonic sensors are widely used in robotics, automation, and distance measurement applications. AVR microcontrollers can interface with ultrasonic sensors like the **HC-SR04** to measure distances using sound waves. This chapter explores how to configure and use ultrasonic sensors with AVR microcontrollers for precise distance measurement.

Key Concepts of Ultrasonic Sensor Interfacing in AVR C

Concept	Description	Example
Ultrasonic Sound Waves	Measures distance based on echo time.	`HC-SR04`
Trigger Pulse	Sends a short pulse to start measurement.	`` `PORTB = (1 << PB1);` ``
Echo Pulse	Measures the return time of the reflected sound wave.	`pulse_width = Timer_Read();`
Timer Counter	Used to measure the duration of the echo pulse.	`TCNT1 = 0;`
Distance Calculation	Converts echo time into distance.	`distance = pulse_width / 58;`

Basic Rules for Using Ultrasonic Sensors in AVR C

Rule	Correct Example	Incorrect Example
Use precise timing for ultrasonic sensors.	`TCNT1 = 0;` before sending a trigger.	Measuring pulse width without reset.
Ensure proper delay between measurements.	`_delay_ms(50);`	Continuously sending trigger signals.
Use external interrupts if needed.	`ISR(INT0_vect) {}`	Polling loop for echo detection.
Convert time to distance accurately.	`distance = pulse_width / 58;`	Using incorrect conversion factor.

Syntax Table

SL	Operation	Syntax/Example	Description
1	**Trigger Ultrasonic Sensor**	`` `PORTB = (1 << PB1);` ``	Sends a pulse to start distance measurement.
2	**Measure Echo Pulse**	`pulse_width = Timer_Read();`	Reads time taken for sound waves to return.
3	**Calculate Distance**	`distance = pulse_width / 58;`	Converts echo time into distance in cm.
4	**Initialize Timer1**	`` `TCCR1B = (1 << CS10);` ``	Configures Timer1 for accurate timing.
5	**Use External Interrupt**	`` `EIMSK = (1 << INT0);` ``	Enables interrupt for precise timing.

Syntax Explanation

1. Triggering the Ultrasonic Sensor

What does it do? Sends a short pulse to the ultrasonic sensor to initiate distance measurement. The pulse tells the sensor to emit ultrasonic waves, which will bounce back from an object.

Syntax:
```
PORTB |= (1 << PB1);
```

Example:
```
void Trigger_Ultrasonic() {
    PORTB |= (1 << PB1);   // Send trigger pulse
    _delay_us(10);
    PORTB &= ~(1 << PB1);  // Stop trigger pulse
}
```

Example Explanation: A 10-microsecond pulse is sent to the ultrasonic sensor's trigger pin to start the measurement process. The sensor then sends out an ultrasonic sound wave, which will reflect off objects and return to the echo pin.

2. Measuring Echo Pulse

What does it do? Measures the duration of the echo pulse received from the ultrasonic sensor. This duration helps determine how far away the object is.
Syntax:
```
pulse_width = Timer_Read();
```

Example:
```
uint16_t Measure_Distance() {
    while (!(PIND & (1 << PD3)));  // Wait for echo start
    TCNT1 = 0;  // Reset timer
    while (PIND & (1 << PD3));  // Wait for echo end
    return TCNT1;  // Return pulse duration
}
```

Example Explanation: The function waits for the echo pulse, resets the timer, and returns the time taken for the sound wave to travel back to the sensor. The echo pin goes HIGH when it detects the returning wave, and the timer starts counting until the pulse ends.

3. Calculating Distance

What does it do? Converts the measured echo time into distance in centimeters. The conversion is based on the speed of sound (343 m/s) and the time it takes for the wave to travel back and forth.
Syntax:
```
distance = pulse_width / 58;
```

Example:
```
uint16_t Calculate_Distance(uint16_t pulse_width) {
    return pulse_width / 58;  // Convert time to cm
}
```
Example Explanation: The time measured by the echo pulse is divided by 58 to convert it into centimeters. This formula is derived from the speed of sound, as the ultrasonic pulse travels to an object and back.

Real-life Applications Project: Ultrasonic Distance Measurement System

Project Overview This project demonstrates how to use an HC-SR04 ultrasonic sensor with an AVR microcontroller to measure distance and display it on an LCD. The microcontroller sends a trigger pulse to the ultrasonic sensor, receives the echo pulse, and calculates the distance based on the travel time of the sound waves.

Required Components

Component	Description
AVR Microcontroller	The main processing unit.
HC-SR04 Sensor	Measures distance using sound waves.
LCD Display	Displays distance values.
Resistors (10kΩ)	Used for pull-up connections.

Circuit Connection Table

Component	AVR Microcontroller Pin	Power Source	Purpose
HC-SR04 Trigger	PB1	5V	Sends trigger pulse.
HC-SR04 Echo	PD3	5V	Reads reflected pulse.
LCD Display	PD4-PD7	5V	Displays distance data.

Project Code

```
#include <avr/io.h>
#include <util/delay.h>
#include "lcd.h"

#define TRIGGER_PIN PB1
#define ECHO_PIN PD3

void Trigger_Ultrasonic() {
    PORTB |= (1 << TRIGGER_PIN);
    _delay_us(10);
    PORTB &= ~(1 << TRIGGER_PIN);
```

```
}

uint16_t Measure_Distance() {
    while (!(PIND & (1 << ECHO_PIN)));  // Wait for
echo start
    TCNT1 = 0;  // Reset timer
    while (PIND & (1 << ECHO_PIN));  // Wait for echo
end
    return TCNT1 / 58;  // Convert to cm
}

int main() {
    LCD_Init();
    DDRB |= (1 << TRIGGER_PIN);  // Set trigger pin as
output
    DDRD &= ~(1 << ECHO_PIN);  // Set echo pin as input
    char buffer[16];
    while (1) {
        Trigger_Ultrasonic();
        uint16_t distance = Measure_Distance();
        LCD_Clear();
        snprintf(buffer, sizeof(buffer), "Distance: %d
cm", distance);
        LCD_Write_String(buffer);
        _delay_ms(500);
    }
}
```

Expected Results

- The system continuously measures distance using the HC-SR04 ultrasonic sensor.
- The measured distance is displayed on an LCD in real-time.
- The system can be expanded to include obstacle detection and automatic control applications.

Chapter 44: Humidity Sensors

Humidity sensors measure the moisture level in the air and are widely used in weather monitoring, industrial automation, and agricultural applications. AVR microcontrollers can interface with **DHT11**, **DHT22**, and **SHT21** humidity sensors to measure relative humidity and temperature.

This chapter covers how to configure and use humidity sensors with AVR microcontrollers for precise environmental monitoring.

Key Concepts of Humidity Sensor Interfacing in AVR C

Concept	Description	Example
Digital Humidity Sensors	Provide direct digital output using protocols like 1-Wire or I2C.	`DHT11, SHT21`
Relative Humidity (RH)	The percentage of water vapor in the air relative to the maximum possible at a given temperature.	`40% RH`
Dew Point Calculation	Used to determine the temperature at which condensation begins.	`Dew Point = f(RH, Temp)`
Temperature Compensation	Adjusts humidity readings based on temperature fluctuations.	`Compensated RH = RH + offset`
Data Integrity Check	Ensures received sensor data is valid using CRC or checksum.	`DHT11_Checksum ();`

Basic Rules for Using Humidity Sensors in AVR C

Rule	Correct Example	Incorrect Example
Use correct timing when reading DHT11/DHT22.	`_delay_ms(1000);`	Reading too frequently without delay.
Check checksum to verify sensor data.	`if (checksum_valid)`	Using data without verifying integrity.

Read data using the correct protocol.	I2C_Read(); for I2C sensors.	Attempting to read digital sensors using ADC.
Store calibration values if needed.	EEPROM_Write ();	Hardcoding sensor offsets in the program.

Syntax Table

SL	Operation	Syntax/Example	Description
1	Initialize DHT Sensor	DHT_Init();	Prepares the sensor for communication.
2	Read Humidity Value	humidity = DHT_Read();	Reads the digital humidity data.
3	Check Data Integrity	if (checksum_va lid)	Ensures the received data is correct.
4	Convert Raw Data	humidity = raw_data / 10;	Converts raw sensor output to RH value.
5	Read Temperature from Sensor	temp = DHT_ReadTemp ();	Retrieves the current temperature value.

Syntax Explanation

1. Initializing the DHT Humidity Sensor

What does it do? Sets up the DHT sensor by configuring the data pin for communication and preparing it to send humidity readings. This ensures proper initialization and avoids miscommunication with the sensor.

Syntax:
DHT_Init();

Example:

```
void DHT_Init() {
    DDRD |= (1 << PD0);  // Set data pin as output
    PORTD |= (1 << PD0); // Pull data pin high
    _delay_ms(1000);     // Wait for sensor
stabilization
}
```

Example Explanation: The function configures the DHT data pin as an output, ensures a high state, and waits for the sensor to stabilize before reading data. This is crucial to ensure accurate readings.

2. Reading Humidity Value

What does it do? Retrieves the relative humidity data from the DHT sensor and processes it for use. The data received is in raw form and may need further processing.
Syntax:
```
humidity = DHT_Read();
```

Example:
```
uint8_t DHT_Read() {
    uint8_t humidity;
    // Communicate with DHT sensor and retrieve data
    return humidity;
}
```

Example Explanation: This function establishes communication with the DHT sensor, receives the humidity value, and returns it for further processing. Proper timing is needed to ensure data integrity.

3. Checking Data Integrity

What does it do? Verifies that the received sensor data is valid using a checksum or error-checking mechanism. This prevents errors in humidity and temperature readings.
Syntax:
```
if (checksum_valid)
```

Example:
```
if (DHT_Checksum() == 1) {
    // Process valid data
} else {
    // Handle error
}
```

Example Explanation: This function ensures that the received data is valid by comparing the checksum received from the sensor with the calculated checksum. If they do not match, the data is considered invalid.

4. Convert Raw Data

What does it do? Converts the raw sensor data into a human-readable format, such as percentage relative humidity. Many sensors output scaled values that need conversion.
Syntax:
```
humidity = raw_data / 10;
```

Example:
```
float Convert_Humidity(uint16_t raw_data) {
    return raw_data / 10.0; // Convert raw value to
percentage
}
```

Example Explanation: Many humidity sensors provide data in a raw format that must be converted into human-readable values. This function divides the raw reading by 10 to obtain the correct relative humidity percentage.

5. Read Temperature from Sensor

What does it do? Retrieves the current temperature reading from the humidity sensor, which can be used for further calculations, including temperature compensation for humidity readings.
Syntax:
```
temp = DHT_ReadTemp();
```

Example:
```
float DHT_ReadTemp() {
    float temperature;
    // Read temperature data from sensor
    return temperature;
}
```

Example Explanation: Many humidity sensors also measure temperature. This function reads the temperature value and returns it for display or calculations such as temperature compensation. Proper reading intervals are necessary to ensure accurate temperature readings.

Real-life Applications Project: Humidity and Temperature Monitoring System

Project Overview This project demonstrates how to use a DHT11 or DHT22 humidity sensor with an AVR microcontroller to measure and display humidity and temperature readings. The system continuously monitors environmental conditions and updates the display in real-time.

Required Components

Component	Description
AVR Microcontroller	The main processing unit.
DHT11/DHT22 Sensor	Measures humidity and temperature.
LCD Display (16x2)	Displays sensor data.
Resistors (10kΩ)	Used as pull-up resistors for data lines.

Circuit Connection Table

Component	AVR Microcontroller Pin	Power Source	Purpose
DHT11/ DHT22	PD0	3.3V or 5V	Measures humidity and temperature.
LCD Display	PD4-PD7, RS=PB0, EN=PB1	5V	Displays humidity and temperature values.

Project Code

```
#include <avr/io.h>
#include <util/delay.h>
#include "lcd.h"
#include "dht.h"


#define DHT_PIN PD0
```

```c
void Display_Data(uint8_t humidity, uint8_t
temperature) {
    char buffer[16];
    LCD_Clear();
    LCD_Set_Cursor(1, 1);
    snprintf(buffer, sizeof(buffer), "Hum: %d%% Temp:
%dC", humidity, temperature);
    LCD_Write_String(buffer);
}

int main() {
    LCD_Init();
    DHT_Init();
    uint8_t humidity, temperature;

    while (1) {
        if (DHT_Read(DHT_PIN, &humidity, &temperature))
{
            Display_Data(humidity, temperature);
        } else {
            LCD_Clear();
            LCD_Write_String("Sensor Error");
        }
        _delay_ms(2000);
    }
}
```

Expected Results
- The AVR microcontroller continuously reads humidity and temperature values from the DHT sensor.
- The measured data is displayed on an LCD screen in real-time.
- If there is a sensor error, the LCD will indicate an issue with data retrieval.
- The system can be expanded for use in weather stations, smart agriculture, or industrial climate monitoring applications.

Chapter 45: Pressure Sensors

Pressure sensors are used to measure air, liquid, or gas pressure in various applications such as weather monitoring, industrial automation, and fluid control systems. AVR microcontrollers can interface with **analog** and **digital** pressure sensors such as **MPX5010**, **BMP280**, and **MPL3115A2** to measure and process pressure data accurately.

This chapter covers how to configure and use pressure sensors with AVR microcontrollers.

Key Concepts of Pressure Sensor Interfacing in AVR C

Concept	Description	Example
Analog Pressure Sensor	Outputs voltage proportional to pressure.	MPX5010, MPX5100
Digital Pressure Sensor	Uses I2C/SPI communication for precise readings.	BMP280, MPL3115A2
Absolute vs. Gauge Pressure	Absolute measures total pressure; Gauge measures relative to atmospheric pressure.	BMP180 (Absolute), MPX5010 (Gauge)
Altitude Calculation	Converts pressure readings to altitude.	Altitude = f(Pressure)
Temperature Compensation	Adjusts pressure readings for temperature changes.	BMP280 includes compensation

Basic Rules for Using Pressure Sensors in AVR C

Rule	Correct Example	Incorrect Example
Use a stable voltage reference for ADC.	= (1 << REFS0);`	Floating ADC reference.
Read digital sensors using I2C/SPI.	I2C_Read();	Attempting to read via ADC.

| Apply calibration for accuracy. | `pressure = raw_value * scale;` | Using raw sensor data directly. |
| Implement filtering for stable readings. | `pressure_avg = (p1 + p2) / 2;` | Using raw data without filtering. |

Syntax Table

SL	Operation	Syntax/Example	Description
1	**Initialize ADC for Analog Sensor**	`` `ADMUX = (1 << REFS0);` ``	Sets AVCC as ADC reference.
2	**Read Analog Pressure Sensor**	`adc_value = ADC_Read();`	Reads the analog output from the sensor.
3	**Convert ADC Value to Pressure**	`pressure = (adc_value / 1023.0) * 10;`	Converts ADC reading to pressure in kPa.
4	**Read Digital Pressure Sensor**	`pressure = I2C_Read();`	Reads pressure using I2C communication.
5	**Calculate Altitude from Pressure**	`altitude = 44330 * (1 - pow(pressure / P0, 0.1903));`	Converts pressure to altitude.

Syntax Explanation
1. Initialize ADC for Analog Sensor
What does it do? Configures the ADC to read analog values from a pressure sensor, converting voltage into digital values.
Syntax:
```
ADMUX |= (1 << REFS0);
```
Example:
```
void ADC_Init() {
    ADMUX |= (1 << REFS0);  // Select AVCC as reference
voltage
    ADCSRA |= (1 << ADEN) | (1 << ADPS2);  // Enable
ADC with prescaler
}
```

Example Explanation: This function ensures that the ADC is properly configured for stable and accurate pressure readings from an analog sensor.

2. Read Analog Pressure Sensor

What does it do? Retrieves the analog voltage level corresponding to pressure from the sensor.
Syntax:
```
adc_value = ADC_Read();
```

Example:
```
uint16_t ADC_Read() {
    ADCSRA |= (1 << ADSC);  // Start conversion
    while (ADCSRA & (1 << ADSC));  // Wait for
conversion
    return ADC;
}
```

Example Explanation: The function starts an ADC conversion, waits until completion, and returns the digital value representing the pressure measurement.

3. Convert ADC Value to Pressure

What does it do? Converts the ADC reading into a meaningful pressure value in kilopascals (kPa).
Syntax:
```
pressure = (adc_value / 1023.0) * 10;
```
Example:
```
float Convert_Pressure(uint16_t adc_value) {
    return (adc_value / 1023.0) * 10.0;  // Convert ADC
value to kPa
}
```
Example Explanation: Since the sensor outputs a voltage proportional to pressure, this function scales the ADC reading to a pressure value.

4. Read Digital Pressure Sensor

What does it do? Reads pressure data from a digital sensor using the I2C communication protocol.
Syntax:
```
pressure = I2C_Read();
```

Example:
```
uint16_t Read_Pressure_I2C() {
    TWI_Start();
    TWI_Write(SENSOR_ADDRESS);
    return TWI_Read();
}
```

Example Explanation: This function communicates with a digital pressure sensor over I2C and retrieves the pressure value for processing.

5. Calculate Altitude from Pressure

What does it do? Converts measured pressure into altitude using the barometric formula. This is useful in weather stations, drones, and aviation applications.
Syntax:
```
altitude = 44330 * (1 - pow(pressure / P0, 0.1903));
```

Example:
```
float Calculate_Altitude(float pressure) {
    const float P0 = 1013.25; // Standard atmospheric
pressure at sea level in hPa
    return 44330 * (1 - pow(pressure / P0, 0.1903));
}
```

Example Explanation: This function takes the measured pressure and applies the barometric formula to estimate the altitude above sea level. The constant P0 represents the atmospheric pressure at sea level. The formula assumes standard atmospheric conditions.

Real-life Applications Project: Digital Pressure Measurement System

Project Overview This project demonstrates how to use a pressure sensor with an AVR microcontroller to measure and display real-time pressure and altitude data. The system continuously monitors atmospheric pressure and converts it into a meaningful altitude value.

Required Components

Component	Description
AVR Microcontroller	The main processing unit.
BMP280 / MPX5010 Sensor	Measures air pressure.
LCD Display	Displays pressure and altitude data.
Resistors (10kΩ)	Used for pull-up connections.

Circuit Connection Table

Component	AVR Microcontroller Pin	Power Source	Purpose
BMP280 (I2C)	SDA = PC4, SCL = PC5	3.3V	Reads pressure digitally.
MPX5010 (Analog)	ADC0 (PA0)	5V	Reads pressure as voltage.
LCD Display	PD4-PD7	5V	Displays pressure and altitude.

Project Code

```
#include <avr/io.h>
#include <util/delay.h>
#include "lcd.h"
#include "i2c.h"
#include "bmp280.h"

#define P0 1013.25  // Sea level standard pressure in hPa
```

```c
void Display_Data(float pressure, float altitude) {
    char buffer[16];
    LCD_Clear();
    LCD_Set_Cursor(1,1);
    snprintf(buffer, sizeof(buffer), "P: %.2f hPa",
pressure);
    LCD_Write_String(buffer);
    LCD_Set_Cursor(2,1);
    snprintf(buffer, sizeof(buffer), "Alt: %.2f m",
altitude);
    LCD_Write_String(buffer);
}

int main() {
    LCD_Init();
    BMP280_Init();
    float pressure, altitude;

    while (1) {
        pressure = BMP280_ReadPressure();
        altitude = 44330 * (1 - pow(pressure / P0,
0.1903));
        Display_Data(pressure, altitude);
        _delay_ms(1000);
    }
}
```

Expected Results

- The AVR microcontroller continuously reads pressure values from an analog or digital sensor.
- The measured pressure data is displayed on an LCD in real-time.
- The altitude is calculated and displayed using the pressure sensor's data.
- The system can be used for weather monitoring, industrial control, or altitude-based navigation applications.

Chapter 46: Sound Sensors

Sound sensors detect audio signals and convert them into electrical signals that can be processed by a microcontroller. AVR microcontrollers can interface with **analog** and **digital** sound sensors like **KY-038**, **LM393**, and **MAX9814** to measure sound intensity, detect specific frequencies, or trigger events based on sound levels.

This chapter explores how to configure and use sound sensors with AVR microcontrollers.

Key Concepts of Sound Sensor Interfacing in AVR C

Concept	Description	Example
Analog Sound Sensor	Outputs voltage proportional to sound intensity.	`KY-038, MAX9814`
Digital Sound Sensor	Provides a HIGH or LOW signal based on a threshold.	`LM393, KY-037`
Frequency Analysis	Detects specific sound frequencies.	`Goertzel Algorithm`
Microphone Amplification	Amplifies weak sound signals for processing.	`MAX9814 Auto Gain Control`
Noise Filtering	Reduces unwanted background noise.	`Low-pass filtering`

Basic Rules for Using Sound Sensors in AVR C

Rule	Correct Example	Incorrect Example
Use a stable power supply for sensors.	`Vcc = 5V regulated`	Using an unstable voltage source.
Filter out unwanted noise.	`Apply low-pass filtering`	Using raw, unfiltered sensor output.
Adjust sensitivity for accurate detection.	`Set threshold using a potentiometer`	Keeping default sensitivity settings.
Use interrupts for real-time detection.	`Attach INT0 to digital output`	Polling sensor in a loop.

Syntax Table

SL	Operation	Syntax/Example	Description
1	Initialize ADC for Sound Sensor	`ADMUX = (1 << REFS0);`	Sets AVCC as ADC reference
2	Read Analog Sound Sensor	`adc_value = ADC_Read();`	Reads the analog output from the sensor.
3	Detect Sound Using Digital Sensor	`if (PIND & (1 << PD2)) {}`	Checks if the sensor detects sound.
4	Filter and Process Sound Data	`filtered_value = LowPassFilter (adc_value);`	Reduces noise in sound signal.
5	Trigger Event on Loud Sound	`if (adc_value > threshold) {}`	Activates an event when sound exceeds threshold.

Syntax Explanation

1. Initialize ADC for Sound Sensor

What does it do? Configures the ADC to read analog values from a sound sensor, converting voltage into digital values. The ADC is necessary for analog sound sensors, as they output varying voltages that represent sound intensity.

Syntax:
```
ADMUX |= (1 << REFS0);
```

Example:
```
void ADC_Init() {
    ADMUX |= (1 << REFS0);   // Select AVCC as reference
voltage
    ADCSRA |= (1 << ADEN) | (1 << ADPS2);   // Enable
ADC with prescaler
}
```
Example Explanation: This function initializes the ADC to use AVCC as the reference voltage. The ADC is enabled, and a prescaler is set to optimize accuracy when reading sensor data.

2. Read Analog Sound Sensor

What does it do? Retrieves the analog voltage level corresponding to sound intensity from the sensor. The ADC conversion allows us to measure how loud a sound is based on voltage fluctuations.
Syntax:
```
adc_value = ADC_Read();
```

Example:
```
uint16_t ADC_Read() {
    ADCSRA |= (1 << ADSC);  // Start conversion
    while (ADCSRA & (1 << ADSC));  // Wait for
conversion
    return ADC;
}
```

Example Explanation: This function starts an ADC conversion, waits until completion, and returns the digital value representing sound intensity. The value can then be used for processing or comparison against thresholds.

3. Detect Sound Using Digital Sensor

What does it do? Reads the digital sound sensor output to determine if a loud sound has been detected. Digital sound sensors use a comparator to generate a HIGH or LOW output based on a predefined threshold.
Syntax:
```
if (PIND & (1 << PD2)) {}
```

Example:
```
if (PIND & (1 << PD2)) {
    PORTB |= (1 << PB0);  // Turn ON LED when loud
sound detected
} else {
    PORTB &= ~(1 << PB0);  // Turn OFF LED
}
```

Example Explanation: If the digital sound sensor detects a loud sound, it outputs a HIGH signal, turning ON an LED to indicate detection. Otherwise, the LED remains OFF.

4. Filter and Process Sound Data

What does it do? Applies a low-pass filter to remove noise and process sound signals more accurately. This step is important to prevent false triggers and improve sensitivity.
Syntax:
```
filtered_value = LowPassFilter(adc_value);
```

Example:
```
float LowPassFilter(float input) {
    static float prev_output = 0;
    float alpha = 0.1;  // Adjust filter strength
    prev_output = alpha * input + (1 - alpha) *
prev_output;
    return prev_output;
}
```
Example Explanation: This function applies a simple low-pass filter to smooth out rapid changes in sound sensor readings, reducing false detections caused by noise.

5. Trigger Event on Loud Sound

What does it do? Triggers an event when the sound sensor detects a sound above a certain threshold. This allows for applications like voice-activated controls or noise detection systems.
Syntax:
```
if (adc_value > threshold) {}
```
Example:
```
uint16_t threshold = 500;
if (ADC_Read() > threshold) {
    PORTB |= (1 << PB0);  // Turn ON LED when loud
sound is detected
} else {
    PORTB &= ~(1 << PB0);  // Turn OFF LED
}
```

Example Explanation: The function continuously reads the sensor value and compares it to a predefined threshold. If the sound level exceeds the threshold, an LED is turned ON to indicate detection.

Real-life Applications Project: Sound-Activated Light System

Project Overview This project demonstrates how to use a sound sensor with an AVR microcontroller to detect sound levels and activate a light or LED when a loud sound is detected.

Required Components

Component	Description
AVR Microcontroller	The main processing unit.
KY-038 Sound Sensor	Detects sound intensity.
LED Indicator	Lights up when sound is detected.
Resistors (10kΩ)	Used for pull-up connections.

Circuit Connection Table

Component	AVR Microcontroller Pin	Power Source	Purpose
KY-038 Analog Output	ADC0 (PA0)	5V	Reads sound intensity.
KY-038 Digital Output	PD2 (INT0)	5V	Detects loud sounds.
LED Indicator	PB0	5V	Turns ON/OFF based on sound.

Project Code

```
#include <avr/io.h>
#include <util/delay.h>
#include "adc.h"

#define SOUND_SENSOR_PIN PA0
#define LED_PIN PB0
#define SOUND_THRESHOLD 500

void Initialize_System() {
```

```
    DDRB |= (1 << LED_PIN);  // Set LED pin as output
    ADC_Init();  // Initialize ADC for reading sound
sensor
}

int main() {
    Initialize_System();
    uint16_t sound_level;

    while (1) {
        sound_level = ADC_Read(SOUND_SENSOR_PIN);
        if (sound_level > SOUND_THRESHOLD) {
            PORTB |= (1 << LED_PIN);  // Turn ON LED
when sound detected
        } else {
            PORTB &= ~(1 << LED_PIN);  // Turn OFF LED
        }
        _delay_ms(100);
    }
}
```

Expected Results

- The AVR microcontroller continuously reads sound intensity values from the sensor.
- If a loud sound is detected, an LED turns ON.
- The system can be used for noise monitoring, security alerts, or voice-activated applications.

Chapter 47: Gas Sensors

Gas sensors are used to detect various gases, such as carbon monoxide (CO), methane (CH4), and LPG, in applications like industrial safety, environmental monitoring, and home security. AVR microcontrollers can interface with both **analog** and **digital** gas sensors, such as **MQ-2**, **MQ-7**, and **MQ-135**, to measure gas concentration and trigger alerts when necessary.
This chapter explores how to configure and use gas sensors with AVR microcontrollers.

Key Concepts of Gas Sensor Interfacing in AVR C

Concept	Description	Example
Analog Gas Sensor	Outputs voltage proportional to gas concentration.	MQ-2, MQ-7
Digital Gas Sensor	Provides HIGH or LOW signal based on threshold.	MQ-135 with comparator
Gas Calibration	Adjusts sensor readings for better accuracy.	Baseline calibration
Threshold-Based Alerts	Triggers actions when gas concentration is high.	Buzzer or LED alert
Preheating Requirement	Some sensors require heating before operation.	MQ series

Basic Rules for Using Gas Sensors in AVR C

Rule	Correct Example	Incorrect Example
Allow sensor preheating time.	Wait for 1-2 minutes on startup	Reading values immediately.
Use stable power supply.	Vcc = 5V regulated	Using an unstable voltage source.
Calibrate sensor before use.	Measure baseline in clean air	Using raw uncalibrated values.
Use filtering to remove noise.	Apply moving average filter	Using raw fluctuating sensor data.

Syntax Table

SL	Operation	Syntax/Example	Description
1	**Initialize ADC for Gas Sensor**	`` `ADMUX = (1 << REFS0);` ``	Sets AVCC as ADC reference.
2	**Read Analog Gas Sensor**	`adc_value = ADC_Read();`	Reads the analog output from the sensor.
3	**Detect Gas Using Digital Sensor**	`if (PIND & (1 << PD2)) {}`	Checks if the sensor detects gas.
4	**Calibrate Gas Sensor**	`baseline = MeasureBaseline();`	Stores baseline gas levels for accuracy.
5	**Trigger Alert on High Gas Level**	`if (adc_value > threshold) {}`	Activates buzzer or LED when gas exceeds threshold.

Syntax Explanation

1. Initialize ADC for Gas Sensor

What does it do? Configures the ADC to read analog values from a gas sensor, converting voltage into digital values. This allows the microcontroller to measure gas concentration by analyzing the sensor's output voltage.

Syntax:
```
ADMUX |= (1 << REFS0);
```
Example:
```
void ADC_Init() {
    ADMUX |= (1 << REFS0);  // Select AVCC as reference
voltage
    ADCSRA |= (1 << ADEN) | (1 << ADPS2);  // Enable
ADC with prescaler
}
```

Example Explanation: The function initializes the ADC by selecting AVCC as the reference voltage and enabling it with a suitable prescaler. This ensures accurate voltage readings from the gas sensor.

2. Read Analog Gas Sensor

What does it do? Retrieves the analog voltage level corresponding to gas concentration from the sensor. The ADC conversion allows measurement of gas concentration changes.
Syntax:
```
adc_value = ADC_Read();
```

Example:
```
uint16_t ADC_Read() {
    ADCSRA |= (1 << ADSC);  // Start conversion
    while (ADCSRA & (1 << ADSC));  // Wait for
conversion
    return ADC;
}
```

Example Explanation: This function initiates an ADC conversion, waits for it to complete, and returns the digital value representing gas concentration. The higher the value, the higher the detected gas concentration.

3. Detect Gas Using Digital Sensor

What does it do? Reads the digital gas sensor output to determine if a gas threshold has been exceeded. If the gas level surpasses a predefined limit, the sensor outputs a HIGH signal.
Syntax:
```
if (PIND & (1 << PD2)) {}
```

Example:
```
if (PIND & (1 << PD2)) {
    PORTB |= (1 << PB0);  // Turn ON LED when gas
```

```
detected
} else {
    PORTB &= ~(1 << PB0);   // Turn OFF LED
}
```

Example Explanation: The function checks if the digital sensor output is HIGH. If it is, the LED turns ON to indicate gas detection; otherwise, the LED remains OFF.

4. Calibrate Gas Sensor

What does it do? Measures a baseline value in clean air to calibrate the sensor. Calibration ensures accurate gas readings by accounting for environmental conditions.
Syntax:
```
baseline = MeasureBaseline();
```

Example:
```
uint16_t MeasureBaseline() {
    uint16_t baseline = 0;
    for (int i = 0; i < 100; i++) {
        baseline += ADC_Read();
        _delay_ms(10);
    }
    return baseline / 100;   // Average baseline value
}
```

Example Explanation: This function takes 100 sensor readings in clean air and calculates the average baseline value. This baseline is used as a reference to detect deviations caused by gas presence.

5. Trigger Alert on High Gas Level

What does it do? Activates an alert (e.g., buzzer or LED) when gas levels exceed a predefined threshold. This is used for safety alerts in case of gas leaks.
Syntax:
```
if (adc_value > threshold) {}
```

Example:
```
uint16_t threshold = 600;
if (ADC_Read() > threshold) {
    PORTB |= (1 << PB1);   // Turn ON buzzer when gas
detected
} else {
    PORTB &= ~(1 << PB1);   // Turn OFF buzzer
}
```

Example Explanation: This function continuously reads the sensor and compares the value to a predefined threshold. If the detected gas level exceeds the threshold, a buzzer is activated to alert users of a possible gas leak.

Real-life Applications Project: Gas Leakage Detection System

Project Overview This project demonstrates how to use a gas sensor with an AVR microcontroller to detect hazardous gas levels and trigger alerts when necessary. The system continuously monitors gas concentration and activates a buzzer or LED if the gas level exceeds a defined threshold.

Required Components

Component	Description
AVR Microcontroller	The main processing unit.
MQ-2 Gas Sensor	Detects various gases (LPG, CO, CH4).
Buzzer	Sounds an alarm when gas is detected.
LED Indicator	Lights up when gas level exceeds threshold.
Resistors (10kΩ)	Used for pull-up connections.

Circuit Connection Table

Component	AVR Microcontroller Pin	Power Source	Purpose
MQ-2 Analog Output	ADC0 (PA0)	5V	Reads gas concentration.
MQ-2 Digital Output	PD2 (INT0)	5V	Detects gas threshold exceeded.

Buzzer	PB1	5V	Activates alarm on gas detection.
LED Indicator	PB0	5V	Lights up when gas detected.

Project Code

```c
#include <avr/io.h>
#include <util/delay.h>
#include "adc.h"

#define GAS_SENSOR_PIN PA0
#define BUZZER_PIN PB1
#define LED_PIN PB0
#define GAS_THRESHOLD 600

void Initialize_System() {
    DDRB |= (1 << BUZZER_PIN) | (1 << LED_PIN);  // Set
buzzer and LED pins as outputs
    ADC_Init();  // Initialize ADC for reading gas
sensor
}
int main() {
    Initialize_System();
    uint16_t gas_level;

    while (1) {
        gas_level = ADC_Read(GAS_SENSOR_PIN);
        if (gas_level > GAS_THRESHOLD) {
            PORTB |= (1 << BUZZER_PIN) | (1 <<
LED_PIN);  // Turn ON buzzer and LED
        } else {
            PORTB &= ~(1 << BUZZER_PIN) & ~(1 <<
LED_PIN);  // Turn OFF buzzer and LED
        }
        _delay_ms(100);
    }
}
```

Chapter 48: Air Quality Monitoring Sensors

Air quality monitoring sensors detect pollutants such as **carbon dioxide (CO2), volatile organic compounds (VOCs), particulate matter (PM2.5, PM10), and oxygen levels**. These sensors are widely used in environmental monitoring, industrial safety, and smart home applications. AVR microcontrollers can interface with **analog and digital air quality sensors**, such as **MQ-135, CCS811, PMS5003**, and **SDS011**, to measure air pollution and take necessary actions.

This chapter explains how to configure and use air quality monitoring sensors with AVR microcontrollers.

Key Concepts of Air Quality Sensor Interfacing in AVR C

Concept	Description	Example
Analog Air Quality Sensors	Outputs voltage proportional to pollutant concentration.	`MQ-135, MQ-9`
Digital Air Quality Sensors	Communicates using I2C/UART for precise readings.	`CCS811, PMS5003`
PM Sensors	Detects particulate matter (PM2.5, PM10) in the air.	`PMS5003, SDS011`
VOC and CO2 Sensors	Measures volatile organic compounds and CO2.	`CCS811, SGP30`
Preheating Requirement	Some sensors require heating before operation.	`MQ series`

Basic Rules for Using Air Quality Sensors in AVR C

Rule	Correct Example	Incorrect Example
Allow sensor preheating before reading.	`Wait for 1-3 minutes`	Reading immediately after power-up.
Use stable power for sensor accuracy.	`Vcc = 5V regulated`	Using an unstable voltage source.
Calibrate sensor before first use.	`Measure baseline in clean air`	Using raw, uncalibrated values.
Read PM sensors with correct timing.	`Read data at regular intervals`	Polling sensor continuously.

Syntax Table

SL	Operation	Syntax/Example	Description
1	**Initialize ADC for Sensor**	`` `ADMUX= (1 << REFSO);` ``	Sets AVCC as ADC reference
2	**Read Analog Air Quality Sensor**	`adc_value = ADC_Read();`	Reads the sensor's analog output.
3	**Read Digital Air Quality Sensor**	`data = UART_Read();`	Reads sensor data over UART/I2C.
4	**Calibrate Sensor Baseline**	`baseline = MeasureBaseli ne();`	Stores baseline air quality data.
5	**Trigger Alert on High Pollution**	`if (adc_value > threshold) {}`	Activates an alert when pollution is high.

Syntax Explanation

3. Read Digital Air Quality Sensor

What does it do? Reads sensor data from a digital air quality sensor using UART or I2C communication protocols. Digital sensors provide precise and pre-processed data.
Syntax:
```
data = UART_Read();
```

Example:
```
uint16_t Read_Digital_Sensor() {
    UART_Start();
    UART_Write(SENSOR_ADDRESS);
    return UART_Read();
}
```

Example Explanation: The function initializes UART communication with the sensor, sends a read request, and retrieves the pollution data. This approach is used for sensors like PMS5003 and CCS811.

4. Calibrate Sensor Baseline

What does it do? Measures a baseline air quality value in clean air to improve accuracy and reduce false alarms.
Syntax:
```
baseline = MeasureBaseline();
```

Example:
```
uint16_t MeasureBaseline() {
    uint16_t baseline = 0;
    for (int i = 0; i < 100; i++) {
        baseline += ADC_Read();
        _delay_ms(10);
    }
    return baseline / 100;   // Average baseline value
}
```
Example Explanation: This function takes multiple sensor readings in clean air and averages them to establish a reference point. This ensures accurate detection of pollution changes.

5. Trigger Alert on High Pollution

What does it do? Activates an alert (e.g., buzzer or LED) when pollution levels exceed a predefined threshold.
Syntax:
```
if (adc_value > threshold) {}
```
Example:
```
uint16_t threshold = 600;
if (ADC_Read() > threshold) {
    PORTB |= (1 << PB1);   // Turn ON buzzer when
pollution detected
} else {
    PORTB &= ~(1 << PB1);   // Turn OFF buzzer
}
```
Example Explanation: This function continuously reads air quality sensor values and compares them to a threshold. If the pollution level is too high, a buzzer or LED is activated to alert users of poor air quality.

Real-life Applications Project: Air Quality Monitoring System

Project Overview This project demonstrates how to use an air quality sensor with an AVR microcontroller to monitor air pollution and trigger an alert when pollution exceeds a threshold.

Required Components

Component	Description
AVR Microcontroller	The main processing unit.
MQ-135 Air Quality Sensor	Detects air pollution levels.
Buzzer	Sounds an alarm when pollution is high.
LCD Display	Displays air quality readings.
Resistors (10kΩ)	Used for pull-up connections.

Circuit Connection Table

Component	AVR Microcontroller Pin	Power Source	Purpose
MQ-135 Analog Output	ADC0 (PA0)	5V	Reads air pollution levels.
LCD Display	PD4-PD7	5V	Displays air quality values.
Buzzer	PB1	5V	Sounds alarm on high pollution.

Project Code

```
#include <avr/io.h>
#include <util/delay.h>
#include "adc.h"

#define AIR_SENSOR_PIN PA0
#define BUZZER_PIN PB1
#define POLLUTION_THRESHOLD 500

void Initialize_System() {
    DDRB |= (1 << BUZZER_PIN);  // Set buzzer pin as
output
    ADC_Init();  // Initialize ADC for reading air
```

```
quality sensor
}

int main() {
    Initialize_System();
    uint16_t air_quality;

    while (1) {
        air_quality = ADC_Read(AIR_SENSOR_PIN);
        if (air_quality > POLLUTION_THRESHOLD) {
            PORTB |= (1 << BUZZER_PIN);  // Turn ON
buzzer when pollution detected
        } else {
            PORTB &= ~(1 << BUZZER_PIN);  // Turn OFF
buzzer
        }
        _delay_ms(1000);
    }
}
```

Expected Results

- The AVR microcontroller continuously reads air quality values from the sensor.
- If pollution levels exceed a predefined threshold, a buzzer sounds an alarm.
- The system can be used for air pollution monitoring in homes, industries, and outdoor environments.

Chapter 49: Force Sensors

Force sensors measure the amount of applied force or pressure and convert it into an electrical signal. These sensors are widely used in robotics, industrial automation, medical devices, and touch-sensitive applications. AVR microcontrollers can interface with **analog and digital force sensors**, such as **FSR (Force-Sensitive Resistor), Load Cells, and Strain Gauges**, to measure and process force data accurately.

This chapter explains how to configure and use force sensors with AVR microcontrollers.

Key Concepts of Force Sensor Interfacing in AVR C

Concept	Description	Example
Analog Force Sensors	Outputs voltage proportional to applied force.	`FSR-402, FSR-406`
Digital Force Sensors	Uses I2C/SPI for precise force readings.	`Load Cell HX711`
Load Cells	Measures force by detecting strain in a material.	`HX711-based Load Cell`
Force-Sensitive Resistors	Resistors that change resistance based on force.	`FSR Sensors`
Strain Gauges	Detects minute changes in resistance under stress.	`Metallic Strain Gauges`

Basic Rules for Using Force Sensors in AVR C

Rule	Correct Example	Incorrect Example
Use proper voltage reference for ADC.	`` `ADMUX = (1 << REFS0);` ``	Using an unstable voltage source.
Calibrate sensor before taking readings.	`Measure baseline in no-load state.`	Using raw, uncalibrated values.
Use amplifiers for load cells.	`Use HX711 amplifier module.`	Directly connecting load cell to ADC.
Apply filtering for stable readings.	`Use moving average filter.`	Using raw fluctuating sensor data.

Syntax Table

SL	Operation	Syntax/Example	Description
1	Initialize ADC for Sensor	`ADMUX= (1 << REFS0);`	Sets AVCC as ADC reference.
2	Read Analog Force Sensor	adc_value = ADC_Read();	Reads the sensor's analog output.
3	Read Digital Force Sensor	data = SPI_Read();	Reads sensor data over SPI/I2C.
4	Calibrate Sensor Baseline	baseline = MeasureBaseline();	Stores baseline force measurement.
5	Trigger Action on High Force	if (force_value > threshold) {}	Activates an event when force is high.

Syntax Explanation

1. Initialize ADC for Force Sensor

What does it do? Configures the ADC to read analog values from a force sensor, converting voltage into digital values.
Syntax:
ADMUX |= (1 << REFS0);

Example:
```
void ADC_Init() {
    ADMUX |= (1 << REFS0);  // Select AVCC as reference
voltage
    ADCSRA |= (1 << ADEN) | (1 << ADPS2);  // Enable
ADC with prescaler
}
```

Example Explanation: The function initializes the ADC by selecting AVCC as the reference voltage and enabling it with a prescaler. This ensures accurate voltage readings from the sensor.

2. Read Analog Force Sensor

What does it do? Retrieves the analog voltage level corresponding to the applied force from the sensor.
Syntax:
```
adc_value = ADC_Read();
```

Example:
```
uint16_t ADC_Read() {
    ADCSRA |= (1 << ADSC);   // Start conversion
    while (ADCSRA & (1 << ADSC));   // Wait for
conversion
    return ADC;
}
```

Example Explanation: This function initiates an ADC conversion, waits for it to complete, and returns the digital value representing the force measurement.

3. Read Digital Force Sensor

What does it do? Reads sensor data from a digital force sensor using SPI or I2C communication protocols. Digital sensors provide precise and pre-processed data.
Syntax:
```
data = SPI_Read();
```

Example:
```
uint16_t Read_Digital_Sensor() {
    SPI_Start();
    SPI_Write(SENSOR_ADDRESS);
    return SPI_Read();
}
```

Example Explanation: The function initializes SPI communication with the sensor, sends a read request, and retrieves the force data. This approach is used for sensors like HX711-based load cells.

4. Calibrate Sensor Baseline

What does it do? Measures a baseline force value in a no-load state to improve accuracy and reduce false readings.
Syntax:
```
baseline = MeasureBaseline();
```

Example:
```
uint16_t MeasureBaseline() {
    uint16_t baseline = 0;
    for (int i = 0; i < 100; i++) {
        baseline += ADC_Read();
        _delay_ms(10);
    }
    return baseline / 100;   // Average baseline value
}
```
Example Explanation: This function takes multiple sensor readings with no force applied and averages them to establish a reference point. This ensures accurate detection of force variations.

5. Trigger Action on High Force

What does it do? Activates an event (e.g., buzzer, LED, or motor stop) when the applied force exceeds a predefined threshold.
Syntax:
```
if (force_value > threshold) {}
```
Example:
```
uint16_t threshold = 700;
if (ADC_Read() > threshold) {
    PORTB |= (1 << PB1);   // Turn ON buzzer when high force detected
} else {
    PORTB &= ~(1 << PB1);   // Turn OFF buzzer
}
```
Example Explanation: This function continuously reads force sensor values and compares them to a threshold. If the force level exceeds the threshold, an alert (such as a buzzer or LED) is activated to indicate excessive force.

Real-life Applications Project: Force Measurement System

Project Overview This project demonstrates how to use a force sensor with an AVR microcontroller to measure applied force and trigger an event when force exceeds a threshold.

Required Components

Component	Description
AVR Microcontroller	The main processing unit.
FSR-402 Force Sensor	Detects applied force.
Buzzer	Sounds an alarm when force is high.
LCD Display	Displays force readings.
Resistors (10kΩ)	Used for pull-up connections.

Circuit Connection Table

Component	AVR Microcontroller Pin	Power Source	Purpose
FSR-402 Analog Output	ADC0 (PA0)	5V	Reads applied force levels.
LCD Display	PD4-PD7	5V	Displays force values.
Buzzer	PB1	5V	Sounds alarm on high force.

Project Code

```c
#include <avr/io.h>
#include <util/delay.h>
#include "adc.h"


#define FORCE_SENSOR_PIN PA0
#define BUZZER_PIN PB1
#define FORCE_THRESHOLD 700


void Initialize_System() {
    DDRB |= (1 << BUZZER_PIN);  // Set buzzer pin as output
    ADC_Init();  // Initialize ADC for reading force sensor
}
```

```
int main() {
    Initialize_System();
    uint16_t force_level;

    while (1) {
        force_level = ADC_Read(FORCE_SENSOR_PIN);
        if (force_level > FORCE_THRESHOLD) {
            PORTB |= (1 << BUZZER_PIN);   // Turn ON
buzzer when force detected
        } else {
            PORTB &= ~(1 << BUZZER_PIN);   // Turn OFF
buzzer
        }
        _delay_ms(1000);
    }
}
```

Expected Results

- The AVR microcontroller continuously reads force values from the sensor.
- If the force exceeds a predefined threshold, a buzzer sounds an alarm.
- The system can be used for pressure-sensitive applications, robotic touch sensors, and medical monitoring devices.

Chapter 50: Touch Sensors

Touch sensors detect physical contact or proximity and convert this into an electrical signal, allowing AVR microcontrollers to respond to touch inputs. These sensors are commonly used in consumer electronics, smart home systems, and industrial control panels. AVR microcontrollers can interface with capacitive touch sensors, resistive touch panels, and proximity touch sensors for interactive control applications.

This chapter explains how to configure and use touch sensors with AVR microcontrollers.

Key Concepts of Touch Sensor Interfacing in AVR C

Concept	Description	Example
Capacitive Touch Sensors	Detect touch based on changes in capacitance.	TTP223 Module
Resistive Touch Panels	Detect touch position by measuring resistance changes.	4-Wire Touch Screen
Proximity Touch Sensors	Detect nearby objects without physical contact.	TTP229 Module
Capacitive Touch ICs	Dedicated touch sensor ICs with I2C/SPI interface.	AT42QT1070

Basic Rules for Using Touch Sensors in AVR C

Rule	Correct Example	Incorrect Example
Use stable power supply	Use decoupling capacitors	Directly power from noisy supply
Calibrate touch thresholds	Determine touch/no-touch levels	Use fixed arbitrary thresholds
Use software debouncing	Implement touch state filtering	Use raw fluctuating readings
Read sensor data consistently	Use periodic polling/interrupts	Read data irregularly

Syntax Table

SL	Operation	Syntax/Example	Description
1	Initialize Touch Sensor	`TouchSensor_Init();`	Sets up touch sensor pins and settings.
2	Read Capacitive Sensor	`status = Read_Touch();`	Reads touch state (pressed/released).
3	Detect Touch Event	`if (status == TOUCHED)`	Detects if touch occurred.
4	Calibrate Touch Sensor	`Calibrate_Sensor();`	Sets baseline touch threshold.
5	Trigger Action on Touch	`if (touched) { }`	Activates event when touch detected.

Syntax Explanation

1. Initialize Touch Sensor

This step configures the AVR microcontroller pins to interface with the touch sensor. It sets the designated touch pin as an input and enables the internal pull-up resistor to provide a stable input state. This ensures the pin reads "high" when untouched and "low" when touched.
Syntax:
`TouchSensor_Init();`

Example:
```
void TouchSensor_Init() {
    DDRC &= ~(1 << PC0); // Set PC0 as input for touch sensor
    PORTC |= (1 << PC0); // Enable pull-up resistor
}
```

Explanation:
- `DDRC &= ~(1 << PC0);` configures PC0 as an input.
- `PORTC |= (1 << PC0);` activates the pull-up resistor, ensuring the pin defaults to logic high.

2. Read Capacitive Sensor

This step reads the current state of the touch sensor, indicating whether a touch has occurred. The input pin is checked directly, and the result is returned as either TOUCHED (1) or NOT_TOUCHED (0).

Syntax:
```
status = Read_Touch();
```

Example:
```
uint8_t Read_Touch() {
    return (PINC & (1 << PC0)) == 0 ? TOUCHED :
NOT_TOUCHED;
}
```

Explanation:
- PINC & (1 << PC0) checks if PC0 is low (indicating touch).
- When touch occurs, it returns TOUCHED (1). Otherwise, it returns NOT_TOUCHED (0).

3. Detect Touch Event

This step uses the touch state to trigger an action. When the sensor detects touch, the program can activate an output like an LED or a buzzer.

Syntax:
```
if (status == TOUCHED)
```

Example:
```
if (Read_Touch() == TOUCHED) {
    PORTB |= (1 << PB0); // Turn on LED when touch
detected
}
```

Explanation:
- The touch state is read.
- If touch is detected, the LED connected to PB0 is turned on.

4. Calibrate Touch Sensor

Calibration helps establish a baseline value for touch detection, particularly useful in capacitive touch systems where environmental factors may affect readings.
Syntax:
```
Calibrate_Sensor();
```

Example:
```
void Calibrate_Sensor() {
    baseline = Read_Capacitive_Level(); // Assume
function exists to read baseline level
}
```

Explanation:
- A separate function (Read_Capacitive_Level) would read the no-touch state.
- This baseline value helps filter out noise or environmental changes.

5. Trigger Action on Touch

This step continuously monitors the touch sensor and performs an action (like turning on/off an LED) based on touch state.
Syntax:
```
if (touched)
```

Example:
```
if (Read_Touch() == TOUCHED) {
    PORTB |= (1 << PB0); // Turn on LED when touched
} else {
    PORTB &= ~(1 << PB0); // Turn off LED when not
touched
}
```

Explanation:

- Read_Touch() continuously checks the sensor.
- When touch is detected, the LED turns on.
- When no touch is detected, the LED turns off.

Real-life Applications Project: Touch-Controlled Lighting System

Project Overview This project demonstrates how to use a capacitive touch sensor with an AVR microcontroller to control an LED.

Required Components

Component	Description
AVR Microcontroller	Main control unit
TTP223 Touch Sensor	Capacitive touch sensor
LED	Output indicator
Resistors (1kΩ)	Current limiting for LED

Circuit Connection Table

Component	AVR Microcontroller Pin	Power Source	Purpose
TTP223 Output	PC0	5V	Reads touch state
LED	PB0	5V	Indicates touch event

Project Code

```
#include <avr/io.h>
#include <util/delay.h>

#define TOUCH_PIN PC0
#define LED_PIN PB0

#define TOUCHED 1
#define NOT_TOUCHED 0

void Initialize_System() {
    DDRB |= (1 << LED_PIN); // Set LED pin as output
    DDRC &= ~(1 << TOUCH_PIN); // Set touch pin as
```

```
input
    PORTC |= (1 << TOUCH_PIN); // Enable pull-up
resistor
}

uint8_t Read_Touch() {
    return (PINC & (1 << TOUCH_PIN)) == 0 ? TOUCHED :
NOT_TOUCHED;
}

int main() {
    Initialize_System();

    while (1) {
        if (Read_Touch() == TOUCHED) {
            PORTB |= (1 << LED_PIN); // Turn on LED
        } else {
            PORTB &= ~(1 << LED_PIN); // Turn off LED
        }
        _delay_ms(100);
    }
}
```

Expected Results

The AVR microcontroller continuously monitors the touch sensor. When a touch is detected, the LED lights up. When touch is released, the LED turns off.

This system can be extended for touch-activated switches, smart appliances, and interactive panels.

Chapter 51: GPS Sensors

GPS (Global Positioning System) sensors determine geographical location using satellite signals. These sensors are commonly used in vehicle tracking, navigation systems, outdoor robots, and asset tracking applications. AVR microcontrollers can interface with GPS modules to read latitude, longitude, altitude, speed, and timestamp data, which is often transmitted via UART (serial communication).

This chapter explains how to configure and use GPS sensors with AVR microcontrollers.

Key Concepts of GPS Sensor Interfacing in AVR C

Concept	Description	Example
NMEA Data Format	Standard text-based GPS data format	GPGGA, GPRMC
Serial Communication	Data transmission via UART	Neo-6M GPS
Position Fix	GPS acquiring valid location data	3D Fix LED on Neo-6M
Latitude & Longitude	Coordinates describing location	37.7749°N, 122.4194°W
Time & Date	Time-stamped GPS data	2025-03-04 12:34:56

Basic Rules for Using GPS Sensors in AVR C

Rule	Correct Example	Incorrect Example
Use correct baud rate	Set GPS baud to 9600	Using wrong baud rate
Parse only needed data	Extract GPGGA or GPRMC	Processing all NMEA sentences
Ensure continuous reading	Poll UART buffer regularly	Intermittent reads
Check position fix status	Confirm valid GPS fix	Use data without fix check

Syntax Table

SL	Operation	Syntax/Example	Description
1	Initialize UART for GPS	`UART_Init(9600);`	Configures UART at 9600 baud
2	Read GPS Data Line	`GPS_ReadLine(buffer);`	Reads one NMEA line into buffer
3	Parse Latitude & Longitude	`Parse_GPGGA(buffer);`	Extracts position from GPGGA data
4	Check GPS Fix Status	`if (gps_fix)`	Checks if location is valid
5	Display Coordinates	`Display_Coordinates(lat, lon);`	Shows location on LCD/serial

Syntax Explanation

1. Initialize UART for GPS

What does it do? This function sets up the UART hardware on the AVR microcontroller for serial communication with the GPS module. The GPS module continuously transmits data over UART at a standard baud rate (commonly 9600 bps).

Syntax: `UART_Init(9600);`

Example:
```
void UART_Init(unsigned long baud) {
    uint16_t ubrr = F_CPU/16/baud-1;
    UBRR0H = (uint8_t)(ubrr>>8);
    UBRR0L = (uint8_t)ubrr;
    UCSR0B = (1<<RXEN0) | (1<<TXEN0); // Enable RX and TX
    UCSR0C = (1<<UCSZ01) | (1<<UCSZ00); // 8-bit data
}
```

Explanation:
- `F_CPU/16/baud-1` calculates the baud rate divider based on the microcontroller clock.
- `UBRR0H` and `UBRR0L` set the baud rate.
- `RXEN0` and `TXEN0` enable receiving and transmitting data.
- Data is configured for 8-bit length with no parity.

2. Read GPS Data Line

What does it do? This function reads a complete line (sentence) from the GPS module's NMEA data stream. Each line ends with a newline character ('\n').
Syntax: `GPS_ReadLine(buffer);`
Example:

```
void GPS_ReadLine(char* buffer) {
    char c;
    int i = 0;
    do {
        c = UART_Receive();
        buffer[i++] = c;
    } while (c != '\n' && i < MAX_BUFFER_SIZE);
    buffer[i] = '\0';
}
```

Explanation:
- Reads characters one at a time using `UART_Receive()`.
- Stops reading when either a newline character or the buffer limit is reached.
- Stores a null terminator at the end to make the buffer a valid string.

3. Parse Latitude & Longitude

What does it do? This function extracts the latitude and longitude from a GPGGA NMEA sentence, which contains positional data.
Syntax: `Parse_GPGGA(buffer);`
Example:

```
void Parse_GPGGA(char* buffer) {
    char *token = strtok(buffer, ",");
    for (int i = 0; token != NULL; i++) {
        if (i == 2) latitude = atof(token);
        if (i == 4) longitude = atof(token);
        token = strtok(NULL, ",");
    }
}
```

Explanation:
- `strtok()` splits the NMEA sentence into comma-separated tokens.
- `latitude` and `longitude` are extracted from their respective fields.
- These values are converted to floating-point numbers using `atof()`.

4. Check GPS Fix Status

What does it do? Before using the GPS data, the system checks if the GPS module has acquired a satellite fix. Without a fix, position data is unreliable or missing.

Syntax: `if (gps_fix)`
Example:

```
if (gps_fix) {
    Display_Coordinates(latitude, longitude);
}
```

Explanation:
- `gps_fix` is a flag set to 1 when the GPS has a valid fix.
- Only if this flag is true, the coordinates are processed or displayed.

5. Display Coordinates

What does it do? This function displays the latitude and longitude either on a connected LCD, serial terminal, or another display device.

Syntax: `Display_Coordinates(lat, lon);`
Example:

```
void Display_Coordinates(float lat, float lon) {
    printf("Latitude: %.6f\n", lat);
    printf("Longitude: %.6f\n", lon);
}
```

Explanation:

- Uses `printf()` (or an equivalent method for the display) to show latitude and longitude.
- The `.6f` ensures coordinates are displayed with six decimal places, offering better precision.

Real-life Applications Project: GPS Tracking System

Project Overview This project demonstrates how to use a GPS module with an AVR microcontroller to display the current location on a serial monitor.

Required Components

Component	Description
AVR Microcontroller	Main control unit
Neo-6M GPS Module	GPS receiver
Serial Terminal	Displays GPS data

Circuit Connection Table

Component	AVR Pin	Power Source	Purpose
Neo-6M TX	RX (PD0)	5V	GPS to AVR communication
Neo-6M VCC	-	5V	Power GPS module
Neo-6M GND	-	GND	Ground connection

Project Code

```c
#include <avr/io.h>
#include <util/delay.h>
#include <stdlib.h>
#include <stdio.h>

#define F_CPU 16000000UL

void UART_Init(unsigned long baud);
char UART_Receive(void);
void GPS_ReadLine(char* buffer);
```

```c
void Parse_GPGGA(char* buffer);

float latitude, longitude;

int main() {
    char buffer[100];
    UART_Init(9600);

    while (1) {
        GPS_ReadLine(buffer);
        if (strstr(buffer, "$GPGGA")) {
            Parse_GPGGA(buffer);
            printf("Latitude: %.6f, Longitude: %.6f\n",
latitude, longitude);
        }
        _delay_ms(1000);
    }
}
```

Expected Results The AVR microcontroller reads location data from the GPS module and displays latitude and longitude on a serial monitor. This system can be extended to vehicle tracking, outdoor robotics, and navigation systems.

Chapter 52: GSM Module Sensors

GSM modules enable communication between AVR microcontrollers and cellular networks, allowing devices to send SMS, make calls, and access basic GPRS data services. These modules are widely used in remote monitoring systems, IoT projects, vehicle tracking systems, and emergency alert systems.

This chapter explains how to configure and use GSM modules with AVR microcontrollers.

Key Concepts of GSM Module Interfacing in AVR C

Concept	Description	Example
AT Commands	Text commands used to control the module	AT+CMGS (send SMS)
Serial Communication	Communication between GSM and AVR	SIM900, SIM800
SMS Transmission	Sending messages via cellular network	SMS Alert System
Call Control	Initiating or receiving calls	ATD123456789;
Network Registration	Checking if the module is connected	AT+CREG?

Basic Rules for Using GSM Modules in AVR C

Rule	Correct Example	Incorrect Example
Use proper baud rate	Set GSM baud to 9600	Using wrong baud rate
Wait for module to initialize	Delay after power-up	Immediate AT command send
Use proper AT command format	Send "AT\r\n"	Missing terminators
Check response status	Check "OK" reply	Assume command success

Syntax Table

SL	Operation	Syntax/Example	Description
1	Initialize UART for GSM	`UART_Init(9600);`	Configures UART for GSM module
2	Send AT Command	`GSM_SendCommand("AT\r\n");`	Sends an AT command string
3	Read GSM Response	`GSM_ReadResponse(buffer);`	Reads module's response
4	Send SMS	`GSM_SendSMS("12345 67890", "Hello");`	Sends a text message
5	Check Network Status	`GSM_CheckNetwork();`	Verifies connection to network

Syntax Explanation

1. Initialize UART for GSM

What does it do? Initializes the AVR microcontroller's UART (Universal Asynchronous Receiver/Transmitter) to establish serial communication with the GSM module. Most GSM modules, like SIM800 or SIM900, communicate at 9600 baud by default.
Syntax: `UART_Init(9600);`
Example:
```
void UART_Init(unsigned long baud) {
    uint16_t ubrr = F_CPU/16/baud-1;
    UBRR0H = (uint8_t)(ubrr>>8);
    UBRR0L = (uint8_t)ubrr;
    UCSR0B = (1<<RXEN0) | (1<<TXEN0); // Enable RX and TX
    UCSR0C = (1<<UCSZ01) | (1<<UCSZ00); // 8-bit data
}
```
Explanation:
- F_CPU is the clock speed of the microcontroller (usually 16 MHz).
- The formula calculates the baud rate divider.

- The RXEN0 and TXEN0 enable reception and transmission.
- 8-bit data, no parity, 1 stop bit configuration is standard for GSM communication.

2. Send AT Command

What does it do? This function sends a command string to the GSM module. All GSM commands follow the "AT" format, often ending with \r\n.

Syntax: `GSM_SendCommand("AT\r\n");`

Example:

```
void GSM_SendCommand(const char* cmd) {
    while(*cmd) {
        UART_Transmit(*cmd++);
    }
}
```

Explanation:

- `UART_Transmit()` sends a character.
- The `cmd` string is sent character by character.
- Commands must end with \r\n (carriage return + newline) for proper processing by the module.

3. Read GSM Response

What does it do? Reads the GSM module's response after a command is sent. Responses often include status like "OK" or "ERROR" along with data.

Syntax: `GSM_ReadResponse(buffer);`

Example:

```
void GSM_ReadResponse(char* buffer) {
    char c;
    int i = 0;
    while ((c = UART_Receive()) != '\n' && i <
MAX_BUFFER_SIZE - 1) {
        buffer[i++] = c;
    }
    buffer[i] = '\0';
}
```

Explanation:
- Continuously reads characters until a newline is received.
- Stores received characters in `buffer`.
- Ensures the buffer is null-terminated for easy string handling.

4. Send SMS

What does it do? Sends an SMS message to a specified phone number. It configures the module for text mode, specifies the recipient, sends the message body, and finalizes with a special CTRL+Z character (ASCII 26).

Syntax: `GSM_SendSMS("1234567890", "Hello");`

Example:
```
void GSM_SendSMS(const char* number, const char*
message) {
    GSM_SendCommand("AT+CMGF=1\r\n");
    _delay_ms(500);
    GSM_SendCommand("AT+CMGS=\"");
    GSM_SendCommand(number);
    GSM_SendCommand("\"\r\n");
    _delay_ms(500);
    GSM_SendCommand(message);
    UART_Transmit(26); // CTRL+Z to end message
}
```

Explanation:
- `AT+CMGF=1` sets SMS mode to text.
- `AT+CMGS="number"` starts message transmission.
- Message body is sent, then ended with CTRL+Z (ASCII 26).

5. Check Network Status

What does it do? Checks if the GSM module is registered to a cellular network.

Syntax: `GSM_CheckNetwork();`

Example:

```
void GSM_CheckNetwork() {
    GSM_SendCommand("AT+CREG?\r\n");
    char response[50];
    GSM_ReadResponse(response);
    if (strstr(response, ",1") || strstr(response,
",5")) {
        printf("Network Registered\n");
    } else {
        printf("Not Registered\n");
    }
}
```

Explanation:

- AT+CREG? requests network registration status.
- ,1 and ,5 indicate successful registration.
- Other responses mean no network connection.

Real-life Applications Project: SMS Alert System

Project Overview This project demonstrates how to use a GSM module with an AVR microcontroller to send an SMS alert when an event occurs (like sensor trigger).

Required Components

Component	Description
AVR Microcontroller	Main control unit
SIM800 GSM Module	GSM communication
SIM Card	Cellular network access

Circuit Connection Table

Component	AVR Pin	Power Source	Purpose
GSM TX	RX (PD0)	5V	Data from GSM to AVR
GSM RX	TX (PD1)	5V	Data from AVR to GSM
GSM VCC	-	5V	Power GSM module
GSM GND	-	GND	Ground connection

Project Code

```c
#include <avr/io.h>
#include <util/delay.h>
#include <string.h>
#include <stdio.h>

#define F_CPU 16000000UL

void UART_Init(unsigned long baud);
void GSM_SendCommand(const char* cmd);
void GSM_SendSMS(const char* number, const char*
message);

int main() {
    UART_Init(9600);
    _delay_ms(3000);   // Wait for GSM startup

    GSM_SendSMS("1234567890", "System Alert: Event
Detected!");
    while(1);
}
```

Expected Results The AVR microcontroller initializes communication with the GSM module and sends an SMS alert message to a specified phone number when triggered. This setup can be used for security systems, remote monitoring, or emergency alerts.

Chapter 53: Using Accelerometers Sensors

Accelerometers are sensors that measure acceleration forces in one or more axes. These forces can be due to movement, vibration, or gravity. AVR microcontrollers can interface with analog and digital accelerometers to capture motion data for applications such as tilt detection, vibration monitoring, gesture control, and impact sensing. This chapter explains how to configure and use accelerometers with AVR microcontrollers.

Key Concepts of Accelerometer Interfacing in AVR C

Concept	Description	Example
Analog Accelerometers	Output analog voltage proportional to acceleration	ADXL335
Digital Accelerometers	Communicate via I2C/SPI interface	ADXL345
Axis Measurement	Measures acceleration along X, Y, Z axes	3-axis accelerometer
Tilt Detection	Detects orientation change	Tilt alarm systems
Vibration Monitoring	Detects abnormal vibrations	Industrial equipment

Basic Rules for Using Accelerometers in AVR C

Rule	Correct Example	Incorrect Example
Use proper ADC reference	`ADMUX	= (1 << REFS0);`
Calibrate sensor at startup	Read offset data initially	Skip calibration
Apply filtering for noise	Use moving average filter	Use raw noisy data
Use appropriate interface	Analog read for ADXL335	I2C for ADXL345

Syntax Table

SL	Operation	Syntax/Example	Description
1	Initialize ADC for Analog Accelerometer	`ADC_Init();`	Sets up ADC for analog data
2	Read Analog Axis Data	`x = ADC_Read(0);`	Reads analog value for X-axis
3	Initialize I2C for Digital Accelerometer	`I2C_Init();`	Prepares I2C communication
4	Read Digital Axis Data	`x = ReadRegister(AD XL345_X_ADDR);`	Reads digital data for X-axis
5	Detect Tilt	`if (x > THRESHOLD)`	Compares acceleration to threshold

Syntax Explanation

1. Initialize ADC for Analog Accelerometer

What does it do? Configures the ADC (Analog-to-Digital Converter) to read voltage output from the analog accelerometer. Each axis (X, Y, Z) produces a voltage proportional to acceleration in that direction.

Syntax: `ADC_Init();`

Example:

```
void ADC_Init() {
    ADMUX |= (1 << REFS0);   // Use AVCC as reference
voltage
    ADCSRA |= (1 << ADEN) | (1 << ADPS2);   // Enable
ADC and set prescaler to divide clock
}
```

Explanation:

- REFS0 selects AVCC as the reference voltage.
- ADEN enables the ADC hardware.
- ADPS2 sets the ADC prescaler, adjusting speed for optimal readings.

2. Read Analog Axis Data

What does it do? Reads a voltage value from the specified ADC channel (X, Y, or Z) and returns the digital equivalent.
Syntax: x = ADC_Read(0);
Example:

```
uint16_t ADC_Read(uint8_t channel) {
    ADMUX = (ADMUX & 0xF8) | (channel & 0x07);  //
Select desired channel
    ADCSRA |= (1 << ADSC);  // Start conversion
    while (ADCSRA & (1 << ADSC));  // Wait for
conversion to complete
    return ADC;  // Return the digital value
}
```

Explanation:
- ADMUX selects the appropriate axis channel (0 for X, 1 for Y, etc.).
- ADSC starts the conversion.
- The loop waits until conversion finishes.
- The digital value (0-1023 for 10-bit ADC) is returned.

3. Initialize I2C for Digital Accelerometer

What does it do? Configures the AVR microcontroller's I2C hardware to communicate with a digital accelerometer (like ADXL345).
Syntax: I2C_Init();
Example:

```
void I2C_Init() {
    TWSR = 0x00;  // Set prescaler to 1
    TWBR = 0x47;  // Set SCL frequency to 100kHz
(assuming 16 MHz CPU clock)
    TWCR = (1 << TWEN);  // Enable I2C
}
```

Explanation:
- Prescaler set to 1 (no division).
- TWBR controls the actual clock rate.
- TWEN enables I2C hardware.

4. Read Digital Axis Data

What does it do? Reads the acceleration data (one axis) from a register in a digital accelerometer via I2C.

Syntax: `x = ReadRegister(ADXL345_X_ADDR);`

Example:

```
uint8_t ReadRegister(uint8_t reg) {
    I2C_Start(ADXL345_ADDRESS);
    I2C_Write(reg);   // Send register address
    I2C_Start(ADXL345_ADDRESS | 0x01);   // Repeated
start for read
    uint8_t data = I2C_ReadNACK();   // Read single byte
    I2C_Stop();
    return data;
}
```

Explanation:
- Starts communication with the sensor.
- Writes the target register address (X, Y, or Z axis data).
- Repeated start to switch to read mode.
- Reads the data byte and stops communication.

5. Detect Tilt

What does it do? Compares the acceleration reading from a given axis to a pre-defined threshold. If the value exceeds the threshold, it indicates the device is tilted beyond the allowed angle.

Syntax: `if (x > THRESHOLD)`

Example:

```
#define THRESHOLD 500
if (x > THRESHOLD) {
    PORTB |= (1 << PB0);   // Turn on warning LED
}
```

Explanation:
- Compares the current X-axis reading to the threshold.
- If tilt is detected (value exceeds threshold), an LED or buzzer is activated.
- This is useful for basic tilt or vibration detection systems.

Real-life Applications Project: Tilt Detection Alarm System

Project Overview This project uses an accelerometer to detect when a device tilts beyond a threshold angle and activates an alarm (LED or buzzer).

Required Components

Component	Description
AVR Microcontroller	Main processing unit
ADXL335 Accelerometer	Analog 3-axis accelerometer
Buzzer or LED	Alarm indicator
Resistors	Current limiting

Circuit Connection Table

Component	AVR Pin	Power Source	Purpose
ADXL335 X Output	ADC0	5V	Reads X-axis acceleration
ADXL335 Y Output	ADC1	5V	Reads Y-axis acceleration
ADXL335 Z Output	ADC2	5V	Reads Z-axis acceleration
LED/Buzzer	PB0	5V	Alarm output

Project Code

```
#include <avr/io.h>
#include <util/delay.h>

#define THRESHOLD 500

void ADC_Init() {
```

```
    ADMUX |= (1 << REFS0);
    ADCSRA |= (1 << ADEN) | (1 << ADPS2);
}

uint16_t ADC_Read(uint8_t channel) {
    ADMUX = (ADMUX & 0xF8) | (channel & 0x07);
    ADCSRA |= (1 << ADSC);
    while (ADCSRA & (1 << ADSC));
    return ADC;
}

int main() {
    DDRB |= (1 << PB0);
    ADC_Init();

    while (1) {
        uint16_t x = ADC_Read(0);
        if (x > THRESHOLD) {
            PORTB |= (1 << PB0);
        } else {
            PORTB &= ~(1 << PB0);
        }
        _delay_ms(500);
    }
}
```

Expected Results

The microcontroller reads acceleration data from the X-axis. If the
value exceeds a set threshold, the LED lights up indicating tilt. This
can be expanded for multi-axis detection or vibration monitoring.

Chapter 54: Gyroscopes Sensors

Gyroscope sensors measure angular velocity, i.e., the rate of rotation around one or more axes. These sensors are widely used in motion detection, balancing systems, robotics, drones, and gaming controllers. AVR microcontrollers can interface with analog and digital gyroscopes to capture rotation data for real-time processing. This chapter explains how to configure and use gyroscopes with AVR microcontrollers.

Key Concepts of Gyroscope Interfacing in AVR C

Concept	Description	Example
Analog Gyroscopes	Output voltage proportional to rotation rate	LPR5150AL
Digital Gyroscopes	Communicate via I2C/SPI interface	MPU-6050
Angular Velocity	Measures rotation rate around X, Y, Z axes	3-axis gyroscope
Drift Compensation	Corrects sensor drift over time	Complementary Filter
Combining with Accelerometer	Enhances orientation estimation	IMU (Inertial Measurement Unit)

Basic Rules for Using Gyroscopes in AVR C

Rule	Correct Example	Incorrect Example
Use stable voltage reference	`ADMUX= (1 << REFS0);`	
Calibrate at startup	Read baseline at rest	Use raw data directly
Filter data	Apply complementary filter	Use unprocessed data
Use correct communication interface	Analog for LPR5150AL	I2C for MPU-6050

Syntax Table

SL	Operation	Syntax/Example	Description
1	Initialize ADC for Analog Gyroscope	`ADC_Init();`	Sets up ADC for analog sensor
2	Read Analog Gyro Data	`rateX = ADC_Read(0);`	Reads analog data for X-axis rotation
3	Initialize I2C for Digital Gyroscope	`I2C_Init();`	Prepares I2C communication
4	Read Digital Gyro Data	`rateX = ReadGyroRegister(M PU6050_XRATE_ADDR);`	Reads digital rotation rate for X-axis
5	Detect Excess Rotation	`if (rateX > THRESHOLD)`	Detects when rotation rate exceeds threshold

Syntax Explanation

1. Initialize ADC for Analog Gyroscope

What does it do? Configures the ADC (Analog-to-Digital Converter) to read voltage from analog gyroscope axes. Each axis produces a voltage proportional to angular velocity (rotation rate).

Syntax: ADC_Init();

Example:

```
void ADC_Init() {
    ADMUX |= (1 << REFS0);  // Use AVCC as reference
voltage
    ADCSRA |= (1 << ADEN) | (1 << ADPS2);  // Enable
ADC with prescaler
}
```

Explanation:
- REFS0 selects AVCC as the reference voltage.
- ADEN enables the ADC module.
- ADPS2 sets the prescaler to adjust the ADC clock speed for better accuracy.

2. Read Analog Gyro Data

What does it do? Reads a voltage value from a specific gyroscope axis (X, Y, or Z), representing angular velocity in that axis.

Syntax: `rateX = ADC_Read(0);`

Example:

```
uint16_t ADC_Read(uint8_t channel) {
    ADMUX = (ADMUX & 0xF8) | (channel & 0x07);  //
Select appropriate channel
    ADCSRA |= (1 << ADSC);  // Start conversion
    while (ADCSRA & (1 << ADSC));  // Wait until
conversion completes
    return ADC;  // Return digital value
}
```

Explanation:
- ADMUX selects the desired ADC channel (0 for X-axis, 1 for Y-axis, etc.).
- ADSC starts the conversion process.
- Returns a 10-bit value (0-1023) representing rotation rate.

3. Initialize I2C for Digital Gyroscope

What does it do? Configures the AVR microcontroller's I2C hardware to communicate with a digital gyroscope (like MPU-6050).

Syntax: `I2C_Init();`

Example:

```
void I2C_Init() {
    TWSR = 0x00;  // Set prescaler to 1
    TWBR = 0x47;  // Set SCL frequency (100 kHz)
    TWCR = (1 << TWEN);  // Enable I2C module
}
```

Explanation:
- TWSR sets no prescaler.
- TWBR controls clock rate based on CPU clock (16 MHz assumed).
- TWEN enables I2C hardware.

4. Read Digital Gyro Data

What does it do? Reads angular velocity (rotation rate) data from a specified register in a digital gyroscope.
Syntax: `rateX = ReadGyroRegister(MPU6050_XRATE_ADDR);`
Example:

```
uint8_t ReadGyroRegister(uint8_t reg) {
    I2C_Start(MPU6050_ADDRESS);
    I2C_Write(reg);  // Send register address
    I2C_Start(MPU6050_ADDRESS | 0x01);  // Switch to
read mode
    uint8_t data = I2C_ReadNACK();  // Read data from
register
    I2C_Stop();
    return data;
}
```

Explanation:
- Starts I2C communication with the gyroscope.
- Writes the register address to read (X, Y, or Z rate).
- Issues repeated start to switch to read mode.
- Reads the data byte and terminates communication.

5. Detect Excess Rotation

What does it do? Compares the measured angular velocity to a predefined threshold. If the rate exceeds the threshold, it triggers an alert.
Syntax: `if (rateX > THRESHOLD)`
Example:

```
#define THRESHOLD 300
if (rateX > THRESHOLD) {
    PORTB |= (1 << PB0);  // Trigger alarm (LED/buzzer)
}
```

Explanation:

- THRESHOLD defines the maximum safe rotation rate.
- If the rotation rate exceeds the threshold, the system activates an alert.
- This is useful for detecting sudden rotational movements in drones, vehicles, or machinery.

Real-life Applications Project: Gyroscope-based Rotation Alert System

Project Overview This project uses a gyroscope to detect excessive rotation and activates an alarm if the rotation rate exceeds a safe limit.

Required Components

Component	Description
AVR Microcontroller	Main processing unit
LPR5150AL Gyroscope	Analog 2-axis gyroscope
Buzzer or LED	Alarm indicator
Resistors	Current limiting

Circuit Connection Table

Component	AVR Pin	Power Source	Purpose
Gyro X Output	ADC0	5V	Reads X-axis rotation rate
Gyro Y Output	ADC1	5V	Reads Y-axis rotation rate
Buzzer/LED	PB0	5V	Alarm output

Project Code

```
#include <avr/io.h>
#include <util/delay.h>

#define THRESHOLD 300

void ADC_Init() {
    ADMUX |= (1 << REFS0);
```

```
    ADCSRA |= (1 << ADEN) | (1 << ADPS2);
}


uint16_t ADC_Read(uint8_t channel) {
    ADMUX = (ADMUX & 0xF8) | (channel & 0x07);
    ADCSRA |= (1 << ADSC);
    while (ADCSRA & (1 << ADSC));
    return ADC;
}

int main() {
    DDRB |= (1 << PB0);
    ADC_Init();

    while (1) {
        uint16_t rateX = ADC_Read(0);
        if (rateX > THRESHOLD) {
            PORTB |= (1 << PB0);
        } else {
            PORTB &= ~(1 << PB0);
        }
        _delay_ms(500);
    }
}
```

Expected Results

The microcontroller monitors rotation rate from the X-axis. If the rate exceeds a set threshold, an alarm is triggered.

Chapter 55: Controlling LEDs

Controlling LEDs with AVR microcontrollers is a fundamental and essential skill for embedded systems development. LEDs (Light Emitting Diodes) can be used as indicators, visual feedback, or status indicators in various projects. AVR microcontrollers can control LEDs using digital output pins, either by turning them on/off directly or through pulse width modulation (PWM) to adjust brightness.

This chapter explains how to configure and use AVR microcontroller pins to control LEDs.

Key Concepts of LED Control with AVR C

Concept	Description	Example
Digital Output Pin	Configuring a pin to output high/low logic	PORTB
Direct Control	Simple on/off control	Indicator LEDs
PWM Control	Adjusting brightness using PWM	Dimming LEDs
Multi-LED Patterns	Sequencing multiple LEDs	LED chase effect
Current Limiting	Using resistors to protect LEDs	220Ω resistor

Basic Rules for Using LEDs with AVR C

Rule	Correct Example	Incorrect Example
Set pin as output	`DDRB	= (1 << PB0);`
Use current limiting resistor	220Ω resistor	Direct connection
Logical control	`PORTB	= (1 << PB0);`
Use proper drive current	Drive low-power LEDs only	Driving high-current LEDs directly

Syntax Table

SL	Operation	Syntax/Example	Description
1	Set Pin as Output	`` `DDRB= (1 << PB0);` ``	
2	Turn LED ON	`` `PORTB = (1 << PB0);` ``	
3	Turn LED OFF	`PORTB &= ~(1 << PB0);`	Sets pin low to turn LED off
4	Toggle LED	`PORTB ^= (1 << PB0);`	Inverts pin state (on/off)
5	PWM Brightness Control	`OCR0A = brightness;`	Sets PWM duty cycle for brightness

Syntax Explanation

1. Set Pin as Output

What does it do? This operation sets a specified pin as an output pin, allowing it to drive external devices such as LEDs.
Syntax: `DDRB |= (1 << PB0);`
Example:
`DDRB |= (1 << PB0); // Set PB0 as output`

Explanation:
- DDRB is the Data Direction Register for port B.
- PB0 refers to the 0th pin of port B.
- `1 << PB0` sets only bit 0, leaving other pins unchanged.
- This makes PB0 an output pin, required for controlling an LED.

2. Turn LED ON

What does it do? This sets the output pin high, which applies 5V to the pin, turning the connected LED on.
Syntax: `PORTB |= (1 << PB0);`

Example:
```
PORTB |= (1 << PB0);   // Set PB0 high to turn LED ON
```

Explanation:
- PORTB is the output register for port B.
- 1 << PB0 sets the PB0 pin to logic HIGH.
- This causes current to flow through the LED (if properly wired), turning it on.

3. Turn LED OFF

What does it do? This clears (sets low) the specified pin, turning the connected LED off.
Syntax: PORTB &= ~(1 << PB0);
Example:
```
PORTB &= ~(1 << PB0);   // Clear PB0 to turn LED OFF
```

Explanation:
- PORTB is the output register for port B.
- ~(1 << PB0) creates a mask that clears only PB0.
- The result is the pin is pulled to 0V (LOW), turning the LED off.

4. Toggle LED

What does it do? This inverts the current state of the output pin, switching the LED between on and off.
Syntax: PORTB ^= (1 << PB0);
Example:
```
PORTB ^= (1 << PB0);   // Toggle PB0
```
Explanation:
- PORTB is the output register for port B.
- ^= performs bitwise XOR, which flips the current state of PB0.
- If PB0 was high, it becomes low; if low, it becomes high.
- This allows the LED to blink.

5. PWM Brightness Control

What does it do? This operation sets the duty cycle of a PWM signal on a timer-controlled pin, allowing the LED brightness to be adjusted.

Syntax: `OCR0A = brightness;`

Example:

```
OCR0A = 128;  // Set PWM duty cycle to 50%
```

Explanation:

- OCR0A is the Output Compare Register for Timer0.
- The timer automatically toggles the output pin according to the value in OCR0A.
- A higher value means a higher duty cycle, making the LED brighter.
- Requires configuring Timer0 in Fast PWM mode.

Real-life Applications Project: LED Blinking and Dimming System

Project Overview This project demonstrates how to control LEDs with AVR microcontroller, including simple blinking and PWM dimming.

Required Components

Component	Description
AVR Microcontroller	Main control unit
LED	Visual indicator
Resistor (220Ω)	Current limiting resistor

Circuit Connection Table

Component	AVR Pin	Power Source	Purpose
LED Anode	PB0	5V	LED control output
Resistor	Between LED and Ground	5V	Limits LED current

Project Code

```c
#include <avr/io.h>
#include <util/delay.h>

void LED_Init() {
    DDRB |= (1 << PB0);   // Set PB0 as output
}

void LED_Blink() {
    PORTB ^= (1 << PB0);   // Toggle LED state
    _delay_ms(500);
}

int main() {
    LED_Init();
    while (1) {
        LED_Blink();
    }
}
```

Expected Results

The LED connected to PB0 blinks on and off every 500 milliseconds,
demonstrating simple LED control with an AVR microcontroller.

Chapter 56: Using 7-Segment Displays

7-segment displays are commonly used in electronic devices to display numeric values. These displays consist of seven LEDs arranged in a figure-eight shape. By turning on or off specific segments, a 7-segment display can represent any digit from 0 to 9.

AVR microcontrollers can easily control 7-segment displays, either individually or multiplexed to show multiple digits. This chapter covers the use of both common anode and common cathode 7-segment displays, explaining how to control each segment and how to multiplex multiple displays for showing multi-digit values.

Key Concepts of 7-Segment Display Interfacing in AVR C

Concept	Description	Example
7-Segment Display	Displays numbers by lighting up specific segments.	Common Cathode/Anode
Common Cathode Display	All segments share a common cathode pin, and each segment is lit by applying a high signal to the segment pin.	74LS47 IC
Common Anode Display	All segments share a common anode pin, and each segment is lit by applying a low signal to the segment pin.	7-Segment Display (Basic)
Multiplexing	The technique used to drive multiple displays by switching between them rapidly, making them appear to display at once.	Two 7-segment Displays
Port Control	Using AVR I/O pins to control the segments of the display.	PORTB for segment control

Basic Rules for Using 7-Segment Displays in AVR C

Rule	Correct Example	Incorrect Example
Use appropriate segment pattern for digits	PORTB = 0x3F; for digit 0	Incorrect bit patterns
Set up the I/O pins as output	DDRB = 0xFF; for setting all Port B pins as output	Setting pins as input
Apply multiplexing for multiple digits	Use a short delay (_delay_ms(5);) between digits	No delay (flickering effect)
Correctly set the data direction for I/O pins	`DDRB= (1 << PB0);` to set pin as output	Not configuring pins properly

Syntax Table

SL	Operation	Syntax/Example	Description	
1	Initialize Port for 7-Segment Display	DDRB = 0xFF;	Set all pins of PORTB as output	
2	Display a Digit	PORTB = segment_data ;	Send the correct bit pattern to display digit	
3	Multiplex Multiple Digits	multiplex_di splay(digit1 , digit2);	Display two digits using multiplexing	
4	Control Segment Pin	`PORTB	= (1 << PB0);`	Light up a specific segment

Syntax Explanation

1. Initialize Port for 7-Segment Display

What does it do?
This function configures the AVR microcontroller's port (in this case, PORTB) to control the segments of the 7-segment display. All pins of PORTB are set as output to ensure they can be used to control the display.

Syntax:
```
DDRB = 0xFF;
```
Example:
```
void init_ports() {
    DDRB = 0xFF;   // Set all pins of PORTB as output
for 7-segment display
}
```

Explanation:
- DDRB: The **Data Direction Register** for **Port B**.
- Setting DDRB = 0xFF means all 8 bits in PORTB are set as output (0xFF is binary 11111111). This enables all the pins connected to the 7-segment display to be set as outputs so they can control each segment (A-G) of the display.

2. Display a Digit on 7-Segment Display

What does it do?
This function sends a bit pattern to PORTB, which lights up the appropriate segments to display a specific digit (0-9).
Syntax:
```
PORTB = segment_data;
```
Example:
```
void display_digit(uint8_t digit) {
    uint8_t segment_data = get_segment_data(digit);
    PORTB = segment_data;   // Display the number on the
7-segment display
}
```

Explanation:
- get_segment_data(digit): This function returns the bit pattern corresponding to the input digit. For example, for the digit 0, it might return 0x3F (binary 00111111), which lights up all segments except 'G' to form a '0'.
- PORTB: Sends the bit pattern to control the display.

This bit pattern can be customized depending on whether you're using a **common anode** or **common cathode** display.

3. Multiplex Multiple Digits

What does it do?
This function is used to display multiple digits (e.g., two 7-segment displays for "12") using multiplexing. The digits are switched rapidly to give the illusion that they are displayed at once.

Syntax:
```
multiplex_display(digit1, digit2);
```

Example:
```
void multiplex_display(uint8_t digit1, uint8_t digit2)
{
    DisplayDigit(0, digit1);   // Display first digit
    _delay_ms(5);   // Short delay to maintain display
    DisplayDigit(1, digit2);   // Display second digit
}
```

Explanation:
- `DisplayDigit(0, digit1)`: Updates the first digit display with `digit1`.
- `_delay_ms(5)`: The short delay allows each digit to remain visible to the human eye.
- `DisplayDigit(1, digit2)`: Updates the second digit display with `digit2`.

Multiplexing works by turning on one digit at a time, rapidly switching between them to give the appearance of both digits being displayed simultaneously.

4. Control Segment Pin

What does it do?
This function lights up a specific segment on the 7-segment display. It can be used for debugging or custom displays.

Syntax:
```
PORTB |= (1 << PB0);
```

Example:
```
void light_up_segment_A() {
    PORTB |= (1 << PB0);  // Light up segment 'A' of
the 7-segment display
}
```

Explanation:
- PORTB: Controls the pins connected to the segments of the 7-segment display.
- (1 << PB0): This operation shifts the number 1 to the left by PB0 bits (e.g., for PB0, it becomes 0b00000001).
- PORTB |= (1 << PB0): Sets PB0 high, which turns on segment 'A' (if using a **Common Cathode** display).

5. Full Digital Clock (Multiplexing Two Digits)

What does it do?
This example continuously updates two 7-segment displays to show a digital clock's minutes count (from 00 to 99). This showcases the multiplexing technique.

Syntax:
```
multiplex_display(tens, ones);
```
Example:
```
void multiplex_display(uint8_t digit1, uint8_t digit2)
{
    DisplayDigit(0, digit1);  // Display the tens place
    _delay_ms(5);  // Delay for visibility
    DisplayDigit(1, digit2);  // Display the ones place
}
```
Explanation:
- multiplex_display() takes two arguments: digit1 (the tens digit) and digit2 (the ones digit).
- Each digit is displayed sequentially, with a very brief delay (_delay_ms(5)) to ensure each is visible for the human eye.
- This function demonstrates how you can update two displays in a controlled multiplexed fashion, allowing you to display multi-digit values on just two displays.

Real-life Applications Project: 7-Segment Display Digital Clock

Project Overview
In this project, we will use two 7-segment displays to show a two-digit number (from 00 to 99), which could be used as a simple counter or digital clock display.

Required Components

Component	Description
AVR Microcontroller	Main processing unit
Two 7-Segment Displays	Display the two digits
Resistors (220Ω)	Used for current limiting on segments
Button (optional)	For incrementing the counter value

Circuit Connection Table

Component	AVR Pin	Power Source	Purpose
7-Segment Display 1	PORTB	5V	Controls first digit
7-Segment Display 2	PORTC	5V	Controls second digit

Project Code

```
#include <avr/io.h>
#include <util/d


elay.h>


#define THRESHOLD 300


void init_ports() {
    DDRB = 0xFF;  // Set all pins of PORTB as output
    DDRC = 0xFF;  // Set all pins of PORTC as output
}


uint8_t get_segment_data(uint8_t digit) {
    uint8_t segment_map[10] = {
        0x3F, // 0
```

```
        0x06, // 1
        0x5E, // 2
        0x6E, // 3
        0x76, // 4
        0x7B, // 5
        0x7F, // 6
        0x07, // 7
        0x7F, // 8
        0x7E  // 9
    };
    return segment_map[digit];
}

void display_digit(uint8_t digit, uint8_t port) {
    uint8_t segment_data = get_segment_data(digit);
    if (port == 0) {
        PORTB = segment_data;
    } else {
        PORTC = segment_data;
    }
}

void multiplex_display(uint8_t digit1, uint8_t digit2)
{
    display_digit(digit1, 0);  // Display the first
digit
    _delay_ms(5);  // Short delay for visibility
    display_digit(digit2, 1);  // Display the second
digit
}

int main() {
    uint8_t tens = 0, ones = 0;
    init_ports();

    while (1) {
        multiplex_display(tens, ones);
```

```
        _delay_ms(100);   // Update every 100ms
        ones++;
        if (ones == 10) {
            ones = 0;
            tens++;
            if (tens == 10) {
                tens = 0;
            }
        }
    }
}
```

Expected Results

The program should continuously display a two-digit number on the
two 7-segment displays, counting from 00 to 99.

Chapter 57: Interfacing LCD Displays

LCDs (Liquid Crystal Displays) are widely used in embedded systems for displaying information in a user-friendly manner. They provide a simple way to show textual information, sensor readings, or status messages. In this chapter, we'll cover how to interface a standard **16x2 LCD** with an **AVR microcontroller** (like the ATmega series). This chapter will discuss the control of the LCD, initialization, sending data/commands, and displaying strings on the screen.

The 16x2 LCD display consists of 2 lines with 16 characters in each line, and it uses a parallel interface, which is quite straightforward for microcontroller communication. We will look into the proper wiring, essential commands, and write functions for interfacing and controlling the display.

Key Concepts of LCD Interfacing in AVR C

Concept	Description	Example
LCD (Liquid Crystal Display)	A flat-panel display that can show text and numbers. The 16x2 LCD has 2 rows with 16 characters each.	16x2 LCD display
RS (Register Select Pin)	A control pin used to select between data and command modes.	PORTB0
RW (Read/Write Pin)	A control pin that determines whether data is written to or read from the LCD.	PORTB1
E (Enable Pin)	A control pin used to latch the data or command into the LCD by sending a high pulse.	PORTB2
Data Pins	Pins used to send the 8-bit data to the LCD. This can be in 8-bit or 4-bit mode.	PORTD
LCD Commands	Instructions for controlling the LCD, like clearing the display or moving the cursor.	0x01 (clear), 0x0C (display on)

Basic Rules for Using LCD with AVR C

Rule	Correct Example	Incorrect Example
Properly initialize the LCD	lcd_init();	Forgetting to call lcd_init()
Use commands to control the LCD (e.g., clear, cursor)	lcd_command(0x 01);	Sending invalid commands to LCD
Use appropriate delays after sending commands	_delay_ms(2); after clearing the display	Not adding delays causing instability
Set the correct data direction for I/O pins	`DDRB= 0x07;` to configure control pins as outputs	Forgetting to set data direction

Syntax Table

SL	Operation	Syntax/Example	Description
1	Initialize LCD	lcd_init();	Initializes the LCD with the appropriate settings
2	Send a Command to LCD	lcd_command(0x38);	Sends a command to control the LCD
3	Display a Character	lcd_data('A');	Displays a single character
4	Display a String	lcd_string(" Hello");	Displays a string on the LCD
5	Clear the LCD Display	lcd_clear();	Clears the display and resets the cursor position

Syntax Explanation

1. Initialize LCD

What does it do?
This function initializes the LCD by setting the display mode, clearing the screen, and enabling the LCD for use. It configures control pins and ensures that the display is ready for operations.
Syntax:
lcd_init();

Example:
```
void lcd_init() {
    _delay_ms(15);          // Wait for LCD to power up
    lcd_command(0x38);      // Set 8-bit mode and 2-line
display
    lcd_command(0x0C);      // Display on, cursor off,
blink off
    lcd_command(0x01);      // Clear the display
    _delay_ms(2);           // Wait for display to clear
}
```

Explanation:
- `_delay_ms(15)`: Wait for 15ms to ensure that the LCD has powered up.
- `lcd_command(0x38)`: Sets the display to 8-bit mode and 2-line format.
- `lcd_command(0x0C)`: Turns the display on with no cursor or blinking.
- `lcd_command(0x01)`: Clears the screen.
- `_delay_ms(2)`: Provides a short delay to allow the LCD to process the clear command.

2. Send a Command to LCD

What does it do?
This function sends a command (instruction) to the LCD, such as clearing the display or changing the cursor position.
Syntax:
```
lcd_command(command);
```
Example:
```
void lcd_command(uint8_t command) {
    PORTB &= ~(1 << PB0);        // RS = 0 for command
mode
    PORTB &= ~(1 << PB1);        // RW = 0 for write mode
    PORTD = command;             // Send the command to
the LCD
    PORTB |= (1 << PB2);         // Pulse the Enable pin
```

```
        _delay_ms(2);           // Wait for the command
to be processed
        PORTB &= ~(1 << PB2);   // Disable Enable pin
}
```

Explanation:
- PORTB &= ~(1 << PB0): Selects command mode by setting RS to 0.
- PORTB &= ~(1 << PB1): Selects write mode by setting RW to 0.
- PORTD = command: Sends the command byte to the LCD.
- PORTB |= (1 << PB2): Pulses the Enable pin to latch the command.
- _delay_ms(2): Wait for the LCD to process the command.
- PORTB &= ~(1 << PB2): Disables the Enable pin after the command is latched.

3. Display a Character

What does it do?
This function sends a character to the LCD for display.
Syntax:
```
lcd_data(data);
```
Example:
```
void lcd_data(uint8_t data) {
        PORTB |= (1 << PB0);        // RS = 1 for data mode
        PORTB &= ~(1 << PB1);       // RW = 0 for write
mode
        PORTD = data;               // Send the data byte
to the LCD
        PORTB |= (1 << PB2);        // Pulse the Enable pin
        _delay_ms(2);               // Wait for the data to
be processed
        PORTB &= ~(1 << PB2);       // Disable Enable pin
}
```

Explanation:

- `PORTB |= (1 << PB0)`: Selects data mode by setting RS to 1.
- `PORTB &= ~(1 << PB1)`: Selects write mode by setting RW to 0.
- `PORTD = data`: Sends the data byte to the LCD.
- `PORTB |= (1 << PB2)`: Pulses the Enable pin to latch the data.
- `_delay_ms(2)`: Waits for the data to be processed.
- `PORTB &= ~(1 << PB2)`: Disables the Enable pin after the data is latched.

4. Display a String

What does it do?
This function sends a string of characters to the LCD for display.
Syntax:
```
lcd_string("Hello World");
```
Example:
```
void lcd_string(const char *str) {
    while (*str) {                    // Loop until the null
terminator
        lcd_data(*str);               // Display the current
character
        str++;                        // Move to the next
character
    }
}
```

Explanation:

- `while (*str)`: Loops through each character of the string until it reaches the null terminator.
- `lcd_data(*str)`: Displays the current character.
- `str++`: Moves to the next character in the string.

5. Clear the LCD Display

What does it do?
This function clears the LCD display and resets the cursor to the home position.

Syntax:
```
lcd_clear();
```

Example:
```
void lcd_clear() {
    lcd_command(0x01);    // Send the clear display
command
    _delay_ms(2);         // Wait for the display to
clear
}
```

Explanation:
- `lcd_command(0x01)`: Sends the clear screen command to the LCD.
- `_delay_ms(2)`: Waits for the LCD to clear the display before performing any other operations.

Real-life Application Project: Temperature Monitoring System

In this section, we will create a **Temperature Monitoring System** using an **LM35** temperature sensor and a **16x2 LCD** to display the temperature in Celsius.

Required Components

Component	Description
AVR Microcontroller	Main processing unit

LM35 Sensor | Temperature sensor | | **16x2 LCD Display** | Display the temperature | | **Resistor (220Ω)** | Current limiting for the sensor |

Circuit Connection Table

Component	AVR Pin	Description
LM35 Sensor	ADC0	Analog temperature reading
16x2 LCD	PORTB	Controls the LCD

Project Code

```c
#include <avr/io.h>
#include <util/delay.h>
#include <stdio.h>

void lcd_init();
void lcd_command(uint8_t command);
void lcd_data(uint8_t data);
void lcd_string(const char *str);
void lcd_clear();
void adc_init();
uint16_t adc_read(uint8_t channel);

int main(void) {
    uint16_t adc_value;
    float temperature;
    char temp_str[10];

    // Initialize the LCD and ADC
    lcd_init();
    adc_init();

    while (1) {
        // Read the analog value from LM35
        adc_value = adc_read(0); // Assuming LM35 is
connected to ADC0
        temperature = (adc_value * 5.0 / 1024.0) *
100.0; // Convert ADC value to temperature

        // Display the temperature on the LCD
        sprintf(temp_str, "Temp: %.2f C", temperature);
```

```c
        lcd_clear();
        lcd_string(temp_str);

        _delay_ms(1000); // Wait before updating
    }
}

void lcd_init() {
    // LCD initialization code (same as previous
examples)
}

void lcd_command(uint8_t command) {
    // Command function code (same as previous
examples)
}

void lcd_data(uint8_t data) {
    // Data function code (same as previous examples)
}

void lcd_string(const char *str) {
    // String function code (same as previous examples)
}

void lcd_clear() {
    // Clear function code (same as previous examples)
}

void adc_init() {
    // ADC initialization code
    // Set ADC prescaler and reference voltage
    ADMUX = 0x00;   // Use VCC as reference, ADC0 as
input
    ADCSRA |= (1 << ADEN) | (1 << ADPS2) | (1 <<
ADPS1);
}
```

```
uint16_t adc_read(uint8_t channel) {
    ADMUX = (ADMUX & 0xF0) | (channel & 0x0F);   // Set
ADC channel
    ADCSRA |= (1 << ADSC);   // Start conversion
    while (ADCSRA & (1 << ADSC));   // Wait for
conversion to finish
    return ADC;   // Return the ADC result
}
```

Expected Results

The system will continuously display the temperature readings from the LM35 sensor on the LCD. The output will be updated every second.

Chapter 58: Working with OLED Displays

OLED (Organic Light Emitting Diode) displays are widely used in electronic devices for their vibrant colors, low power consumption, and clear visual output. Unlike traditional LCD displays, OLEDs don't require a backlight, as each pixel emits its own light. This allows for deep blacks and high contrast.

AVR microcontrollers can easily interface with OLED displays through communication protocols like I2C or SPI. In this chapter, we'll explore how to interface an OLED display with an AVR microcontroller using the I2C protocol to display text and images.

Key Concepts of OLED Display Interfacing in AVR C

Concept	Description	Example
OLED Display	A type of display that uses organic LEDs to create bright images.	128x64 OLED Display (I2C)
I2C Communication	A two-wire communication protocol used for connecting peripherals.	SDA, SCL lines for communication
OLED Driver	A chip (e.g., SSD1306) that controls the OLED display.	SSD1306, SH1106
Screen Resolution	The number of pixels on the screen. Common resolutions include 128x64 or 128x32.	128x64 pixels
Text and Graphics Display	Methods used to show text or simple graphics on the OLED screen.	Print text, draw lines, shapes

Basic Rules for Using OLED Displays in AVR C

Rule	Correct Example	Incorrect Example
Use the correct I2C address for OLED	0x78 for the SSD1306 I2C address	Using wrong address like 0x3C
Initialize I2C communication properly	i2c_init();	Not initializing I2C before use
Use the right library for the OLED driver	Include ssd1306.h for SSD1306 driver	Using an unsupported driver or library
Send display data with correct commands	ssd1306_write_data(0xFF);	Sending invalid commands for the driver

Syntax Table

SL	Operation	Syntax/Example	Description
1	Initialize I2C Communication	i2c_init();	Initializes the I2C bus
2	Initialize OLED Display	ssd1306_init();	Initializes the OLED display
3	Write Command to OLED	ssd1306_write_command(0xAE);	Sends command to the OLED (e.g., turn off)
4	Write Data to OLED	ssd1306_write_data(0xFF);	Sends data to the OLED display
5	Clear OLED Display	ssd1306_clear();	Clears the OLED screen
6	Print Text to OLED	ssd1306_print("Hello World!");	Prints text to the OLED screen

Syntax Explanation

1. Initialize I2C Communication

What does it do?
This function initializes the I2C communication between the AVR microcontroller and the OLED display. It sets the correct baud rate, enables the I2C peripheral, and ensures communication readiness.

Syntax:
```
i2c_init();
```
Example:
```
void i2c_init() {
    // Set up the I2C clock frequency, enable I2C
    TWSR = 0x00;                    // Prescaler value
    TWBR = 0x48;                    // Set bit rate for
the clock
    TWCR = (1 << TWEN) | (1 << TWSTA);   // Enable I2C
and send start condition
}
```

Explanation:
- TWBR is the **bit rate register** that controls the I2C clock speed.
- TWSR is the **TWI status register** that contains the prescaler value for I2C clock speed.
- TWCR is the **TWI control register** used to enable the I2C bus.

2. Initialize OLED Display

What does it do?
This function sends initialization commands to the OLED display to prepare it for use. These commands configure the display resolution, contrast, and other parameters.

Syntax:
```
ssd1306_init();
```
Example:
```
void ssd1306_init() {
    ssd1306_write_command(0xAE); // Turn off display
    ssd1306_write_command(0xD5); // Set display clock
divide ratio
    ssd1306_write_command(0x80); // Set recommended
ratio
    ssd1306_write_command(0xA8); // Set multiplex ratio
    ssd1306_write_command(0x3F); // Set multiplex to 63
(for 128x64)
    ssd1306_write_command(0xD3); // Set display offset
```

```
    ssd1306_write_command(0x00); // No offset
    ssd1306_write_command(0x40); // Set display start
line
    ssd1306_write_command(0x8D); // Enable charge pump
    ssd1306_write_command(0x14); // Charge pump setting
    ssd1306_write_command(0xAF); // Turn on display
}
```

Explanation:

- Each `ssd1306_write_command()` sends a specific command to the OLED display.
- The commands control various settings such as the clock speed, offset, charge pump, and display start line.
- The final command 0xAF turns the display on.

3. Write Command to OLED

What does it do?

This function sends a command byte to the OLED, which instructs the display on how to behave. Commands control various features such as display settings, contrast, and other hardware settings.

Syntax:

```
ssd1306_write_command(command);
```

Example:

```
void ssd1306_write_command(uint8_t command) {
    i2c_start();   // Start the I2C communication
    i2c_write(0x78);   // I2C address + write mode
    i2c_write(0x00);   // Command mode
    i2c_write(command); // Send the actual command
    i2c_stop();   // Stop I2C communication
}
```

Explanation:

- The function first initiates I2C communication (`i2c_start()`).
- The I2C address of the OLED is sent (0x78 for write mode).
- 0x00 tells the OLED that we are sending a command, not data.
- The command byte is then transmitted, followed by the `i2c_stop()` to terminate communication.

4. Write Data to OLED

What does it do?
This function sends data to the OLED, which will be displayed on the screen. Typically, data is pixel information (binary values representing whether a pixel should be on or off).

Syntax:
```
ssd1306_write_data(data);
```

Example:
```c
void ssd1306_write_data(uint8_t data) {
    i2c_start();      // Start I2C communication
    i2c_write(0x78);  // I2C address + write mode
    i2c_write(0x40);  // Data mode
    i2c_write(data);  // Send data byte
    i2c_stop();       // Stop I2C communication
}
```

Explanation:
- Similar to the write_command() function, but instead of sending a command byte, 0x40 indicates that we're sending data to be displayed.
- Each data byte represents one pixel column on the display, with 0xFF meaning all pixels are on and 0x00 meaning all pixels are off.

5. Display Text on OLED

What does it do?
This function displays a string of characters on the OLED screen.

Syntax:
```
ssd1306_print("Hello, World!");
```

Example:
```c
void ssd1306_print(const char* str) {
    while (*str) {
        ssd1306_write_data(*str);  // Write each
character
```

```
        str++;
    }
}
```

Explanation:
- The function loops through each character of the input string.
- For each character, `ssd1306_write_data()` is called to write it to the OLED.

Real-life Application Project: OLED Temperature Monitor

Project Overview
 This project uses an OLED display to show the temperature readings from an LM35 sensor. The temperature is displayed in real-time on the OLED screen.

Required Components

Component	Description
AVR Microcontroller	Controls the system
OLED Display	Displays temperature
LM35 Temperature Sensor	Reads temperature data
Resistors (220Ω)	

Circuit Connection Table

Component	AVR Pin	Purpose
LM35 Sensor	ADC0	Reads temperature data
OLED Display	SDA, SCL	Communicates with display

Project Code

```
#include <avr/io.h>
#include <util/delay.h>

void i2c_init() {
    // I2C initialization code here
}
```

```c
void ssd1306_init() {
    // OLED initialization code here
}

void ssd1306_write_command(uint8_t command) {
    // Send command to OLED code here
}

void ssd1306_write_data(uint8_t data) {
    // Send data to OLED code here
}

void ssd1306_print(const char* str) {
    // Print text to OLED code here
}

uint16_t read_adc(uint8_t channel) {
    // Read ADC value from LM35
    return ADC;  // Return the ADC value
}

int main() {
    uint16_t temperature;
    char buffer[10];
    i2c_init();
    ssd1306_init();
    while (1) {
        temperature = read_adc(0);  // Read temperature
from LM35
        sprintf(buffer, "Temp: %dC", temperature);  //
Convert ADC to temperature
        ssd1306_print(buffer);  // Display temperature
on OLED
        _delay_ms(1000);  // Update every 1 second
    }
}
```

Chapter 59: Working with TFT Displays

TFT (Thin Film Transistor) displays are widely used in modern electronic devices due to their ability to show full-color graphics and offer high resolutions. Unlike OLED displays, TFT displays require a backlight to illuminate the pixels, but they still offer vibrant and sharp images. TFTs are available in various sizes and resolutions, with the most common being 320x240 pixels or 128x160 pixels.

AVR microcontrollers can interface with TFT displays using communication protocols like SPI. In this chapter, we will explore how to interface a TFT display with an AVR microcontroller using the SPI protocol and display text, shapes, and images.

Key Concepts of TFT Display Interfacing in AVR C

Concept	Description	Example
TFT Display	A type of display that uses a matrix of thin-film transistors for pixel control.	320x240 TFT Display
SPI Communica tion	A synchronous serial communication protocol for fast data transmission.	MOSI, SCK, CS pins
TFT Driver	A chip (e.g., ILI9341) that controls the TFT display.	ILI9341, ST7735
Screen Resolution	The number of pixels on the screen. Common resolutions include 320x240 or 128x160.	320x240 pixels
Color Depth	The number of colors that can be displayed, usually 16-bit or 18-bit.	16-bit (RGB565)
Graphics and Text Display	Methods to display graphical elements and text on the TFT screen.	Draw lines, circles, text

Basic Rules for Using TFT Displays in AVR C

Rule	Correct Example	Incorrect Example
Initialize SPI communication properly	`spi_init();`	Not initializing SPI before use
Use the correct TFT driver for the display	Include `ili9341.h` for ILI9341 driver	Using an unsupported driver or library
Set the correct screen orientation	`tft_set_orientat ion(0);`	Using wrong orientation parameters
Use the correct color format (RGB565)	`tft_draw_pixel(x , y, RGB(255, 0, 0));`	Using unsupported color formats

Syntax Table

SL	Operation	Syntax/Example	Description
1	Initialize SPI Communication	`spi_init();`	Initializes the SPI bus
2	Initialize TFT Display	`tft_init();`	Initializes the TFT display
3	Set TFT Orientation	`tft_set_orientati on(0);`	Set display orientation (portrait/landscape)
4	Draw Pixel on TFT	`tft_draw_pixel(x, y, color);`	Draws a pixel at (x, y) with specified color
5	Draw Line on TFT	`tft_draw_line(x1, y1, x2, y2, color);`	Draws a line from (x1, y1) to (x2, y2)
6	Print Text on TFT	`tft_print("Hello, World!");`	Prints text to the TFT screen

Syntax Explanation

1. Initialize SPI Communication

What does it do?
This function initializes the SPI communication between the AVR microcontroller and the TFT display. It configures the SPI speed, mode, and selects the correct pins.

Syntax:
```
spi_init();
```

Example:
```
void spi_init() {
    // Set the SPI parameters (Master mode, MSB first,
clock speed)
    DDRB |= (1 << PB5) | (1 << PB7) | (1 << PB4); //
Set MOSI, SCK, and CS pins as output
    SPCR = (1 << SPE) | (1 << MSTR) | (1 << SPR0); //
Enable SPI, master mode, clock speed
}
```

Explanation:
- **DDRB**: The **Data Direction Register** for port B, where the pins for SPI are defined (MOSI, SCK, and CS).
  - PB5, PB7, and PB4 are set as output pins (MOSI, SCK, and CS).
- **SPCR**: The **SPI Control Register** that sets up the configuration for the SPI communication.
  - SPE: Enables the SPI module.
  - MSTR: Configures the microcontroller as the SPI master.
  - SPR0: Configures the SPI clock speed. A value of 0x01 sets the clock speed to a prescaler of 16.

2. Initialize TFT Display
What does it do?
This function sends the necessary initialization commands to the TFT display to set up the screen, including the resolution, orientation, and color format.

Syntax:
```
tft_init();
```
Example:
```
void tft_init() {
    spi_init();  // Initialize SPI
    tft_reset(); // Reset TFT display
    tft_send_command(0x01); // Software reset command
    tft_send_command(0x28); // Display off command
    tft_send_command(0x11); // Exit sleep mode command
    tft_send_command(0x29); // Display on command
}
```

Explanation:
- The TFT initialization sequence involves multiple steps where commands are sent to configure the display's settings.
    - `tft_reset()`: Resets the TFT display to ensure it starts in a known state.
    - `tft_send_command(0x01)`: Sends a **software reset** command to the TFT.
    - `tft_send_command(0x28)`: Turns the display off.
    - `tft_send_command(0x11)`: Exits sleep mode to wake up the display.
    - `tft_send_command(0x29)`: Turns the display on.

3. Set TFT Orientation

What does it do?
This function sets the orientation of the TFT screen to either portrait or landscape mode.
Syntax:
```
tft_set_orientation(orientation);
```
Example:
```
void tft_set_orientation(uint8_t orientation) {
    if (orientation == 0) {
        tft_send_command(0x36); // Set to Portrait mode
        tft_send_data(0x48);    // Data to set portrait
orientation
    } else {
```

```
        tft_send_command(0x36); // Set to Landscape
mode
        tft_send_data(0x28);     // Data to set
landscape orientation
    }
}
```

Explanation:
- The tft_set_orientation() function allows you to set the display's orientation.
  - **0** for portrait orientation.
  - **1** for landscape orientation.
- tft_send_command(0x36) sends the orientation command.
- The **data byte** (0x48 for portrait and 0x28 for landscape) is used to set the orientation.

4. Draw Pixel on TFT

What does it do?
This function draws a single pixel at the specified (x, y) coordinates with the given color.
Syntax:
```
tft_draw_pixel(x, y, color);
```
Example:
```
void tft_draw_pixel(uint16_t x, uint16_t y, uint16_t
color) {
    tft_send_command(0x2A); // Set column address
    tft_send_data(x >> 8);   // MSB of x-coordinate
    tft_send_data(x & 0xFF); // LSB of x-coordinate
    tft_send_command(0x2B); // Set row address
    tft_send_data(y >> 8);   // MSB of y-coordinate
    tft_send_data(y & 0xFF); // LSB of y-coordinate
    tft_send_command(0x2C); // Write data to memory
    tft_send_data(color >> 8); // MSB of color
    tft_send_data(color & 0xFF); // LSB of color
}
```

Explanation:

- **0x2A**: Command to set the **column address** of the TFT screen (defines the horizontal position of the pixel).
- **0x2B**: Command to set the **row address** (defines the vertical position).
- **0x2C**: Command to write the color data into the display's memory at the specified pixel location.
- **color** is typically passed as a 16-bit color value (RGB565), with the higher 8 bits representing the red component and the lower 8 bits representing the green and blue components.

5. Print Text on TFT

What does it do?
This function prints a string of text onto the TFT display.
Syntax:
```
tft_print("Hello, World!");
```
Example:
```
void tft_print(const char*

 str) {
    while (*str) {
        tft_draw_char(*str, current_x, current_y,
color);
        str++;
        current_x += char_width;  // Move the cursor to
the right for the next character
        if (current_x >= screen_width) {
            current_x = 0;  // Reset X position if end
of screen is reached
            current_y += char_height;  // Move to the
next line
        }
    }
}
```

Explanation:

- The function loops through each character of the string.
- For each character, `tft_draw_char()` is used to draw it at the current cursor position (`current_x, current_y`).
- **current_x** and **current_y** track the position of the cursor on the screen, and they are updated after each character is printed.
- **char_width** and **char_height** are used to determine how much space each character occupies.

Real-life Application Project: TFT Temperature and Humidity Display

Project Overview

In this project, we will use a TFT display to show the temperature and humidity readings from a DHT11 sensor in real-time. The data will be updated every second.

Required Components

Component	Description
AVR Microcontroller	Controls the system
TFT Display	Displays temperature and humidity
DHT11 Temperature and Humidity Sensor	Measures temperature and humidity
Resistors (220Ω)	For sensor connection

Circuit Connection Table

Component	AVR Pin	Purpose
DHT11 Sensor	PD2	Reads data from sensor
TFT Display	MOSI, SCK, CS	SPI communication

Project Code

```
#include <avr/io.h>
#include <util/delay.h>
#include <stdio.h>
#include "tft.h"
```

```c
void spi_init() {
    // SPI initialization code
}

void tft_init() {
    // TFT initialization code
}

void tft_print(const char* str) {
    // Print text to TFT
}

uint8_t read_dht11() {
    // Read data from DHT11 sensor
    return 25;  // Example temperature value (25°C)
}

int main() {
    char buffer[20];

    spi_init();
    tft_init();

    while (1) {
        uint8_t temperature = read_dht11();  // Read
temperature from DHT11
        sprintf(buffer, "Temp: %dC", temperature);  //
Convert to string
        tft_print(buffer);  // Display temperature on
TFT
        _delay_ms(1000);  // Update every 1 second
    }
}
```

Chapter 60: Working with a Buzzer

A buzzer is a small, electromechanical device that produces an audible sound when energized. It is widely used in embedded systems to provide audible alerts or feedback to users. Buzzers are typically categorized into two types: **active buzzers** and **passive buzzers**. An active buzzer generates sound as soon as power is applied, whereas a passive buzzer requires an external signal (such as a frequency) to produce sound.

In this chapter, we will learn how to interface both types of buzzers with an AVR microcontroller, using basic GPIO operations for active buzzers and PWM (Pulse Width Modulation) to control the tone of passive buzzers.

Key Concepts of Buzzer Interfacing in AVR C

Concept	Description	Example
Active Buzzer	A buzzer that emits sound when powered on (no driving signal needed).	5V active buzzer
Passive Buzzer	A buzzer that requires a frequency signal to produce sound.	5V passive buzzer (PWM control)
PWM (Pulse Width Modulation)	A technique for generating varying signals to control sound frequency.	Tone generation via PWM
Tone Frequency	The frequency of the sound produced by the buzzer, measured in Hz.	1000 Hz, 2000 Hz
Microcontroller Pin	The I/O pin used to control the buzzer.	Port B Pin 3

Basic Rules for Using Buzzers in AVR C

Rule	Correct Example	Incorrect Example
Choose the correct type of buzzer	Use a PWM pin for a passive buzzer	Trying to drive a passive buzzer directly from a digital pin
Initialize the pin properly	`DDRB= (1 << PB3);`	Not configuring the pin as output
Use proper frequency for tone generation	OCR0A = 128;	Using a fixed value without considering frequency
Activate buzzer correctly	`PORTB = (1 << PB3);`	Trying to drive an active buzzer without turning it on
Use appropriate delay for duration of sound	_delay_ms(1000);	Not adding any delay to control sound duration

Syntax Table

SL	Operation	Syntax/Example	Description
1	Set Buzzer Pin as Output	`DDRB= (1 << PB3);`	Set PB3 as an output pin for buzzer control
2	Turn On Active Buzzer	`PORTB = (1 << PB3);`	Turn on an active buzzer (high voltage)
3	Turn Off Active Buzzer	PORTB &= ~(1 << PB3);	Turn off an active buzzer (low voltage)
4	Generate Sound on Passive Buzzer	OCR0A = 128;	Set PWM frequency to generate sound on a passive buzzer
5	Start PWM for Tone	`TCCR0A = (1 << COM0A0);`	Start PWM signal on the passive buzzer pin
6	Stop PWM for Tone	TCCR0A &= ~(1 << COM0A0);	Stop PWM signal for the passive buzzer

Syntax Explanation

1. Set Buzzer Pin as Output

What does it do?

This function sets up a specific I/O pin of the AVR microcontroller as an output, which is necessary for controlling the buzzer. In this case, we configure pin PB3 (port B, pin 3) as an output pin to control the buzzer.

Syntax:

```
DDRB |= (1 << PB3);
```

Example:

```
void buzzer_init() {
    DDRB |= (1 << PB3);   // Set PB3 as output pin for buzzer
}
```

Explanation:

- **DDRB**: This is the **Data Direction Register** for port B. By writing 1 to a bit in this register, the corresponding pin is set to output mode.
- **(1 << PB3)**: This is a bitwise operation that shifts 1 to the left by 3 positions (because PB3 is pin 3). This ensures that only pin 3 is set as an output, leaving other pins unaffected.
- **DDRB |=**: The |= operator ensures that the bit corresponding to PB3 is set to 1, configuring it as an output pin.

2. Turn On Active Buzzer

What does it do?

This function turns on an **active buzzer** by setting the corresponding output pin high, which provides the voltage necessary to generate sound.

Syntax:

```
PORTB |= (1 << PB3);
```

Example:

```
void buzzer_on() {
    PORTB |= (1 << PB3);   // Turn on active buzzer (set pin high)
}
```

Explanation:
- **PORTB**: This is the **Data Register** for port B. Writing a 1 to a bit in this register sets the corresponding pin high (providing voltage to the buzzer).
- **(1 << PB3)**: This shifts 1 to the left by 3 positions, corresponding to pin PB3. This operation sets PB3 high.
- **PORTB |=**: The |= operator ensures that the bit corresponding to PB3 is set to 1, powering the buzzer and turning it on.

3. Turn Off Active Buzzer

What does it do?
This function turns off the active buzzer by setting the corresponding output pin low, cutting off the voltage and stopping the sound.

Syntax:
```
PORTB &= ~(1 << PB3);
```
Example:
```
void buzzer_off() {
    PORTB &= ~(1 << PB3);  // Turn off active buzzer
(set pin low)
}
```

Explanation:
- **PORTB**: This is the **Data Register** for port B. Writing a 0 to a bit in this register sets the corresponding pin low (removing voltage from the buzzer).
- **~(1 << PB3)**: The ~ operator inverts the bit corresponding to PB3. Instead of setting the bit to 1, it sets it to 0 (low).
- **PORTB &=**: The &= operator ensures that only the PB3 bit is cleared (set to 0), turning off the buzzer.

4. Generate Sound on Passive Buzzer

What does it do?
This function sets the frequency of the tone that will be generated by the **passive buzzer** using PWM. The frequency is controlled by the value stored in the **OCR0A** register, which determines the duration of each high and low cycle of the PWM signal.

Syntax:
```
OCR0A = 128;
```

Example:
```
void buzzer_generate_tone(uint8_t frequency) {
    OCR0A = frequency;   // Set PWM frequency for tone
generation
}
```

Explanation:
- **OCR0A**: This is the **Output Compare Register A** for **Timer/Counter 0**. It controls the duty cycle and frequency of the PWM signal generated by the timer.
- **frequency**: The value assigned to **OCR0A** determines the frequency of the generated sound. For example, a value of 128 corresponds to a specific tone frequency, while higher or lower values change the pitch of the sound.
- **PWM Signal**: The microcontroller uses the value in **OCR0A** to control the frequency of the PWM signal that drives the passive buzzer. Higher values correspond to lower frequencies (lower-pitched sounds), while lower values correspond to higher frequencies (higher-pitched sounds).

5. Start PWM for Tone

What does it do?
This function starts the PWM signal on the **OC0A** pin, which is used to drive the passive buzzer. The PWM signal alternates between high and low states at a frequency determined by the **OCR0A** register.

Syntax:
```
TCCR0A |= (1 << COM0A0);
```

Example:

```
void buzzer_start_pwm() {
    TCCR0A |= (1 << COM0A0);  // Enable PWM on OC0A pin
}
```

Explanation:
- **TCCR0A**: This is the **Timer/Counter Control Register A**. It configures the behavior of **Timer/Counter 0** and determines how the PWM signal is generated.
- **COM0A0**: This bit in **TCCR0A** controls the **Compare Output Mode A** for Timer/Counter 0. Setting this bit to 1 enables PWM output on the **OC0A** pin.
- **TCCR0A |=**: The |= operator ensures that the **COM0A0** bit is set to 1, starting the PWM signal.

6. Stop PWM for Tone

What does it do?
This function stops the PWM signal, turning off the tone generated by the passive buzzer.

Syntax:

```
TCCR0A &= ~(1 << COM0A0);
```

Example:

```
void buzzer_stop_pwm() {
    TCCR0A &= ~(1 << COM0A0);  // Disable PWM on OC0A
pin
}
```

Explanation:
- **TCCR0A**: This is the **Timer/Counter Control Register A**. It manages the settings for Timer/Counter 0.
- **COM0A0**: This bit controls the **Compare Output Mode A** for Timer/Counter 0. Clearing this bit stops the PWM signal from being output on the **OC0A** pin.
- **TCCR0A &=**: The &= operator ensures that the **COM0A0** bit is cleared (set to 0), stopping the PWM signal and turning off the buzzer.

Real-life Application Project: Security System with Buzzer

Project Overview

In this project, a buzzer will be used to alert the user when a security sensor (e.g., a motion sensor) is triggered. The buzzer will sound for a specific duration, notifying the user of a potential intrusion.

Required Components

Component	Description
AVR Microcontroller	Controls the buzzer and sensor
Passive Buzzer	Generates sound for alert
Sensor	Detects motion or other events

Circuit Connection Table

Component	AVR Pin	Purpose
Buzzer	PB3	Controls buzzer sound
Sensor	PD2	Detects event trigger

Project Code

```c
#include <avr/io.h>
#include <util/delay.h>

void buzzer_init() {
    DDRB |= (1 << PB3);   // Set PB3 as output pin for
buzzer
}

void buzzer_on() {
    PORTB |= (1 << PB3);   // Turn on active buzzer
}

void buzzer_off() {
    PORTB &= ~(1 << PB3);   // Turn off active buzzer
}

uint8_t read_sensor() {
    return PIND & (1 << PD2);   // Read sensor input
```

```
(motion detection)
}

int main() {
    buzzer_init();  // Initialize buzzer control pin

    while (1) {
        if (read_sensor()) {  // If sensor is triggered
(motion detected)
            buzzer_on();        // Activate buzzer
            _delay_ms(1000);    // Sound the buzzer for 1
second
            buzzer_off();       // Deactivate buzzer
        }
    }
}
```

Expected Results

When the sensor is triggered (e.g., motion detected), the buzzer will sound for one second and then turn off. This process will repeat as long as the sensor continues to detect an event.

Chapter 61: Generating Sounds with PWM

Generating sounds using a microcontroller involves producing audio signals of different frequencies. One common method to achieve this is by utilizing **Pulse Width Modulation (PWM)**. PWM can be used to produce audio tones by varying the duty cycle of a square wave, which controls the frequency and the tone of the sound emitted by a speaker or buzzer.

In this chapter, we will explore how to use PWM to generate different tones and sounds with an **AVR microcontroller**. We will also cover the basics of how to configure **timers** and **output compare modes** to generate a PWM signal that can drive an external buzzer or speaker.

Key Concepts of Sound Generation Using PWM in AVR
Pulse Width Modulation (PWM)
 A method of generating a square wave signal by varying the duty cycle. It can be used for tone generation with a buzzer or speaker.
Timer/Counter
 An AVR internal module that can be used to generate PWM signals. Timers are crucial for controlling the frequency of the PWM signal.
Frequency
 The rate at which a signal oscillates, measured in Hz. It determines the pitch of the sound produced.
Duty Cycle
 The proportion of time the PWM signal is high within one cycle. This can be adjusted to control the volume or loudness of the sound.
Speaker/Buzzer
 An output device that converts electrical signals into sound. Passive buzzers require a PWM signal to emit tones.

Basic Rules for Generating Sound in AVR C

Rule	Correct Example	Incorrect Example
Use a timer to generate PWM signal	`TCCR0A = (1 << COM0A0);`	Not configuring timer correctly for PWM
Set the appropriate frequency for sound	OCR0A = 128;	Using a fixed, incorrect value for tone
Control the duty cycle for tone modulation	OCR0A = 128;	Not adjusting duty cycle for tonal variation
Start and stop PWM signal properly	`TCCR0A = (1 << COM0A0);`	Forgetting to stop the PWM signal after use
Use delay functions for sound duration	_delay_ms(500);	Not adding delays for sound duration

Syntax Table

SL	Operation	Syntax/Example	Description
1	Initialize Timer for PWM	`TCCR0A = (1 << COM0A0);`	Configure Timer0 for PWM output
2	Set Frequency (Tone)	OCR0A = 128;	Set the frequency of the tone
3	Start PWM	`TCCR0A = (1 << COM0A0);`	Enable PWM on the output pin
4	Stop PWM	TCCR0A &= ~(1 << COM0A0);	Disable PWM and stop sound
5	Set Timer for PWM (prescaler)	`TCCR0B = (1 << CS00);`	Set Timer0 prescaler for correct timing
6	Set Duty Cycle (Volume control)	OCR0B = 128;	Control the duty cycle for sound volume

Syntax Explanation

1. Initialize Timer for PWM

What does it do?
This function configures the **AVR's Timer** to operate in **PWM mode**. The **Timer** is used to generate a square wave signal with a specific frequency, which will be output to a pin connected to a buzzer or speaker.
Syntax:
```
TCCR0A |= (1 << COM0A0);
```
Example:
```
void pwm_init() {
    TCCR0A |= (1 << COM0A0);   // Set Timer0 to PWM
mode, output on OC0A (Pin)
}
```

Explanation:
- **TCCR0A**: This is the **Timer/Counter Control Register A**. By setting the **COM0A0** bit, we configure the timer to generate a PWM signal on the output compare pin (**OC0A**).
- **COM0A0**: This bit controls the **Compare Output Mode** for **Timer0**, specifically the **OC0A** pin. Setting it to 1 enables PWM output.

2. Set Frequency (Tone)

What does it do?
This function sets the frequency of the **PWM signal** generated by the **Timer**. The frequency of the tone is determined by the value stored in the **OCR0A** register, which defines the period of the PWM signal.
Syntax:
```
OCR0A = 128;
```
Example:
```
void set_frequency(uint8_t frequency) {
    OCR0A = frequency;   // Set PWM frequency for tone
generation
}
```

Explanation:
- **OCR0A**: This is the **Output Compare Register A** for **Timer0**. It holds the value that determines the frequency of the PWM signal. A lower value in **OCR0A** corresponds to a higher frequency, while a higher value corresponds to a lower frequency.
- **Frequency**: The value you set in **OCR0A** directly affects the frequency of the sound produced. Typically, for audio applications, this would be set to a value corresponding to the desired pitch of the sound (e.g., 1000 Hz for a standard tone).

3. Start PWM

What does it do?
This function starts the **PWM signal** generation. When the PWM mode is enabled and the frequency is set, this function begins outputting the PWM signal at the configured frequency to drive the speaker or buzzer.

Syntax:
```
TCCR0A |= (1 << COM0A0);
```

Example:
```
void start_pwm() {
    TCCR0A |= (1 << COM0A0);   // Start PWM on OC0A pin
(e.g., PB3)
}
```

Explanation:
- **TCCR0A**: This register controls the operation of **Timer0**.
- **COM0A0**: Setting this bit to 1 enables the **OC0A** pin for PWM output.
- **PWM Output**: The signal will alternate between high and low at the frequency determined by **OCR0A**. The buzzer or speaker will produce sound based on this signal.

4. Stop PWM

What does it do?
This function stops the **PWM signal** from being output, thus silencing the buzzer or speaker. Stopping the PWM signal prevents further tone generation.

Syntax:
```
TCCR0A &= ~(1 << COM0A0);
```

Example:
```
void stop_pwm() {
    TCCR0A &= ~(1 << COM0A0);  // Disable PWM on OC0A
pin (e.g., PB3)
}
```

Explanation:
- **TCCR0A**: This register controls the timer settings.
- **COM0A0**: Clearing this bit (set to 0) disables PWM output on the **OC0A** pin, effectively stopping the tone generation.

5. Set Timer for PWM (prescaler)

What does it do?
This function configures the **prescaler** of **Timer0** to adjust the speed at which the timer counts. The prescaler determines how quickly the timer counts up, and thus how frequently the PWM signal is generated.

Syntax:
```
TCCR0B |= (1 << CS00);
```

Example:
```
void set_prescaler() {
    TCCR0B |= (1 << CS00);  // Set prescaler for Timer0
to 1 (no prescaling)
}
```

Explanation:
- **TCCR0B**: This register controls the clock source and prescaler for **Timer0**.
- **CS00**: Setting this bit to 1 configures **Timer0** to use the system clock with no prescaling, meaning the timer will increment with every clock cycle.

6. Set Duty Cycle (Volume control)

What does it do?
This function adjusts the **duty cycle** of the **PWM signal**, controlling the "volume" or "loudness" of the sound. The duty cycle defines the proportion of time the signal is high versus low during one cycle.

Syntax:
```
OCR0B = 128;
```

Example:
```
void set_duty_cycle(uint8_t duty) {
    OCR0B = duty;  // Adjust duty cycle for volume
control
}
```

Explanation:

- **OCR0B**: This is the **Output Compare Register B** for **Timer0**. It controls the duty cycle of the PWM signal. A value of 128 corresponds to a **50% duty cycle**, which means the signal is high for half of the period and low for the other half.
- **Duty Cycle**: A higher duty cycle means the signal stays high longer, resulting in a louder sound. A lower duty cycle reduces the loudness.

Real-life Application Project: Musical Tone Generator

Project Overview
In this project, we use a **PWM signal** to generate **musical tones** on a passive buzzer. The AVR microcontroller will output different tones by adjusting the frequency of the PWM signal.

Required Components

Component	Description
AVR Microcontroller	Controls the PWM signal for sound generation
Passive Buzzer	Emits sound based on PWM signal
Push Buttons	Allows user to change tones or start the song

Circuit Connection Table

Component	AVR Pin	Purpose
Buzzer	PB3	Outputs PWM signal for sound
Button1	PD2	Selects tone 1
Button2	PD3	Selects tone 2

Project Code

```c
#include <avr/io.h>
#include <util/delay.h>

void pwm_init() {
    TCCR0A |= (1 << COM0A0);   // Set Timer0 to PWM mode
on OC0A
    TCCR0B |= (1 << CS00);     // No prescaling
}

void set_frequency(uint8_t frequency) {
    OCR0A = frequency;   // Set PWM frequency
}

void start_pwm() {
    TCCR0A |= (1 << COM0A0);   // Start PWM
}

void stop_pwm() {
    TCCR0A &= ~(1 << COM0A0);   // Stop PWM
}

int main() {
    pwm_init();   // Initialize PWM
    uint8_t frequency = 128;   // Default frequency for
tone 1

    while (1) {
        if (PIND & (1 << PD2)) {   // Button1 pressed
(tone 1)
```

```
            frequency = 128;   // Set frequency for tone
1 (e.g., 1000 Hz)
        }
        if (PIND & (1 << PD3)) {   // Button2 pressed
(tone 2)
            frequency = 64;    // Set frequency for tone
2 (e.g., 2000 Hz)
        }

        set_frequency(frequency);  // Adjust frequency
        start_pwm();               // Start sound
generation
        _delay_ms(500);            // Play tone for 500
ms
        stop_pwm();                // Stop sound
        _delay_ms(500);            // Delay between
tones
    }
}
```

Expected Results

The microcontroller will generate different tones when the buttons
are pressed. The user can switch between tones with different
frequencies, and the buzzer will emit a corresponding sound. The
tone will play for 500 milliseconds before stopping.

Chapter 62: Controlling DC Motors

DC motors are widely used in various robotic and mechanical applications. They are simple to interface with microcontrollers like the **AVR** and can be controlled to rotate in either direction, speed, and at specific intervals. In this chapter, we will explore how to control a **DC motor** using an AVR microcontroller by manipulating the **PWM** signal and using an **H-Bridge circuit** to control the direction of rotation.

The basic operation of a DC motor involves two primary factors:

1. **Speed Control**: Achieved by varying the voltage applied to the motor, often done using **PWM**.
2. **Direction Control**: The motor's direction is controlled by switching the polarity of the voltage applied to the motor.

We will use an **H-Bridge circuit** to change the direction and **PWM** to control the motor's speed.

Key Concepts of DC Motor Control in AVR

Concept	Description	Example
DC Motor	A type of electric motor that runs on DC power, used in many applications.	Small hobby DC motor
PWM	A technique used to control the speed of a motor by adjusting the duty cycle of a square wave signal.	Speed control of the motor
H-Bridge	A circuit used to control the direction of the DC motor by switching the polarity of the voltage.	L298, L293D H-Bridge IC
Motor Driver	A component that amplifies the signal from the microcontroller to drive the motor.	L298 Motor Driver IC
Speed Control	The motor speed is controlled by varying the duty cycle of the PWM signal.	Using OCR0A to adjust speed
Direction Control	The direction of rotation is controlled by setting the state of H-Bridge inputs.	Changing inputs to H-Bridge pins

Basic Rules for Controlling DC Motors in AVR C

Rule	Correct Example	Incorrect Example
Use PWM for motor speed control	OCR0A = 128;	Not using PWM for speed control
Use H-Bridge for direction control	`PORTB = (1 << PB0);`	Not controlling direction with H-Bridge
Initialize timers for PWM	`TCCR0A = (1 << COM0A0);`	Forgetting to initialize PWM timers
Set direction pins before changing speed	`PORTB = (1 << PB1);`	Changing speed without controlling direction
Use delays for motor running time	_delay_ms(1000);	Forgetting to add delays for motor operation

Syntax Table

SL	Operation	Syntax/Example	Description
1	Initialize PWM Timer	`TCCR0A = (1 << COM0A0);`	Set Timer0 for PWM mode on OC0A pin
2	Set PWM Frequency/Speed	OCR0A = 128;	Set the PWM duty cycle (motor speed)
3	Initialize Direction Pins	`DDRB = (1 << PB0)	Set direction pins to output
4	Set Motor Direction	`PORTB = (1 << PB0);`	Set direction of motor (forward or reverse)
5	Start PWM Signal	`TCCR0A = (1 << COM0A0);`	Start PWM signal for motor speed
6	Stop PWM Signal	TCCR0A &= ~(1 << COM0A0);	Stop PWM signal to halt the motor
7	Control Motor with Delay	_delay_ms(1000);	Add delay to control motor running time

Syntax Explanation

1. Initialize PWM Timer

What does it do?
This function configures the AVR's **Timer0** to generate a PWM signal on the OC0A pin, which is connected to the motor driver. The PWM signal controls the speed of the motor by adjusting the duty cycle.

Syntax:
```
TCCR0A |= (1 << COM0A0);
```

Example:
```
void pwm_init() {
    TCCR0A |= (1 << COM0A0);  // Set Timer0 for PWM
mode on OC0A pin
    TCCR0B |= (1 << CS00);    // Set prescaler to no
prescaling (max frequency)
}
```

Explanation:
- **TCCR0A**: This register controls the behavior of **Timer0**. Setting **COM0A0** enables **PWM** on the **OC0A** pin.
- **CS00**: Setting this bit to 1 configures **Timer0** to run with no prescaling, allowing for the highest frequency of PWM output.

2. Set PWM Frequency/Speed

What does it do?
This function sets the **duty cycle** of the PWM signal, which in turn controls the speed of the motor. The value in **OCR0A** determines how long the signal stays high during each cycle.

Syntax:
```
OCR0A = 128;
```

Example:
```
void set_motor_speed(uint8_t speed) {
    OCR0A = speed;  // Set PWM duty cycle to control
speed
}
```

Explanation:
- **OCR0A**: This register controls the PWM frequency. The value you set in **OCR0A** represents the duty cycle, with 0 meaning 0% duty cycle (motor off) and 255 meaning 100% duty cycle (motor at full speed).
- **Speed**: A value of 128 gives a duty cycle of approximately **50%**, resulting in the motor running at half speed.

3. Initialize Direction Pins

What does it do?
This function configures the **direction control pins** of the motor driver (H-Bridge). These pins control the polarity of the voltage applied to the motor, thus determining the direction of rotation.
Syntax:
```
DDRB |= (1 << PB0) | (1 << PB1);
```
Example:
```
void motor_direction_init() {
    DDRB |= (1 << PB0) | (1 << PB1);  // Set PB0 and
PB1 as output pins
}
```

Explanation:
- **DDRB**: This register controls the **data direction** for **PORTB** pins. Setting **PB0** and **PB1** as outputs allows the microcontroller to control the motor's direction by setting the states of these pins.
- **PB0 and PB1**: These pins are connected to the direction control inputs of the **H-Bridge**.

4. Set Motor Direction

What does it do?
This function sets the motor's direction by controlling the state of the direction control pins of the **H-Bridge**. By setting **PB0** and **PB1** to either high or low, we can make the motor spin in different directions.

Syntax:
```
PORTB |= (1 << PB0);
```
Example:
```
void set_motor_direction(uint8_t direction) {
    if (direction == 1) {
        PORTB |= (1 << PB0);   // Forward direction
        PORTB &= ~(1 << PB1);
    } else {
        PORTB |= (1 << PB1);   // Reverse direction
        PORTB &= ~(1 << PB0);
    }
}
```

Explanation:
- **PORTB**: This register controls the **output** of **PORTB** pins. Setting **PB0** high while clearing **PB1** will make the motor rotate in the forward direction. Conversely, setting **PB1** high while clearing **PB0** will make the motor rotate in reverse.

5. Start PWM Signal

What does it do?
This function starts the PWM signal generation on the motor driver, which will drive the motor at the specified speed.
Syntax:
```
TCCR0A |= (1 << COM0A0);
```
Example:
```
void start_pwm() {
    TCCR0A |= (1 << COM0A0);   // Start PWM on OC0A pin
(motor driver)
}
```

Explanation:
- **TCCR0A**: Setting the **COM0A0** bit to 1 enables the PWM output on **OC0A**, allowing the motor to start rotating at the specified speed.

6. Stop PWM Signal

What does it do?
This function stops the PWM signal from being generated, effectively halting the motor's rotation.
Syntax:
```
TCCR0A &= ~(1 << COM0A0);
```
Example:
```
void stop_pwm() {
    TCCR0A &= ~(1 << COM0A0);  // Stop PWM on OC0A pin
(motor driver)
}
```

Explanation:
- **TCCR0A**: Clearing the **COM0A0** bit disables the PWM signal on **OC0A**, which stops the motor from rotating.

7 Control Motor with Delay

What does it do?
This function introduces a delay between motor operations, allowing the motor to run for a specified amount of time before stopping or changing direction.
Syntax:
```
_delay_ms(1000);
```
Example:
```
void run_motor_for_time(uint16_t time) {
    _delay_ms(time);  // Delay for the specified time
}
```

Explanation:
- **_delay_ms(time)**: This function adds a delay in milliseconds to control how long the motor runs before performing another action, such as changing direction or stopping.

Real-life Application Project: DC Motor Control with PWM

Project Overview
This project uses a **DC motor** connected to an **AVR microcontroller** to create a simple motor control system. The motor speed is controlled using PWM, and the direction of the motor is toggled using an H-Bridge. The user can switch between forward, reverse, and control the motor speed using a potentiometer or push buttons.

Required Components

Component	Description
AVR Microcontroller	Controls the motor driver and PWM
DC Motor	The motor that will be controlled
Motor Driver (L298)	Controls direction and amplifies PWM signal
Push Buttons	To toggle direction or change speed
Potentiometer	To adjust motor speed (optional)

Circuit Connection Table

Component	AVR Pin	Purpose
DC Motor	OUT1, OUT2	Connected to motor driver
Button1	PD2	Switches motor direction
Button2	PD3	Adjusts motor speed
Potentiometer	ADC0	Adjusts motor speed (optional)

Project Code

```
#include <avr/io.h>
#include <util/delay.h>

void pwm_init() {
    TCCR0A |= (1 << COM0A0);   // Set Timer0 for PWM
mode on OC0A pin
    TCCR0B |= (1 << CS00);     // Set prescaler to no
prescaling (max frequency)
}

void set_motor_speed(uint8_t speed) {
```

```c
    OCR0A = speed;   // Set PWM duty cycle to control
speed
}

void motor_direction_init() {
    DDRB |= (1 << PB0) | (1 << PB1);   // Set PB0 and
PB1 as output pins
}

void set_motor_direction(uint8_t direction) {
    if (direction == 1) {
        PORTB |= (1 << PB0);   // Forward direction
        PORTB &= ~(1 << PB1);
    } else {
        PORTB |= (1 << PB1);   // Reverse direction
        PORTB &= ~(1 << PB0);
    }
}

void start_pwm() {
    TCCR0A |= (1 << COM0A0);   // Start PWM on OC0A pin
}

void stop_pwm() {
    TCCR0A &= ~(1 << COM0A0);   // Stop PWM on OC0A pin
}

int main() {
    pwm_init();              // Initialize PWM
    motor_direction_init();  // Initialize motor
direction control

    while (1) {
        set_motor_direction(1);   // Set motor direction
to forward
        set_motor_speed(128);     // Set motor speed to
50%
```

```
        start_pwm();                  // Start motor

        _delay_ms(1000);              // Run motor for 1
second
        stop_pwm();                   // Stop motor

        _delay_ms(1000);              // Delay before next
operation

        set_motor_direction(0);  // Set motor direction
to reverse
        set_motor_speed(255);     // Set motor speed to
100%
        start_pwm();                  // Start motor

        _delay_ms(1000);              // Run motor for 1
second
        stop_pwm();                   // Stop motor

        _delay_ms(1000);              // Delay before next
operation
    }
}
```

Expected Results

The motor will run forward and backward, with the speed controlled by PWM. Each direction will be maintained for 1 second before switching to the next.

Chapter 63: Servo Motor Control

A **servo motor** is a type of motor that provides precise control over its position. Unlike standard motors, servo motors can rotate to a specific angle with high accuracy. This makes them ideal for applications where precise motion control is necessary, such as in robotics, cameras, and hobby projects.

In this chapter, we will explore how to control a **servo motor** using an **AVR microcontroller**. The servo motor is controlled by generating a **Pulse Width Modulation (PWM)** signal, where the width of the pulse determines the position of the servo.

Key Concepts of Servo Motor Control with AVR

Concept	Description	Example
Servo Motor	A motor that can be controlled to rotate to a specific angle.	SG90, MG90S
PWM Signal	A signal used to control the position of the servo by varying pulse width.	Duty cycle from 1ms to 2ms
Control Angle	The angle of rotation of the servo motor, typically between 0° and 180°.	0° for minimum, 180° for maximum
Timer/Counter	The AVR's internal timer used to generate PWM signals.	Timer0, Timer1
Duty Cycle	The proportion of the time the PWM signal is high, determines the servo position.	1ms for 0°, 2ms for 180°

Basic Rules for Servo Motor Control in AVR C

Rule	Correct Example	Incorrect Example
Use a timer to generate a PWM signal	`TCCR0A = (1 << COM0A0);`	Forgetting to configure the timer
Set the PWM frequency for servo control	OCR0A = 128;	Using incorrect values for servo control
Adjust the duty cycle to change servo angle	OCR0A = 180;	Using a constant PWM signal for all angles
Enable the timer to output PWM	`TCCR0A = (1 << COM0A0);`	Forgetting to enable the PWM signal

Syntax Table

SL	Operation	Syntax/Example	Description
1	Initialize Timer for PWM	`TCCR0A = (1 << COM0A0);`	Configure Timer0 for PWM output
2	Set PWM Frequency (Servo Angle)	OCR0A = 128;	Set PWM signal width to control servo angle
3	Start PWM Signal	`TCCR0A = (1 << COM0A0);`	Enable PWM signal for servo control
4	Set Timer Prescaler	`TCCR0B = (1 << CS00);`	Set timer prescaler for correct timing
5	Stop PWM Signal	TCCR0A &= ~(1 << COM0A0);	Disable PWM signal when servo is idle

Syntax Explanation

1. Initialize Timer for PWM

What does it do?
 This function configures the **AVR's Timer** to operate in **PWM mode**, which is necessary for generating the signal to control the servo motor. The duty cycle of this PWM signal will determine the position of the servo.

Syntax:
```
TCCR0A |= (1 << COM0A0);
```

Example:
```
void pwm_init() {
    TCCR0A |= (1 << COM0A0);  // Set Timer0 to PWM mode
on OC0A (Pin)
}
```

Explanation:
- **TCCR0A**: This register controls the operation of **Timer0**. By setting the **COM0A0** bit, we configure the timer to generate a PWM signal on the output compare pin (**OC0A**).
- **COM0A0**: This bit is used to enable the PWM output on **OC0A**. When this bit is set, Timer0 will output a PWM signal, which is required to control the servo.

2. Set PWM Frequency (Servo Angle)

What does it do?
This function adjusts the **duty cycle** of the PWM signal, which determines the position of the servo motor. A longer pulse (greater duty cycle) corresponds to a larger rotation angle.
Syntax:
```
OCR0A = 128;
```
Example:
```
void set_servo_angle(uint8_t angle) {
    OCR0A = angle;  // Set PWM duty cycle for the servo
motor
}
```
Explanation:
- **OCR0A**: This is the **Output Compare Register A** for **Timer0**. The value in **OCR0A** determines the width of the pulse, which in turn controls the angle of the servo motor. The servo angle is typically controlled by a PWM signal with a period of 20ms. A pulse width between **1ms** and **2ms** corresponds to an angle range from **0° to 180°**.
- **Angle**: The value you write into **OCR0A** adjusts the PWM signal width to rotate the servo to the desired angle. For example, a value of 128 may correspond to a position around **90°** for a typical servo.

3. Start PWM Signal

What does it do?
This function enables the **PWM signal**, allowing the servo to start responding to the PWM pulses by rotating to the desired position.
Syntax:
```
TCCR0A |= (1 << COM0A0);
```
Example:
```
void start_pwm() {
    TCCR0A |= (1 << COM0A0);  // Enable PWM on OC0A pin
(e.g., PB3)
}
```

Explanation:
- **TCCR0A**: This register controls the behavior of **Timer0**. The **COM0A0** bit, when set, generates the PWM signal on the output pin **OC0A** (PB3 on many AVR microcontrollers).
- **PWM Output**: The signal will alternate between high and low at the frequency determined by the timer, and the duty cycle of the signal will control the servo position.

4. Set Timer Prescaler

What does it do?
This function configures the **prescaler** of **Timer0** to adjust the frequency of the PWM signal. The prescaler allows the timer to count at a slower rate, making it possible to achieve the required PWM period.
Syntax:
```
TCCR0B |= (1 << CS00);
```
Example:
```
void set_prescaler() {
    TCCR0B |= (1 << CS00);  // Set prescaler for Timer0
to 1 (no prescaling)
}
```

Explanation:
- **TCCR0B**: This register controls the clock source and prescaler for **Timer0**.
- **CS00**: Setting this bit to 1 configures **Timer0** to use the system clock with no prescaling. This means the timer will increment with every clock cycle, giving the desired PWM period.

5. Stop PWM Signal

What does it do?
This function stops the PWM signal from being output, thus stopping the movement of the servo motor.

Syntax:
```
TCCR0A &= ~(1 << COM0A0);
```

Example:
```
void stop_pwm() {
    TCCR0A &= ~(1 << COM0A0);   // Disable PWM on OC0A
pin (e.g., PB3)
}
```

Explanation:
- **TCCR0A**: This register controls the operation of **Timer0**.
- **COM0A0**: Clearing this bit disables PWM output on the **OC0A** pin, effectively stopping the servo motor from moving.

Real-life Application Project: Servo Arm Controller

Project Overview

In this project, we will use a servo motor to control the position of an arm. The **AVR microcontroller** will output a PWM signal to the servo motor, and the angle of the arm will be controlled by adjusting the duty cycle of the PWM signal.

Required Components

Component	Description
AVR Microcontroller	Controls the PWM signal for servo control
Servo Motor	Moves based on PWM signal
Potentiometer	Adjusts the angle of the servo motor
Resistors (220Ω)	For current limiting

Circuit Connection Table

Component	AVR Pin	Purpose
Servo Motor	PB3 (OC0A)	Outputs PWM signal for servo control
Potentiometer	ADC0	Adjusts the angle of the servo

Project Code

```c
#include <avr/io.h>
#include <util/delay.h>

void pwm_init() {
    TCCR0A |= (1 << COM0A0);  // Set Timer0 to PWM mode
on OC0A
    TCCR0B |= (1 << CS

00);   // No prescaling
}

void set_servo_angle(uint8_t angle) {
    OCR0A = angle;  // Set PWM duty cycle for the servo
motor
}

int main() {
    uint16_t adc_value;
    uint8_t angle;

    pwm_init();  // Initialize PWM

    while (1) {
        adc_value = ADC;  // Read ADC value from
potentiometer
```

```
        angle = (adc_value * 180) / 1023;   // Convert
ADC value to angle
        set_servo_angle(angle);   // Set servo position
based on potentiometer value
        _delay_ms(100);   // Small delay for stability
    }
}
```

Expected Results

When the potentiometer is adjusted, the servo motor will rotate to
the corresponding angle, allowing precise control over its position.

Chapter 64: Using Stepper Motors

A **stepper motor** is a type of motor that moves in discrete steps, offering precise control over the rotation angle. Stepper motors are commonly used in applications where accurate positioning is essential, such as in 3D printers, CNC machines, and robotic arms. Unlike DC motors, which rotate continuously, stepper motors rotate in fixed increments, and the number of steps is directly related to the motor's internal gear mechanism.

In this chapter, we will explore how to control a **stepper motor** using an **AVR microcontroller**. We will generate the control signals to drive the stepper motor through its steps, enabling precise movement.

Key Concepts of Stepper Motor Control with AVR

Concept	Description	Example
Stepper Motor	A motor that rotates in discrete steps, allowing precise control.	28BYJ-48, NEMA 17
Step Sequence	The specific order of pulses that determine the direction and position.	Full-step, half-step, microstepping
Control Pins	The pins on the microcontroller used to control the motor.	4 control pins for 4-phase stepper motor
Pulse Width	The width of the pulse that determines the step increment.	Typically 10-20ms for each pulse
Stepper Driver	A driver circuit that amplifies the control signals to drive the motor.	ULN2003, A4988

Basic Rules for Stepper Motor Control in AVR C

Rule	Correct Example	Incorrect Example
Use a proper step sequence to control rotation	`step_sequence();`	Forgetting to sequence the steps

Use a delay to control stepper motor speed	_delay_ms(10);	Using no delay, causing erratic movement
Set the control pins for each step	`PORTB = (1 << PB0);`	Forgetting to set the appropriate pins
Ensure the stepper driver is properly wired	Use ULN2003 with correct pin connections	Incorrect wiring of stepper motor driver

Syntax Table

SL	Operation	Syntax/Example	Description
1	Set Control Pin High	`PORTB = (1 << PB0);`	Set pin PB0 high to energize a coil
2	Set Control Pin Low	PORTB &= ~(1 << PB0);	Set pin PB0 low to de-energize a coil
3	Delay between Steps	_delay_ms(10);	Delay to control stepper motor speed
4	Initialize Stepper Motor Pins	DDRB = 0x0F;	Set the direction of the pins
5	Step Sequence Function	step_sequence();	Execute the step sequence for rotation

Syntax Explanation

1. Set Control Pin High

What does it do?
This function sets the microcontroller's control pin high, supplying voltage to one of the coils of the stepper motor. This causes the motor to energize and take a step in a specific direction.

Syntax:
PORTB |= (1 << PB0);

Example:
```
void stepper_step(uint8_t pin) {
    PORTB |= (1 << pin);  // Set the pin high to
energize the coil
}
```

Explanation:

- **PORTB**: This is the register that controls the output state of **PORTB** pins.
- **PB0**: The microcontroller pin connected to one of the stepper motor's coils. This pin is set high to energize the corresponding coil.
- **(1 << PB0)**: This bitwise operation shifts 1 to the left by PB0 positions, which isolates the pin for modification.
- The **OR** operation (|=) sets the bit corresponding to **PB0** to 1, turning on the coil.

2. Set Control Pin Low

What does it do?
 This function sets the microcontroller's control pin low, de-energizing one of the coils of the stepper motor. This causes the motor to stop energizing the corresponding coil.

Syntax:
```
PORTB &= ~(1 << PB0);
```

Example:
```
void stepper_off(uint8_t pin) {
    PORTB &= ~(1 << pin);  // Set the pin low to de-energize the coil
}
```

Explanation:

- **PORTB**: Again, this is the register controlling the **PORTB** pins.
- **(1 << PB0)**: The bitwise operation shifts 1 to the left by PB0 positions.
- **NOT Operation (~)**: The **NOT (~)** operator inverts the bits, turning the target bit (PB0) to 0.
- The **AND** operation (&=) ensures that **PB0** is cleared to 0, turning off the coil.

3. Delay Between Steps

What does it do?
This function creates a delay between each step of the motor. The delay time controls the speed of the stepper motor. A longer delay results in slower motor movement.

Syntax:
```
_delay_ms(10);
```

Example:
```
void stepper_move() {
    _delay_ms(10);   // Delay between steps
}
```

Explanation:
- **_delay_ms()**: This function, provided by the **util/delay.h** library, creates a delay in milliseconds. The value 10 means the delay will last for 10 milliseconds.
- The delay allows the motor to complete each step at a controlled speed. Reducing the delay results in faster motor movement.

4. Initialize Stepper Motor Pins

What does it do?
This function configures the AVR microcontroller's pins as output pins for controlling the stepper motor. The direction and control of these pins are essential for stepping the motor in the desired sequence.

Syntax:
```
DDRB = 0x0F;
```

Example:
```
void init_stepper() {
    DDRB = 0x0F;   // Set the lower 4 bits of PORTB as output
}
```

Explanation:

- **DDRB**: This is the Data Direction Register for **PORTB**. It defines whether the pins on **PORTB** are input or output.
- **0x0F**: The hexadecimal value 0x0F corresponds to 00001111 in binary, meaning the lower 4 bits (PB0 to PB3) are set as output, and the higher bits are set as input.

5. Step Sequence Function

What does it do?
 This function controls the stepping of the motor by following a specific sequence of energizing the coils. The sequence determines the direction and speed of rotation.
Syntax:
```
step_sequence();
```
Example:
```
void step_sequence() {
    // Step Sequence for a 4-phase stepper motor (e.g.,
full-step sequence)
    PORTB |= (1 << PB0);   // Coil 1 energized
    _delay_ms(10);
    PORTB &= ~(1 << PB0);

    PORTB |= (1 << PB1);   // Coil 2 energized
    _delay_ms(10);
    PORTB &= ~(1 << PB1);

    PORTB |= (1 << PB2);   // Coil 3 energized
    _delay_ms(10);
    PORTB &= ~(1 << PB2);

    PORTB |= (1 << PB3);   // Coil 4 energized
    _delay_ms(10);
    PORTB &= ~(1 << PB3);
}
```

Explanation:

- The function follows a sequence where each coil is energized one after the other.
- The delay between each step ensures that the motor steps at a controlled rate.
- This type of sequence is commonly used for **full-step** control of the motor. For more precise control, half-step or microstepping sequences can be used.

Real-life Application Project: Stepper Motor Positioning System

Project Overview

This project uses a **stepper motor** to position a camera mount at specific angles. By controlling the stepper motor with an AVR microcontroller, the camera can be positioned at different angles based on user input.

Required Components

Component	Description
AVR Microcontroller	Controls the stepper motor
Stepper Motor	Moves based on control signals
Stepper Motor Driver	Amplifies control signals for the motor
Push Buttons	User input for controlling motor position

Circuit Connection Table

Component	AVR Pin	Purpose
Stepper Motor	PB0, PB1, PB2, PB3	Controls stepper motor coils
Button1	PD2	Increase motor position
Button2	PD3	Decrease motor position

Project Code

```
#include <avr/io.h>
#include <util/delay.h>

void init_stepper() {
    DDRB = 0x0F;  // Set lower 4 pins of PORTB as
output
```

```c
}

void step_sequence() {
    PORTB |= (1 << PB0);
    _delay_ms(10);
    PORTB &= ~(1 << PB0);

    PORTB |= (1 << PB1);
    _delay_ms(10);
    PORTB &= ~(1 << PB1);

    PORTB |= (1 << PB2);
    _delay_ms(10);
    PORTB &= ~(1 << PB2);

    PORTB |= (1 << PB3);
    _delay_ms(10);
    PORTB &= ~(1 << PB3);
}

int main() {
    init_stepper();  // Initialize stepper motor
control pins

    while (1) {
        step_sequence();  // Execute motor step
sequence
        if (PIND & (1 << PD2)) {  // If button 1 is
pressed
            // Increase motor position
        }
        if (PIND & (1 << PD3)) {  // If button 2 is
pressed
            // Decrease motor position
        }
    }
}
```

Chapter 65: Implementing Relays

A **relay** is an electrically operated switch that allows you to control high-power devices like motors, lights, or household appliances using low-power signals from microcontrollers like the AVR. Relays are often used in automation systems, home appliances, and industrial equipment to switch on or off devices based on a control signal.

In this chapter, we will explore how to interface a relay with an AVR microcontroller. We will control the relay using a microcontroller pin and use it to switch on and off a high-power device, such as a light or motor, using a transistor as a driver to handle the current.

Key Concepts of Relay Control with AVR

Concept	Description	Example
Relay	An electromechanical switch that controls high-power devices.	5V Relay, SPDT Relay
Relay Driver	A transistor used to amplify the current from the microcontroller.	NPN Transistor (e.g., 2N2222)
Control Pin	The pin on the AVR that controls the relay through a transistor.	PORTB, PB0
Relay Coil	The coil inside the relay that is energized to activate the switch.	Usually controlled via a transistor
Contact Rating	The maximum voltage and current the relay can safely switch.	10A at 250V AC
Diode Protection	A diode placed across the relay coil to protect against voltage spikes.	1N4007 Diode

Basic Rules for Relay Control in AVR C

Rule	Correct Example	Incorrect Example
Use a transistor to drive the relay coil	Use a transistor (e.g., 2N2222) between the AVR pin and relay	Directly driving the relay from the AVR pin
Use a diode across the relay coil for protection	Place a diode like 1N4007 across the relay coil	Forgetting to use a flyback diode
Ensure the control pin is properly configured	Set the AVR pin as output with `DDRB = (1 << PB0);`	Not configuring the control pin as output
Properly choose the relay's contact rating	Choose a relay rated for the voltage and current of the load	Choosing a relay with too low a contact rating

Syntax Table

SL	Operation	Syntax/Example	Description
1	Set Relay Control Pin as Output	`DDRB = (1 << PB0);`	Set PB0 as an output pin
2	Activate Relay (Turn ON)	`PORTB = (1 << PB0);`	Set PB0 high to activate the relay coil
3	Deactivate Relay (Turn OFF)	PORTB &= ~(1 << PB0);	Set PB0 low to deactivate the relay coil
4	Initialize Relay Driver Pin	`DDRC = (1 << PC0);`	Set PC0 as output pin for transistor driver
5	Turn ON Transistor (Relay Driver)	`PORTC = (1 << PC0);`	Set PC0 high to turn on transistor driver

Syntax Explanation

1. Set Relay Control Pin as Output

What does it do?
This command configures the control pin on the AVR microcontroller as an output pin. This pin will be used to send the control signal to the transistor, which in turn will activate the relay.

Syntax:
```
DDRB |= (1 << PB0);
```
Example:
```
void init_relay() {
    DDRB |= (1 << PB0);   // Set PB0 as output pin for
relay control
}
```

Explanation:
- **DDRB**: This is the **Data Direction Register** for **PORTB**. Setting a bit to 1 configures the corresponding pin as an output.
- **PB0**: Refers to **pin 0** of **PORTB**. This is the control pin that will be used to activate the relay.
- **(1 << PB0)**: A bitwise operation that shifts 1 to the left by PB0 positions, isolating this pin and configuring it as an output.

2. Activate Relay (Turn ON)

What does it do?
This command sets the control pin high, which sends a signal to the transistor and energizes the relay's coil, activating the switch and turning on the connected device.

Syntax:
```
PORTB |= (1 << PB0);
```
Example:
```
void activate_relay() {
    PORTB |= (1 << PB0);   // Set PB0 high to energize
relay coil
}
```

Explanation:

- **PORTB**: This is the **Data Register** for **PORTB**, which controls the output state of the pins. Setting a bit to 1 turns on the output on that pin.
- **(1 << PB0)**: The **bitwise shift** operation sets **PB0** high, turning on the relay.

3. Deactivate Relay (Turn OFF)

What does it do?
This command sets the control pin low, which turns off the transistor, de-energizing the relay's coil, and switching off the connected device.

Syntax:
```
PORTB &= ~(1 << PB0);
```
Example:
```
void deactivate_relay() {
    PORTB &= ~(1 << PB0);   // Set PB0 low to turn off
relay coil
}
```

Explanation:

- **PORTB**: This is the **Data Register** for **PORTB**.
- **(1 << PB0)**: The **bitwise shift** isolates **PB0**.
- **~(1 << PB0)**: The **NOT (~)** operator inverts the bit, turning it into 0 to ensure that the relay is de-energized.
- **&=**: The **AND operation** ensures only the selected bit is cleared, while others remain unchanged.

4. Initialize Relay Driver Pin

What does it do?
This function configures the pin connected to the **transistor** (relay driver) as an output. The transistor is necessary because the relay requires more current than the microcontroller can supply directly.

Syntax:
```
DDRC |= (1 << PC0);
```

Example:
```
void init_transistor_driver() {
    DDRC |= (1 << PC0);   // Set PC0 as output for
transistor driver
}
```

Explanation:
- **DDRC**: This is the **Data Direction Register** for **PORTC**. Setting a bit to 1 configures the corresponding pin as output.
- **PC0**: Refers to **pin 0** of **PORTC**, which is used to control the transistor.
- **(1 << PC0)**: This **bitwise shift** sets the **PC0** pin to output.

5. Turn ON Transistor (Relay Driver)

What does it do?
This function turns on the transistor by setting its control pin high. The transistor amplifies the signal from the microcontroller and drives the relay coil.

Syntax:
```
PORTC |= (1 << PC0);
```
Example:
```
void turn_on_transistor() {
    PORTC |= (1 << PC0);   // Set PC0 high to activate
transistor
}
```

Explanation:
- **PORTC**: The **Data Register** for **PORTC** controls the output state of the pin.
- **(1 << PC0)**: The **bitwise shift** operation sets **PC0** high, turning on the transistor and enabling the relay to function.

Real-life Application Project: Home Automation System

Project Overview

This project uses an **AVR microcontroller** and **relay** to control a light in a home automation system. The relay is controlled through the microcontroller to turn the light on and off using a push button.

Required Components

Component	Description
AVR Microcontroller	Controls the relay
Relay	Switches the light on/off
Transistor	Drives the relay coil
Button	User input for turning light on/off
Diode	Protects the relay from voltage spikes
Light	The device being controlled

Circuit Connection Table

Component	AVR Pin	Purpose
Relay	PB0	Controls relay coil
Transistor	PC0	Drives relay coil
Button	PD2	Turn light on/off

Project Code

```
#include <avr/io.h>
#include <util/delay.h>

void init_relay() {
    DDRB |= (1 << PB0);  // Set PB0 as output to
control relay
    DDRC |= (1 << PC0);  // Set PC0 as output

  to control transistor
    DDRD &= ~(1 << PD2); // Set PD2 as input for button
    PORTD |= (1 << PD2); // Enable pull-up resistor on
PD2
}
```

```c
void activate_relay() {
    PORTB |= (1 << PB0);   // Set PB0 high to energize
relay coil
    PORTC |= (1 << PC0);   // Set PC0 high to activate
transistor
}

void deactivate_relay() {
    PORTB &= ~(1 << PB0);   // Set PB0 low to turn off
relay coil
    PORTC &= ~(1 << PC0);   // Set PC0 low to deactivate
transistor
}

int main() {
    init_relay();   // Initialize relay and control pins

    while (1) {
        if (!(PIND & (1 << PD2))) {   // If button is
pressed (active low)
            activate_relay();   // Turn on the light
        } else {
            deactivate_relay();   // Turn off the light
        }
        _delay_ms(100);   // Small delay to debounce
button
    }
}
```

Expected Results

When the button is pressed, the relay will activate, turning on the light.
When the button is released, the relay will deactivate, turning off the
light. This will implement a simple light control system.

Chapter 66: Bluetooth Modules

Bluetooth technology is widely used for wireless communication between devices over short distances. It's an ideal solution for creating wireless communication systems, such as remote controls, sensors, and data transfer applications. Integrating a Bluetooth module with an AVR microcontroller can enable wireless communication between the AVR and Bluetooth-enabled devices like smartphones, laptops, and other microcontrollers.

In this chapter, we will explore how to interface a **Bluetooth module** (e.g., **HC-05** or **HC-06**) with an AVR microcontroller, using the **Serial Communication (USART)** protocol. We'll discuss how to send and receive data wirelessly using Bluetooth, and create a simple system to control devices or send data via Bluetooth.

Key Concepts of Bluetooth Communication with AVR

Concept	Description	Example
Bluetooth Module	A wireless module that supports Bluetooth communication.	HC-05, HC-06, Bluetooth 4.0 (BLE) modules
USART (UART)	A protocol for serial communication used for communication between devices.	Asynchronous serial communication
Baud Rate	The speed at which data is transmitted over the serial interface.	9600, 115200
Bluetooth Pairing	The process of establishing a connection between two Bluetooth devices.	Bluetooth device pairing with HC-05/HC-06
TX and RX Pins	The pins for transmitting and receiving data via serial communication.	TX (transmit), RX (receive)

Basic Rules for Using Bluetooth Modules in AVR C

Rule	Correct Example	Incorrect Example
Set the correct baud rate for Bluetooth communication	`ubrr = 103; // 9600 baud rate`	Using an incorrect baud rate
Use the correct TX and RX pins	`TX -> PD1, RX -> PD0`	Incorrectly connecting TX and RX pins
Initialize USART communication	`USART_init();`	Forgetting to initialize USART before using it
Ensure proper pairing of Bluetooth devices	Pair the smartphone with the Bluetooth module (e.g., HC-05)	Not pairing the Bluetooth module with the device
Use serial communication functions for sending/receiving data	`USART_Transmit(data);`	Using non-standard communication functions

Syntax Table

SL	Operation	Syntax/Example	Description
1	Initialize USART	`USART_init();`	Initializes USART communication for Bluetooth
2	Transmit Data over USART	`USART_Transmit(data);`	Sends data byte via serial communication
3	Receive Data from USART	`data = USART_Receive();`	Receives data byte from the Bluetooth device
4	Set Baud Rate	`UBRR = 103;`	Sets the baud rate for communication (9600 bps)
5	Enable UART Receive Interrupt	`USART_RXCIE = 1;`	Enables UART RX interrupt to detect incoming data

Syntax Explanation

1. Initialize USART Communication

What does it do?
This function sets up the USART communication between the AVR microcontroller and the Bluetooth module. It configures the baud rate, data frame format, and other necessary settings for serial communication.

Syntax:
```
USART_init();
```

Example:
```
void USART_init() {
    unsigned int ubrr = 103;  // Set the baud rate to
9600 (for 16 MHz clock)
    UBRRH = (unsigned char)(ubrr >> 8);  // Set the
high byte of the baud rate
    UBRRL = (unsigned char)ubrr;         // Set the low
byte of the baud rate
    UCSRB = (1 << RXEN) | (1 << TXEN);   // Enable
receiver and transmitter
    UCSRC = (1 << UCSZ1) | (1 << UCSZ0); // 8-bit data
frame
}
```

Explanation:
- **UBRR**: The **USART Baud Rate Register** holds the value that determines the communication speed (baud rate). The value 103 corresponds to 9600 baud when using a 16 MHz clock.
- **UCSRB**: The **USART Control and Status Register B** enables the transmitter (TX) and receiver (RX).
- **UCSRC**: The **USART Control and Status Register C** sets the data frame format. In this case, it's set to 8-bit data (no parity, 1 stop bit).

2. Transmit Data over USART

What does it do?

This function sends a data byte via USART. It is used to send characters or commands from the AVR to the Bluetooth module or to other devices.

Syntax:

```
USART_Transmit(data);
```

Example:

```
void USART_Transmit(unsigned char data) {
    while (!(UCSRA & (1 << UDRE)))  // Wait until the
transmit buffer is empty
        ;
    UDR = data;  // Put data into the buffer, which
sends it to the Bluetooth module
}
```

Explanation:

- **UCSRA**: The **USART Control and Status Register A** contains the **USART Data Register Empty (UDRE)** flag, which indicates whether the transmit buffer is empty and ready to accept data.
- **UDR**: The **USART Data Register** holds the data that is transmitted or received via the USART interface.

3. Receive Data from USART

What does it do?

This function reads a data byte that has been received by the USART from the Bluetooth module. It's used to get data sent from a connected Bluetooth device.

Syntax:

```
data = USART_Receive();
```

Example:

```
unsigned char USART_Receive(void) {
    while (!(UCSRA & (1 << RXC)))  // Wait for data to
be received
        ;
    return UDR;  // Get and return received data from
the data register
}
```

Explanation:

- **UCSRA**: The **USART Control and Status Register A** contains the **USART Receive Complete (RXC)** flag, which indicates when data has been received and is ready to be read from the data register.
- **UDR**: The **USART Data Register** contains the received data byte.

4. Set Baud Rate

What does it do?

This command sets the baud rate for the USART communication. Baud rate determines how fast data is transmitted between the AVR and Bluetooth module.

Syntax:

```
UBRR = 103;
```

Example:

```
void USART_set_baud_rate() {
    unsigned int ubrr = 103;   // 9600 baud rate (for 16 MHz clock)
    UBRRH = (unsigned char)(ubrr >> 8);   // Set the high byte
    UBRRL = (unsigned char)ubrr;           // Set the low byte
}
```

Explanation:

- **UBRR**: This register sets the baud rate for the communication. For 9600 baud with a 16 MHz system clock, 103 is the value used to configure the baud rate.

Real-life Application Project: Wireless Temperature Monitoring System

Project Overview

This project uses an AVR microcontroller and Bluetooth module (HC-05) to wirelessly transmit temperature data from a temperature sensor (e.g., LM35) to a smartphone. The smartphone can receive the temperature data over Bluetooth and display it on a mobile app.

Required Components

Component	Description
AVR Microcontroller	Controls the system and manages communication
Bluetooth Module (HC-05)	Provides wireless communication between AVR and smartphone
LM35 Temperature Sensor	Measures the ambient temperature
Smartphone	Receives and displays temperature data
Resistors	For sensor and voltage dividers

Circuit Connection Table

Component	AVR Pin	Purpose
LM35 Temperature Sensor	ADC0	Reads the temperature
Bluetooth HC-05	TX -> PD1, RX -> PD0	Communication with smartphone

Project Code

```
#include <avr/io.h>
#include <util/delay.h>
#include <stdio.h>

void USART_init() {
    unsigned int ubrr = 103;   // 9600 baud rate for 16
MHz clock
    UBRRH = (unsigned char)(ubrr >> 8);
    UBRRL = (unsigned char)ubrr;
    UCSRB = (1 << RXEN) | (1 << TXEN);  // Enable
receiver and transmitter
    UCSRC = (1 << UCSZ1) | (1 << UCSZ0); // 8-bit data
frame
}

void USART_Transmit(unsigned char data) {
    while (!(UCSRA & (1 << UDRE)))  // Wait until the
transmit buffer is empty
```

```c
        ;
    UDR = data;   // Send data
}

unsigned char USART_Receive(void) {
    while (!(UCSRA & (1 << RXC)))

 // Wait for data to be received
        ;
    return UDR;   // Get received data
}

uint16_t read_temperature() {
    // Placeholder for reading LM35 temperature sensor
    // Return a sample ADC value representing
temperature
    return 25;   // Return 25°C as a placeholder
}

int main() {
    USART_init();   // Initialize USART communication
    char buffer[16];
    uint16_t temperature;

    while (1) {
        temperature = read_temperature();   // Read
temperature from LM35
        sprintf(buffer, "Temp: %dC", temperature);   //
Format the temperature
        for (int i = 0; buffer[i] != '\0'; i++) {
            USART_Transmit(buffer[i]);   // Send the
temperature via Bluetooth
        }
        _delay_ms(1000);   // Wait for 1 second before
updating
    }
}
```

Chapter 67: Wi-Fi and ESP8266 with AVR

Wi-Fi technology is a popular method for enabling wireless internet connectivity in embedded systems. The **ESP8266** is a low-cost Wi-Fi module commonly used in microcontroller-based projects to enable wireless communication. By connecting the **ESP8266** with an **AVR microcontroller**, you can enable Wi-Fi connectivity and create projects that require internet access, such as IoT (Internet of Things) applications, remote control systems, and data logging systems.

In this chapter, we will explore how to interface the **ESP8266 Wi-Fi module** with an **AVR microcontroller** using **Serial Communication (USART)**. We'll walk through the steps to set up the ESP8266, send AT commands to the module for network connection, and use it for basic tasks like sending data over the internet.

Key Concepts of Wi-Fi Communication with ESP8266 and AVR

Concept	Description	Example
ESP8266 Module	A low-cost Wi-Fi module used for adding wireless connectivity to embedded systems.	ESP8266 (NodeMCU, ESP-01, etc.)
USART (UART)	A communication protocol for transmitting data serially between devices.	UART used to send AT commands to ESP8266
AT Commands	A set of text-based commands used to configure and control the ESP8266 module.	AT+CWJAP, AT+CIPSTART, AT+CIPSEND
Baud Rate	The rate at which data is transmitted serially.	115200, 9600 baud
Wi-Fi Network	A wireless network that allows devices to connect to the internet.	SSID and Password for network connection
TCP/IP Communication	A set of protocols used for communication over the internet.	Sending HTTP requests via ESP8266

Basic Rules for Using ESP8266 in AVR C

Rule	Correct Example	Incorrect Example
Set the correct baud rate for ESP8266	`USART_init(115200);`	Using the wrong baud rate for ESP8266 communication
Use proper AT commands to control ESP8266	`send_AT_command("AT+CWJAP=\"SSID\",\"password\"");`	Sending incorrect AT commands
Wait for ESP8266 response	`while (USART_Receive() != 'OK')`	Not checking for module's response
Use a stable power supply for ESP8266	Ensure stable 3.3V for ESP8266	Using a 5V supply or unstable power
Use USART functions correctly for data transfer	`USART_Transmit(data);`	Not properly sending or receiving data

Syntax Table

SL	Operation	Syntax/Example	Description
1	Initialize USART	`USART_init(115200);`	Initializes USART with the baud rate for ESP8266
2	Send AT Command	`send_AT_command("AT+CWJAP=\"SSID\",\"password\"");`	Sends an AT command to ESP8266 to connect to Wi-Fi
3	Receive Data from USART	`USART_Receive();`	Receives data from the ESP8266 or sends data via USART
4	Transmit Data over USART	`USART_Transmit(data);`	Transmit a byte of data to the ESP8266
5	Check for ESP8266 response	`if (USART_Receive() == 'OK')`	Checks if the ESP8266 returned a successful response

Syntax Explanation

1. Initialize USART Communication

What does it do?

This function sets up the USART communication between the AVR microcontroller and the ESP8266. It configures the baud rate, enabling the communication required to send and receive data from the ESP8266.

Syntax:

```
USART_init(115200);
```

Example:

```c
void USART_init(unsigned int baud) {
    unsigned int ubrr = F_CPU/16/baud-1;   // Calculate the value for UBRR
    UBRRH = (unsigned char)(ubrr>>8);       // Set the high byte of UBRR
    UBRRL = (unsigned char)ubrr;            // Set the low byte of UBRR
    UCSRB = (1<<RXEN) | (1<<TXEN);          // Enable receiver and transmitter
    UCSRC = (1<<UCSZ1) | (1<<UCSZ0);        // Set frame format: 8 data bits, 1 stop bit
}
```

Explanation:

- **UBRR**: This register sets the baud rate for USART. It is calculated based on the microcontroller's clock frequency and desired baud rate.
- **UCSRB**: The **USART Control and Status Register B** enables both the receiver (RX) and transmitter (TX).
- **UCSRC**: The **USART Control and Status Register C** sets the frame format to 8-bit data with 1 stop bit.

2. Send AT Command to ESP8266

What does it do?

This function sends an AT command to the ESP8266 to control its behavior, such as connecting to a Wi-Fi network or setting up a socket for communication.

Syntax:

```
send_AT_command("AT+CWJAP=\"SSID\",\"password\"");
```

Example:

```c
void send_AT_command(char* command) {
    while (*command) {
        USART_Transmit(*command);   // Send each
character of the command
        command++;
    }
    USART_Transmit('\r');           // Carriage return
for command termination
    USART_Transmit('\n');           // Newline character
}
```

Explanation:

- This function iterates through each character of the AT command and sends it over USART to the ESP8266.
- The AT command AT+CWJAP="SSID","password" is used to connect the ESP8266 to a Wi-Fi network.
- \r (carriage return) and \n (newline) are used to terminate the AT command.

3. Receive Data from ESP8266

What does it do?

This function waits for data to be received from the ESP8266 and then reads the data byte from the USART receive buffer.

Syntax:

```
USART_Receive();
```

Example:

```c
unsigned char USART_Receive(void) {
```

```
    while (!(UCSRA & (1<<RXC)))  // Wait for data to be
received
        ;
    return UDR;  // Get and return the received byte
}
```

Explanation:
- The function waits until the **RXC** (USART Receive Complete) flag is set, indicating that the received byte is available in the **UDR** (USART Data Register).
- It then returns the byte received from the ESP8266.

4. Transmit Data over USART

What does it do?
This function transmits a byte of data to the ESP8266, allowing communication from the AVR microcontroller to the Wi-Fi module.
Syntax:
```
USART_Transmit(data);
```
Example:
```
void USART_Transmit(unsigned char data) {
    while (!(UCSRA & (1<<UDRE)))  // Wait for the
transmit buffer to be empty
        ;
    UDR = data;  // Send the data byte to the transmit
buffer
}
```

Explanation:
- The function checks the **UDRE** (USART Data Register Empty) flag, which indicates that the transmit buffer is ready for new data.
- It then writes the data byte into the **UDR** (USART Data Register), which transmits it via the serial interface.

5. Check for ESP8266 Response

What does it do?

This function checks the response from the ESP8266 after sending an AT command. Typically, the ESP8266 responds with OK if the command is successful, or ERROR if there's an issue.

Syntax:

```
if (USART_Receive() == 'OK')
```

Example:

```c
int check_esp_response(void) {
    char response[3];
    int i = 0;
    while (i < 3) {
        response[i] = USART_Receive();   // Receive each character
        i++;
    }
    response[i] = '\0';   // Null-terminate the response string
    if (strcmp(response, "OK") == 0) {
        return 1;   // Successful response
    }
    return 0;   // Error in response
}
```

Explanation:

- This function reads three characters from the USART buffer to check the response from the ESP8266.
- If the response is OK, it indicates that the command was successful, and the function returns 1. If the response is anything else, it returns 0 indicating an error.

Real-life Application Project: Web Server on ESP8266
Project Overview
This project uses the **ESP8266** to create a simple web server, where the
AVR microcontroller will send temperature readings (from a sensor like
the LM35)over Wi-Fi to a webpage.
Required Components

Component	Description
AVR Microcontroller	Controls the system
ESP8266 Wi-Fi Module	Provides Wi-Fi connectivity
LM35 Temperature Sensor	Reads temperature
Resistor (220Ω)	Current-limiting resistor for LM35

Circuit Connection Table

Component	AVR Pin	Purpose
LM35 Sensor	ADC0	Reads temperature
ESP8266 TX/RX	USART TX/RX	Serial Communication

Project Code

```
#include <avr/io.h>
#include <util/delay.h>

void USART_init(unsigned int baud) {
    // USART initialization code
}

void send_AT_command(char* command) {
    // Send AT command to ESP8266
}

unsigned char USART_Receive(void) {
    // USART receive function
}

unsigned char USART_Transmit(unsigned char data) {
    // USART transmit function
}
```

```c
uint16_t read_temperature() {
    // Placeholder for reading temperature sensor
    return 25;   // Return a sample temperature value
}

int main(void) {
    USART_init(115200);
    char buffer[50];
    uint16_t temperature;

    while (1) {
        temperature = read_temperature();
        sprintf(buffer, "GET /temperature?value=%d",
temperature);

send_AT_command("AT+CIPSTART=\"TCP\",\"192.168.1.100\",
80");
        send_AT_command("AT+CIPSEND=50");
        for (int i = 0; buffer[i] != '\0'; i++) {
            USART_Transmit(buffer[i]);   // Send HTTP
GET request
        }
        _delay_ms(1000);   // Wait for the next
transmission
    }
}
```

Expected Results

 When the program runs, the AVR microcontroller reads the temperature
from the LM35 sensor and sends it as part of an HTTP request to a web
server via the ESP8266. The web server will receive the temperature data,
and it can display it on a webpage in real-time.

Chapter 68: LoRa Communication

LoRa (Long Range) is a wireless communication technology designed for long-distance communication with low power consumption. LoRa is particularly useful in Internet of Things (IoT) applications, where devices need to communicate over long distances while minimizing power usage. It operates in the unlicensed ISM (Industrial, Scientific, and Medical) frequency bands, making it an ideal choice for remote monitoring systems, smart agriculture, and environmental sensing.

In this chapter, we'll learn how to interface an AVR microcontroller with a **LoRa module** (such as the **SX1278** or **RFM95W**) for long-range wireless communication. We'll go through the steps to set up LoRa communication, send and receive data between two LoRa modules, and understand the basic concepts behind the communication.

Key Concepts of LoRa Communication with AVR

Concept	Description	Example
LoRa Module	A long-range wireless communication module that uses LoRa technology.	SX1278, RFM95W, etc.
SPI Communication	A high-speed communication protocol used to interface with the LoRa module.	SCK, MOSI, MISO, and CS pins
LoRa Transmitter	A LoRa module configured to send data to another LoRa module.	Module set to transmit mode
LoRa Receiver	A LoRa module configured to receive data from a transmitter.	Module set to receive mode
Frequency Band	LoRa operates in ISM bands, such as 433MHz, 868MHz, or 915MHz.	915MHz, 433MHz
Packet Communication	Sending and receiving data in the form of packets with CRC error-checking.	LoRaWAN or custom protocols

Basic Rules for Using LoRa with AVR

Rule	Correct Example	Incorrect Example
Use the correct SPI pins for LoRa module	MOSI, MISO, SCK, CS pins configured correctly	Not connecting SPI pins correctly
Initialize LoRa module properly	LoRa_init();	Not configuring LoRa module before use
Use correct frequency for LoRa operation	LoRa_set_frequency(915000000);	Using an unsupported frequency
Set LoRa transmission power correctly	LoRa_set_tx_power(14);	Not setting transmission power properly
Wait for acknowledgment after sending data	LoRa_receive_ack();	Not checking for acknowledgment

Syntax Table

SL	Operation	Syntax/Example	Description
1	Initialize SPI Communication	SPI_init();	Initializes the SPI interface for communication with LoRa module
2	Initialize LoRa Module	LoRa_init();	Initializes the LoRa module for communication
3	Set Frequency	LoRa_set_frequency(915000000);	Sets the communication frequency (e.g., 915 MHz for US region)
4	Set Transmit Power	LoRa_set_tx_power(14);	Sets the transmit power for long-range communication
5	Send Data Packet	LoRa_send("Hello, LoRa!");	Sends data packet to another LoRa device
6	Receive Data Packet	LoRa_receive();	Receives data from another LoRa device

| 7 | Check for Acknowledgment | LoRa_receiv e_ack(); | Wait for acknowledgment of received data |

Syntax Explanation

1. Initialize SPI Communication

What does it do?

This function sets up the **SPI interface** on the AVR microcontroller, which is necessary to communicate with the LoRa module. SPI (Serial Peripheral Interface) is used to send and receive data between the microcontroller and the LoRa module.

Syntax:

```
SPI_init();
```

Example:

```
void SPI_init() {
    // Set MOSI, SCK, and SS as output, MISO as input
    DDRB |= (1<<PB5) | (1<<PB7) | (1<<PB4);   // Set
SCK, MOSI, and SS as output pins
    DDRB &= ~(1<<PB6);                        // Set
MISO as input
    SPCR = (1<<SPE) | (1<<MSTR) | (1<<SPR0);  // Enable
SPI, Master mode, clock rate fck/16
}
```

Explanation:

- **MOSI**: Master Out Slave In (PB5)
- **MISO**: Master In Slave Out (PB6)
- **SCK**: Serial Clock (PB7)
- **SS**: Slave Select (PB4)
- **SPCR**: SPI Control Register that enables the SPI peripheral, sets the microcontroller as the master, and configures the clock speed.

2. Initialize LoRa Module

What does it do?

This function initializes the LoRa module by setting up necessary parameters like frequency, transmission power, and communication mode.

Syntax:

```
LoRa_init();
```

Example:

```
void LoRa_init() {
    // Reset LoRa module
    LoRa_write_register(REG_OP_MODE, MODE_SLEEP);  // Set module to sleep mode for setup
    LoRa_set_frequency(915000000);  // Set frequency to 915 MHz
    LoRa_set_tx_power(14);  // Set transmission power to 14 dBm
    LoRa_write_register(REG_OP_MODE, MODE_STDBY);  // Set module to standby mode for operation
}
```

Explanation:
- **REG_OP_MODE**: Register used to control the operational mode of the LoRa module.
- **LoRa_set_frequency()**: Function that sets the LoRa module frequency (e.g., 915 MHz).
- **LoRa_set_tx_power()**: Function to adjust the transmission power to optimize range.

3. Set Frequency

What does it do?

This function sets the frequency at which the LoRa module will communicate. LoRa modules can operate on different frequency bands, including 433 MHz, 868 MHz, and 915 MHz, depending on the region.

Syntax:

```
LoRa_set_frequency(915000000);
```

Example:

```
void LoRa_set_frequency(uint32_t frequency) {
    LoRa_write_register(REG_FRF_MSB, (frequency >> 16)
& 0xFF);
    LoRa_write_register(REG_FRF_MID, (frequency >> 8) &
0xFF);
    LoRa_write_register(REG_FRF_LSB, frequency & 0xFF);
}
```

Explanation:

- **REG_FRF_MSB, REG_FRF_MID, REG_FRF_LSB**: Registers that store the frequency data (most significant, middle, and least significant bytes).
- **LoRa_write_register()**: Function that writes data to a specific register on the LoRa module.

4. Set Transmit Power

What does it do?

This function sets the transmit power of the LoRa module, which influences the communication range. The power can be adjusted to optimize the range and power consumption.

Syntax:

```
LoRa_set_tx_power(14);
```

Example:

```
void LoRa_set_tx_power(int8_t power) {
    LoRa_write_register(REG_PA_CONFIG, (uint8_t)(power
& 0x0F));   // Set transmit power
}
```

Explanation:

- **REG_PA_CONFIG**: Register for controlling the transmit power of the LoRa module.
- **power**: The transmit power value (e.g., 14 dBm for maximum power).

5. Send Data Packet

What does it do?
This function sends a data packet to the LoRa receiver. It prepares the data, writes it to the module's FIFO buffer, and triggers the transmission.
Syntax:
```
LoRa_send("Hello, LoRa!");
```
Example:
```
void LoRa_send(const char* message) {
    LoRa_write_register(REG_FIFO, 0x00);   // Prepare
the FIFO buffer for data
    while (*message) {
        LoRa_write_register(REG_FIFO, *message);   //
Send each character of the message
        message++;
    }
    LoRa_write_register(REG_OP_MODE, MODE_TX);   //
Trigger transmission
}
```

Explanation:
- **REG_FIFO**: Register for writing data to the LoRa FIFO buffer.
- **MODE_TX**: The operational mode for transmission.

6. Receive Data Packet

What does it do?
This function waits for an incoming packet from a LoRa transmitter and retrieves the data when received.
Syntax:
```
LoRa_receive();
```
Example:
```
void LoRa_receive(void) {
    LoRa_write_register(REG_OP_MODE, MODE_RX);   // Set
```

```
module to receive mode
    while (LoRa_read_register(REG_IRQ_FLAGS) &
IRQ_RX_DONE) {
        char data = LoRa_read_register(REG_FIFO);   //
Read received data


        // Process received data here
    }
}
```

Explanation:
- **REG_OP_MODE**: Set the module to receive mode.
- **REG_IRQ_FLAGS**: Register for interrupt flags, used to check if a message has been received.
- **REG_FIFO**: FIFO register from which received data is read.

Real-life Application Project: LoRa-based Remote Weather Station
Project Overview
In this project, two LoRa modules are used to create a remote weather station. One module is attached to an **AVR microcontroller** that reads temperature and humidity values from sensors, while the second module sends the data to a remote receiver for display or further processing.
Required Components

Component	Description
AVR Microcontroller	Controls the system
LoRa Module	Long-range wireless communication
DHT22 Sensor	Temperature and humidity sensor
Resistor (220Ω)	Current-limiting resistor for DHT22

Circuit Connection Table

Component	AVR Pin	Purpose
DHT22 Sensor	Any digital pin	Reads temperature and humidity
LoRa Module	SPI pins (MOSI, MISO, SCK, CS)	LoRa communication

Project Code

```c
#include <avr/io.h>
#include <util/delay.h>
#include "LoRa.h"
#include "DHT22.h"

int main() {
    LoRa_init();  // Initialize LoRa module
    DHT22_init();  // Initialize DHT22 sensor

    while (1) {
        float temperature, humidity;
        DHT22_read(&temperature, &humidity);  // Read
temperature and humidity

        char message[100];
        sprintf(message, "Temperature: %.2f, Humidity:
%.2f", temperature, humidity);
        LoRa_send(message);  // Send data over LoRa

        _delay_ms(5000);  // Wait before sending again
    }
}
```

Expected Results

The AVR microcontroller continuously reads temperature and humidity
data from the **DHT22 sensor**. This data is sent wirelessly via the **LoRa
module** to another LoRa receiver, where it can be processed or displayed.

Chapter 69: RF Modules and Communication

Radio Frequency (RF) communication is a key technology used in wireless data transfer. RF modules enable devices to communicate over short or long distances without the need for physical connections. These modules can operate in various frequency bands and are widely used in applications such as remote controls, wireless sensors, home automation, and IoT (Internet of Things) systems.

In this chapter, we will explore how to interface an AVR microcontroller with **RF modules** such as the **nRF24L01+** (a popular 2.4GHz RF module) to send and receive data. We will cover the basic setup, communication protocols, and how to implement wireless data transmission using these modules.

Key Concepts of RF Communication with AVR

Concept	Description	Example
RF Module	A wireless communication module that uses radio waves to transfer data.	nRF24L01+, RF433MHz, HC-12, etc.
SPI Communication	A synchronous serial communication protocol used to interface with RF modules.	SCK, MOSI, MISO, and CS pins
Data Packets	Data transmitted between devices, often with error-checking and CRC.	Wireless sensor data, control commands
Frequency Bands	RF modules operate in different frequency bands such as 433MHz, 868MHz, and 2.4GHz.	433MHz for long-range, 2.4GHz for short-range
Wireless Communication Protocol	A protocol that defines how data is sent and received over RF.	nRF24L01+ protocol, custom protocols
Antenna	Component that helps transmit and receive RF signals for longer distances.	On-board or external antenna

Basic Rules for Using RF Modules with AVR

Rule	Correct Example	Incorrect Example
Use the correct SPI pins for RF modules	`MOSI, MISO, SCK, CS` pins correctly configured	Incorrect SPI pin configuration
Initialize the RF module before transmission	`nrf_init();`	Not configuring the RF module correctly
Set the correct frequency for RF communication	`nrf_set_frequency(2400000000);`	Using an unsupported frequency for your module
Handle data packets properly	`nrf_send_data("Hello, AVR!");`	Not handling data packets or acknowledging reception
Ensure proper antenna connection	Use an external antenna if necessary	Omitting the antenna, resulting in weak signals

Syntax Table

SL	Operation	Syntax/Example	Description
1	Initialize SPI Communication	`SPI_init();`	Initializes SPI for communication with RF module
2	Initialize RF Module	`nrf_init();`	Initializes the RF module for communication
3	Set RF Module Frequency	`nrf_set_frequency(2400000000);`	Sets the RF communication frequency
4	Send Data Packet	`nrf_send_data("Hello, AVR!");`	Sends a data packet wirelessly to the RF receiver
5	Receive Data Packet	`nrf_receive_data();`	Receives a data packet wirelessly from the RF transmitter

6	Set Transmit Power	nrf_set_tx_power(14);	Sets the transmit power to control communication range
7	Check for Acknowledgment	nrf_check_ack();	Checks for acknowledgment from the receiver after sending data

Syntax Explanation

1. Initialize SPI Communication

What does it do?
This function sets up the **SPI interface** between the AVR microcontroller and the RF module. Since the RF module (like nRF24L01+) communicates using SPI, this step is crucial to establish data communication.

Syntax:
```
SPI_init();
```
Example:
```
void SPI_init() {
    // Set MOSI, SCK, and SS as output, MISO as input
    DDRB |= (1<<PB5) | (1<<PB7) | (1<<PB4);  // Set SCK, MOSI, and SS as output pins
    DDRB &= ~(1<<PB6);                        // Set MISO as input
    SPCR = (1<<SPE) | (1<<MSTR) | (1<<SPR0);  // Enable SPI, Master mode, clock rate fck/16
}
```

Explanation:
- **MOSI**: Master Out Slave In (PB5)
- **MISO**: Master In Slave Out (PB6)
- **SCK**: Serial Clock (PB7)
- **SS**: Slave Select (PB4)
- **SPCR**: SPI Control Register for configuring the AVR SPI communication.

2. Initialize RF Module

What does it do?

This function initializes the RF module, setting the necessary parameters such as frequency, mode, and power levels to prepare the module for sending and receiving data.

Syntax:

```
nrf_init();
```

Example:

```
void nrf_init() {
    // Reset RF module and set mode to RX/TX
    nrf_write_register(REG_OP_MODE, MODE_SLEEP);  //
Sleep mode for configuration
    nrf_set_frequency(2400000000);  // Set frequency to
2.4GHz (for nRF24L01+)
    nrf_set_tx_power(14);  // Set transmission power to
14 dBm
    nrf_write_register(REG_OP_MODE, MODE_TX);  // Set
module to transmit mode
}
```

Explanation:

- **REG_OP_MODE**: Register to control the operation mode (e.g., sleep, receive, transmit).
- **nrf_set_frequency()**: Configures the RF module's operating frequency (2.4 GHz is common for nRF modules).
- **nrf_set_tx_power()**: Sets the power level for transmission to determine the communication range.

3. Set RF Module Frequency

What does it do?

This function sets the communication frequency for the RF module, ensuring that both transmitting and receiving modules are tuned to the same frequency.

Syntax:

```
nrf_set_frequency(2400000000);
```
Example:
```
void nrf_set_frequency(uint32_t frequency) {
    nrf_write_register(REG_RF_SETUP, (frequency >> 24)
& 0xFF);  // Most significant byte
    nrf_write_register(REG_RF_SETUP + 1, (frequency >>
16) & 0xFF);  // Second byte
    nrf_write_register(REG_RF_SETUP + 2, (frequency >>
8) & 0xFF);  // Third byte
    nrf_write_register(REG_RF_SETUP + 3, frequency &
0xFF);  // Least significant byte
}
```

Explanation:
- **REG_RF_SETUP**: Register where the frequency value is stored.
- **nrf_write_register()**: Function to write to a specific register of the RF module.

4. Send Data Packet
What does it do?
This function sends a data packet to another RF module. The data is placed in the module's **FIFO** (First In, First Out) buffer, and the module is then instructed to transmit the packet.

Syntax:
```
nrf_send_data("Hello, AVR!");
```
Example:
```
void nrf_send_data(const char* data) {
    // Prepare data for transmission
    while (*data) {
        nrf_write_register(REG_TX_FIFO, *data);  //
Write each byte to the TX FIFO
        data++;
    }
    nrf_write_register(REG_OP_MODE, MODE_TX);  //
Trigger transmission
}
```

Explanation:

- **REG_TX_FIFO**: Register to send data to the RF module's transmit FIFO buffer.
- **MODE_TX**: Transmission mode that instructs the module to start sending data.

5. Receive Data Packet

What does it do?

This function waits for incoming data from another RF module. Once data is received, it is read from the **FIFO** buffer.

Syntax:

```
nrf_receive_data();
```

Example:

```
void nrf_receive_data(void) {
    // Check if data is available
    if (nrf_read_register(REG_IRQ_FLAGS) & IRQ_RX_DONE)
{
        char received_data =
nrf_read_register(REG_RX_FIFO);   // Read received data
        // Process received data here
    }
}
```

Explanation:

- **REG_IRQ_FLAGS**: Register that holds interrupt flags, used to detect if data has been received.
- **REG_RX_FIFO**: Register to read received data from the RF module's FIFO buffer.

6. Set Transmit Power

What does it do?
This function adjusts the transmit power of the RF module. A higher transmit power increases the range of communication but also consumes more energy.

Syntax:
```
nrf_set_tx_power(14);
```

Example:
```
void nrf_set_tx_power(int8_t power) {
    nrf_write_register(REG_RF_SETUP, (power & 0x

0F));  // Set the TX power level
}
```

Explanation:
- **REG_RF_SETUP**: The register that controls various RF module settings, including transmit power.

Real-life Application Project: Wireless Temperature Sensor
Project Overview
In this project, two AVR microcontrollers equipped with **RF modules** are used for wireless communication. One microcontroller is responsible for reading temperature data from a **temperature sensor** (e.g., LM35), and the other microcontroller wirelessly receives this data and displays it on an LCD or processes it further.

Required Components

Component	Description
AVR Microcontroller	Controls both sending and receiving modules
RF Module (nRF24L01+)	Wireless communication
Temperature Sensor (LM35)	Measures the temperature
Resistor (220Ω)	Current-limiting resistor for the sensor

Circuit Connection Table

Component	AVR Pin	Purpose
LM35 Sensor	ADC pin (e.g., ADC0)	Reads temperature data
nRF24L01+	SPI Pins (MOSI, MISO, SCK, CS)	Wireless communication

Project Code

```c
#include <avr/io.h>
#include <util/delay.h>
#include "nrf24l01.h"
#include "LM35.h"

int main() {
    uint16_t temperature;
    char message[50];

    nrf_init();   // Initialize RF module
    LM35_init();  // Initialize temperature sensor

    while (1) {
        temperature = LM35_read();  // Read temperature from LM35
        sprintf(message, "Temp: %d", temperature);  // Format message
        nrf_send_data(message);  // Send temperature data wirelessly
        _delay_ms(5000);  // Wait before sending again
    }
}
```

Expected Results

The temperature data is continuously transmitted from the sender microcontroller to the receiver via the **nRF24L01+** RF module. The receiver can then process or display the data, such as on an LCD screen or send it to a cloud server.

Chapter 70: Gesture Recognition

Gesture recognition has become an essential part of human-computer interaction (HCI), allowing users to control devices without direct physical interaction. This can be achieved through various sensors that detect hand or body movements. In embedded systems, **gesture recognition** is typically achieved using sensors such as accelerometers, gyroscopes, or specialized gesture modules.

In this chapter, we will explore how to interface an **accelerometer** (e.g., **ADXL345**) with an **AVR microcontroller** to recognize basic gestures like tilting, shaking, or swiping. We will cover the concepts of gesture recognition, sensor integration, and the process of recognizing specific gestures to trigger events in a system.

Key Concepts of Gesture Recognition with AVR

Concept	Description	Example
Gesture Recognition	The process of detecting human movements using sensors.	Hand gestures, head movements, etc.
Accelerometer	A sensor that measures the acceleration forces in multiple axes.	ADXL345, MMA8451
Sensor Interface	The communication protocol (e.g., I2C or SPI) used to interface with sensors.	I2C protocol with ADXL345
3D Motion Detection	Detecting movement in 3D space (X, Y, Z axes).	Motion in all directions

Thresholding	The process of setting a threshold value to trigger events based on sensor data.	Detecting a shake or tilt by setting acceleration thresholds
Event Triggering	Using sensor data to trigger actions or events in a system.	Turning on lights or activating motors when specific gestures are detected

Basic Rules for Gesture Recognition with AVR

Rule	Correct Example	Incorrect Example
Use correct communication protocol	Use I2C to interface with ADXL345	Using unsupported communication protocol
Handle sensor initialization properly	`accelerometer_init();`	Forgetting to initialize sensor before use
Set appropriate gesture detection thresholds	`set_threshold(1000);`	Using arbitrary threshold values without calibration
Filter noisy data from the sensor	Apply averaging or low-pass filtering to raw data	Ignoring noise and using unfiltered data

Syntax Table

SL	Operation	Syntax/Example	Description
1	Initialize Sensor	`accelerometer_init();`	Initializes the accelerometer sensor for use
2	Read Sensor Data	`accel_read();`	Reads the current data from the accelerometer (X, Y, Z values)
3	Set Threshold for Gesture Detection	`set_threshold(1000);`	Sets the threshold value for detecting specific gestures

4	Filter Sensor Data	`filter_data();`	Applies filters to sensor data to remove noise or errors
5	Detect Shake Gesture	`detect_shake();`	Detects if the sensor has undergone a shake or vibration event
6	Detect Tilt Gesture	`detect_tilt();`	Detects if the sensor is tilted beyond a certain angle
7	Trigger Action	`trigger_action();`	Executes an action based on a detected gesture

Syntax Explanation

1. Initialize Sensor

What does it do?

This function initializes the accelerometer sensor and configures it for communication with the AVR microcontroller. The sensor's settings, such as output data rate (ODR), full-scale range, and communication protocol, are defined.

Syntax:

```
accelerometer_init();
```

Example:

```
void accelerometer_init() {
    // Initialize I2C communication
    i2c_init();
    // Write configuration settings to the
accelerometer (ADXL345)
    i2c_write(0x53, 0x2D, 0x08);  // Power on the
device
    i2c_write(0x53, 0x31, 0x08);  // Set data rate
}
```

Explanation:

- **i2c_write(address, register, value)**: Sends a command to configure the accelerometer, such as powering it on and setting the data rate.
- **0x53**: I2C address for the ADXL345 accelerometer.
- **0x2D, 0x31**: Configuration registers for the device.

2. Read Sensor Data

What does it do?

This function reads the X, Y, and Z-axis acceleration data from the accelerometer. The sensor outputs acceleration values as digital data, which the AVR microcontroller processes to determine motion.

Syntax:

```
accel_read();
```

Example:

```
void accel_read() {
    int16_t x = i2c_read(0x53, 0x32);   // Read X-axis data
    int16_t y = i2c_read(0x53, 0x34);   // Read Y-axis data
    int16_t z = i2c_read(0x53, 0x36);   // Read Z-axis data
}
```

Explanation:

- **i2c_read(address, register)**: Reads data from the specified register (X, Y, or Z axis).
- **0x32, 0x34, 0x36**: Registers corresponding to the X, Y, and Z-axis data.

3. Set Threshold for Gesture Detection

What does it do?

This function sets a threshold value for gesture recognition, helping the system to detect specific gestures such as shaking or tilting. When the sensor data exceeds the threshold, the gesture is triggered.

Syntax:

```
set_threshold(1000);
```

Example:
```
void set_threshold(int threshold) {
    // Define a threshold for detecting a shake gesture
    shake_threshold = threshold;
}
```

Explanation:
- **shake_threshold**: A variable storing the threshold value for detecting shakes.
- Threshold values are typically determined based on the sensor's sensitivity and the range of expected motion.

4. Filter Sensor Data

What does it do?
Sensor data is often noisy due to electrical interference or environmental factors. This function applies a filter (e.g., a low-pass filter) to smooth out the raw data and improve accuracy.

Syntax:
```
filter_data();
```

Example:
```
void filter_data() {
    static int16_t x_filtered, y_filtered, z_filtered;
    x_filtered = (x_filtered * 0.8) + (x * 0.2);   //
Low-pass filter for X-axis
    y_filtered = (y_filtered * 0.8) + (y * 0.2);   //
Low-pass filter for Y-axis
    z_filtered = (z_filtered * 0.8) + (z * 0.2);   //
Low-pass filter for Z-axis
}
```

Explanation:
- **Low-pass filter**: Reduces high-frequency noise in the sensor data by averaging the previous data with the new data.
- This approach helps in obtaining smoother readings from the accelerometer.

5. Detect Shake Gesture

What does it do?

This function checks if the accelerometer has experienced a sudden acceleration or vibration, which is characteristic of a shake gesture.

Syntax:

```
detect_shake();
```

Example:

```
void detect_shake() {
    int shake = abs(x) + abs(y) + abs(z);   // Calculate
total acceleration
    if (shake > shake_threshold) {
        trigger_action();   // Trigger an action if the
shake threshold is exceeded
    }
}
```

Explanation:

- **abs()**: Calculates the absolute value of the acceleration on each axis.
- **shake_threshold**: The threshold value set earlier that determines the sensitivity of shake detection.

6. Detect Tilt Gesture

What does it do?

This function detects if the accelerometer has been tilted beyond a certain angle, which can be used for triggering specific actions.

Syntax:

```
detect_tilt();
```

Example:

```
void detect_tilt() {
    if (abs(x) > tilt_threshold || abs(y) >
tilt_threshold) {
```

```
        trigger_action();  // Trigger an action if tilt
is detected
    }
}
```

Explanation:
- **tilt_threshold**: The acceleration value above which the device is considered tilted.
- **abs(x) > tilt_threshold**: Checks if the device has been tilted beyond the set threshold in either the X or Y axis.

7. Trigger Action

What does it do?
This function is called when a specific gesture (shake, tilt, etc.) is detected. It triggers an action such as turning on an LED, controlling a motor, or sending data.

Syntax:
```
trigger_action();
```

Example:
```
void trigger_action() {
    // Perform an action, such as turning on an LED
    PORTB |= (1 << PB0);  // Turn on LED connected to
pin PB0
}
```

Explanation:
- **PORTB**: Control register for setting the state of port B pins (PB0 in this case).
- The actioncould be anything, like controlling an LED, starting a motor, or sending a signal to another device.

Real-life Application Project: Gesture-Controlled Light

Project Overview

This project demonstrates how to use a simple gesture (shake or tilt) to control a light using an AVR microcontroller and an accelerometer sensor. When the user shakes or tilts the sensor, the light will turn on or off.

Required Components

Component	Description
AVR Microcontroller	Controls the system
ADXL345 Accelerometer	Detects the gesture
LED	Light that will be controlled by gestures
Resistor (220Ω)	Current-limiting resistor for LED

Circuit Connection Table

Component	AVR Pin	Purpose
ADXL345 Accelerometer	SDA, SCL	Communication with AVR via I2C
LED	PB0	Controlled via microcontroller

Project Code

```
#include <avr/io.h>
#include <util/delay.h>

void accelerometer_init() {
    // Initialization code for accelerometer here
}

void accel_read() {
    // Read X, Y, Z data from accelerometer here
}

void filter_data() {
    // Filter accelerometer data here
}

void set_threshold(int threshold) {
    shake_threshold = threshold;
}
```

```c
void detect_shake() {
    int shake = abs(x) + abs(y) + abs(z);
    if (shake > shake_threshold) {
        trigger_action();
    }
}

void trigger_action() {
    PORTB |= (1 << PB0);   // Turn on LED
}

int main() {
    DDRB |= (1 << PB0);    // Set PB0 as output (for
LED)
    accelerometer_init();
    set_threshold(1000);

    while (1) {
        accel_read();
        filter_data();
        detect_shake();
        _delay_ms(100);
    }
}
```

Expected Results

In this project, the light will turn on when a shake gesture is detected, and remain on until the gesture is cleared. You can customize the code further to use tilt gestures or other actions for controlling additional devices.

Chapter 71: Speech Processing

Speech processing involves capturing, analyzing, and interpreting human speech to execute specific commands or to convert speech into text. With AVR microcontrollers, it is possible to create basic speech recognition and synthesis systems, although for advanced tasks, more powerful processors are typically used. AVR systems can perform speech recognition and synthesis through integration with speech processing modules or external chips.

In this chapter, we will explore how to interface speech recognition and synthesis modules with an AVR microcontroller. We will also look at how AVR can handle speech signal processing, including techniques for audio playback and voice recognition.

Key Concepts of Speech Processing with AVR

Concept	Description	Example
Speech Recognition	Converting audio input (speech) into commands or text.	Using a module like EasyVR to recognize commands
Speech Synthesis	Converting text or commands into audible speech.	Using a module like Emic-2 to produce speech
Microphone Interface	Capturing audio signals using microphones and analog-to-digital conversion.	ADC to capture microphone signals
Signal Processing	Filtering and processing audio data to enhance clarity or remove noise.	Low-pass filters or noise reduction algorithms
External Speech Modules	Using dedicated hardware for speech recognition or synthesis.	EasyVR, Emic-2 speech synthesis modules

Basic Rules for Speech Processing with AVR

Rule	Correct Example	Incorrect Example
Use a compatible speech module	Use EasyVR for speech recognition	Using incompatible modules without proper communication protocol
Properly interface with microphone	Use ADC to sample microphone input	Using unfiltered or overly noisy input from microphone
Implement necessary signal processing	Apply filters to enhance speech input	Ignoring noise and using raw data directly from the microphone
Use correct libraries for speech synthesis	Include easyvr.h for EasyVR integration	Using unsupported libraries or incorrect configuration

Syntax Table

SL	Operation	Syntax/Example	Description
1	Initialize Speech Module	`easyvr_init();`	Initializes the speech recognition module
2	Capture Audio from Microphone	`microphone_read();`	Captures audio data from a microphone
3	Process Audio Signal	`process_audio_signal();`	Processes the audio signal (e.g., noise reduction, filtering)
4	Recognize Speech Command	`recognize_command();`	Recognizes the spoken command and triggers corresponding action
5	Play Audio (Speech Synthesis)	`play_audio_speech("Hello, world!");`	Plays an audio message through a speech synthesis module
6	Stop Audio Playback	`stop_audio();`	Stops the current audio playback or speech synthesis

Syntax Explanation

1. Initialize Speech Module

What does it do?

This function initializes the speech recognition or synthesis module and prepares it for use. This may involve setting communication protocols like UART, SPI, or I2C, configuring initial settings like baud rates, and loading any necessary data.

Syntax:

```
easyvr_init();
```

Example:

```
void easyvr_init() {
    // Initialize communication with EasyVR module over UART
    uart_init();
    uart_write(0xAA);   // Send start command to EasyVR
    // Load user voice commands
    easyvr_load_commands();
}
```

Explanation:

- **uart_init()**: Initializes the UART (Universal Asynchronous Receiver-Transmitter) for communication with the EasyVR module.
- **uart_write()**: Sends data over UART to the EasyVR module.
- **easyvr_load_commands()**: Loads the predefined voice commands into the EasyVR module.

2. Capture Audio from Microphone

What does it do?

This function reads the audio data from a microphone using an ADC (Analog to Digital Converter). The microphone typically captures analog audio signals, which need to be converted into digital form for processing by the AVR microcontroller.

Syntax:

```
microphone_read();
```

Example:

```
void microphone_read() {
    uint16_t audio_signal = ADC;   // Read ADC value
from microphone
    // Process audio signal here if necessary
}
```

Explanation:

- **ADC**: The ADC register that holds the converted digital value from the microphone's analog signal.
- This function reads the microphone's signal and stores it for further processing.

3. Process Audio Signal

What does it do?

This function processes the captured audio signal, applying necessary filtering or enhancement to improve speech quality. For example, you may apply noise reduction, low-pass filtering, or volume adjustment.

Syntax:

```
process_audio_signal();
```

Example:

```
void process_audio_signal() {
    // Apply a low-pass filter to remove high-frequency
noise
    static int last_signal = 0;
    int filtered_signal = (audio_signal * 0.8) +
(last_signal * 0.2);
    last_signal = filtered_signal;
    // Further processing of filtered_signal can be
done here
}
```

Explanation:

- **Low-pass filter**: Reduces high-frequency noise in the captured audio.
- **filtered_signal**: The signal after applying the low-pass filter, which is smoother and less noisy.

4. Recognize Speech Command

What does it do?

This function uses the speech recognition module (e.g., EasyVR) to recognize a spoken command. The module compares the captured audio to a set of predefined commands and triggers an action based on the recognized command.

Syntax:

```
recognize_command();
```

Example:

```
void recognize_command() {
    uint8_t command = easyvr_recognize();   // Get the recognized command
    if (command == 1) {
        // Execute action for command 1 (e.g., turn on light)
        turn_on_light();
    }
}
```

Explanation:

- **easyvr_recognize()**: A function from the EasyVR library that returns the recognized command number.
- The recognized command triggers specific actions, such as turning on a light or activating a motor.

5. Play Audio (Speech Synthesis)

What does it do?

This function allows the AVR microcontroller to output speech using a speech synthesis module. The module converts text input into audible speech.

Syntax:

```
play_audio_speech("Hello, world!");
```

Example:
```
void play_audio_speech(const char* text) {
    // Send the text to the speech synthesis module for
conversion
    uart_write_text(text);   // Send text via UART to
Emic-2 module
}
```

Explanation:
- **uart_write_text()**: Sends the text message to the Emic-2 module, which converts it into speech and outputs the sound through a speaker.
- **Emic-2**: A text-to-speech module that converts ASCII text into spoken words.

6. Stop Audio Playback

What does it do?
This function stops any ongoing audio playback. This can be useful if the speech synthesis is interrupted or if you need to stop the audio before it finishes.

Syntax:
```
stop_audio();
```
Example:
```
void stop_audio() {
    uart_write(0x00);   // Send stop command to Emic-2
to halt speech playback
}
```

Explanation:
- **uart_write(0x00)**: Sends a command to stop audio playback in the speech synthesis module.

Real-life Application Project: Voice-Controlled Home Automation

Project Overview

In this project, we will build a simple voice-controlled home automation system. Using the EasyVR speech recognition module, an AVR microcontroller will recognize voice commands to control home appliances such as lights and fans.

Required Components

Component	Description
AVR Microcontroller	Controls the system and processes speech commands
EasyVR Module	Recognizes voice commands
Relay	Controls power to home appliances
LED/Light	A simple light to be controlled by voice command

Circuit Connection Table

Component	AVR Pin	Purpose
EasyVR Module	RX, TX	Communication with AVR microcontroller
Relay	PB0	Controls power to appliances
LED/Light	PB1	Controlled via microcontroller

Project Code

```
#include <avr/io.h>
#include <util/delay.h>

void easyvr_init() {
    // Initialize UART and EasyVR module here
}

void recognize_command() {
    uint8_t command = easyvr_recognize();  // Get the
recognized command
    if (command == 1) {
        PORTB |= (1 << PB0);  // Turn on light
    }
    else if (command == 2) {
        PORTB &= ~(1 << PB0); // Turn off light
```

```
    }
}

int main() {
    DDRB |= (1 << PB0);   //

 Set PB0 as output
    easyvr_init();           // Initialize EasyVR module

    while (1) {
        recognize_command();   // Continuously listen
for commands
    }
}
```

Explanation:

- The EasyVR module listens for voice commands. When it
  recognizes a command (e.g., "Turn on the light"), it triggers an
  action by setting or clearing the appropriate pin to control a relay
  and turn on/off an appliance.

Chapter 72: Home Automation

Home automation systems use smart technologies to control various home appliances such as lights, fans, and security devices. AVR microcontrollers can be used as the central controller for home automation systems, allowing users to automate the control of these devices based on certain conditions or commands.

This chapter will explore how to design a home automation system using an AVR microcontroller. We will cover how to interface the AVR with relays, sensors, and communication modules to control appliances, monitor conditions, and enable remote control.

Key Concepts of Home Automation with AVR

Concept	Description	Example
Microcontroller as Controller	Using the AVR microcontroller as the central processing unit of the system.	ATmega328p controlling sensors and relays
Relay Control	Controlling appliances by switching relays connected to high-voltage devices.	Using relays to control lights or fans
Sensors	Detecting environmental factors such as temperature or motion.	DHT11 (temperature/humidity sensor)
Communication Protocols	Allowing remote control or monitoring through wireless communication.	Using RF, Wi-Fi (ESP8266), or Bluetooth
Automation Logic	Setting triggers based on conditions (e.g., time, sensor data).	Automating lights based on motion or time

Basic Rules for Home Automation with AVR

Rule	Correct Example	Incorrect Example
Use relays rated for the appliances	Use a 5V relay to control a 12V fan	Using a 3.3V relay to control a high-power appliance
Properly handle communication protocols	Use UART, I2C, or SPI for communication modules	Using untested or incompatible communication methods
Use appropriate power supplies	Power the relay module and AVR with adequate power	Overloading the microcontroller's output pins
Implement safety precautions	Use a diode for relay flyback protection	Not including any protection for relays

Syntax Table

SL	Operation	Syntax/Example	Description
1	Initialize Relay	`relay_init();`	Initializes the relay control pins for controlling appliances
2	Turn On Appliance	`turn_on_appliance();`	Turns on an appliance via relay
3	Turn Off Appliance	`turn_off_appliance();`	Turns off an appliance via relay
4	Read Sensor Data	`read_sensor();`	Reads the sensor data (e.g., temperature, motion)
5	Send Command Over Wi-Fi/Bluetooth	`send_command("Turn on light");`	Sends commands via communication module to control appliances
6	Monitor Conditions	`monitor_conditions();`	Continuously checks sensor data and makes decisions based on conditions

Syntax Explanation

1. Initialize Relay

What does it do?
This function sets up the GPIO pins to control the relay module. It configures the pin as an output and ensures that the microcontroller is ready to switch the relay on or off.

Syntax:
```
relay_init();
```

Example:
```c
void relay_init() {
    DDRB |= (1 << PB0);   // Set PB0 as output (Relay control)
    PORTB &= ~(1 << PB0); // Initialize relay as off
}
```

Explanation:
- **DDRB**: Data Direction Register for Port B. We set the bit corresponding to PB0 as an output.
- **PORTB**: Data Register for Port B. We clear the bit corresponding to PB0 to turn off the relay initially.

2. Turn On Appliance

What does it do?
This function turns on the appliance by energizing the relay, allowing current to flow to the appliance.

Syntax:
```
turn_on_appliance();
```

Example:
```c
void turn_on_appliance() {
    PORTB |= (1 << PB0);   // Set PB0 high to activate the relay and turn on the appliance
}
```

Explanation:

- **PORTB |= (1 << PB0)**: This sets the bit corresponding to PB0 high, energizing the relay and turning on the connected appliance.

3. Turn Off Appliance

What does it do?
This function turns off the appliance by de-energizing the relay, cutting off current to the appliance.
Syntax:
```
turn_off_appliance();
```
Example:
```
void turn_off_appliance() {
    PORTB &= ~(1 << PB0);   // Set PB0 low to deactivate
the relay and turn off the appliance
}
```

Explanation:

- **PORTB &= ~(1 << PB0)**: This clears the bit corresponding to PB0, which turns off the relay and disconnects power to the appliance.

4. Read Sensor Data

What does it do?
This function reads data from a sensor, such as a temperature or motion sensor, and stores it for processing. The data can be used to trigger specific actions, like turning on lights when motion is detected.
Syntax:
```
read_sensor();
```
Example:
```
uint8_t read_sensor() {
    uint8_t sensor_value = ADC;   // Read ADC value from
sensor
    return sensor_value;
}
```

Explanation:

- **ADC**: The ADC register contains the converted digital value from the sensor.
- **sensor_value**: Holds the value read from the sensor (e.g., temperature, light intensity, or motion).

5. Send Command Over Wi-Fi/Bluetooth

What does it do?

This function sends commands to a remote device, like a smartphone or a server, to control home appliances remotely via Wi-Fi or Bluetooth.

Syntax:

```
send_command("Turn on light");
```

Example:

```
void send_command(const char *command) {
    uart_send_string(command);   // Send command via
UART to Wi-Fi/Bluetooth module
}
```

Explanation:

- **uart_send_string()**: Sends the command string to a Bluetooth or Wi-Fi module, which then relays it to the remote device for execution.

6. Monitor Conditions

What does it do?

This function continuously monitors sensor data and evaluates it to make decisions. For example, if the motion sensor detects movement, the function could turn on the lights.

Syntax:

```
monitor_conditions();
```

Example:

```
void monitor_conditions() {
    uint8_t motion_detected = read_sensor();  // Read
motion sensor data
    if (motion_detected) {
        turn_on_appliance();  // Turn on the light if
motion is detected
    } else {
        turn_off_appliance(); // Turn off the light if
no motion is detected
    }
}
```

Explanation:

- The function reads data from the sensor and checks if motion is detected.
- Based on the result, it triggers actions like turning appliances on or off.

Real-life Application Project: Wi-Fi-Controlled Home Automation System

Project Overview

In this project, we will create a Wi-Fi-based home automation system using an AVR microcontroller and an ESP8266 Wi-Fi module. This system will allow us to control household appliances remotely, such as turning lights on/off or controlling a fan. The system will also monitor environmental conditions (e.g., temperature) using a sensor, and automate actions based on those conditions.

Required Components

Component	Description
AVR Microcontroller	Main controller for the system
ESP8266 Wi-Fi Module	Enables remote control via a smartphone or computer
Relay	Controls appliances by switching power
DHT11 Temperature/Humidity Sensor	Reads room temperature and humidity

Component	AVR Pin	Purpose
LED/Light		To be controlled by the system (example appliance)

Circuit Connection Table

Component	AVR Pin	Purpose
ESP8266 Wi-Fi Module	RX, TX	Communication with the AVR microcontroller
Relay	PB0	Controls power to appliances
DHT11 Sensor	PD0	Reads room temperature and humidity
LED/Light	PB1	Example appliance for control

Project Code

```c
#include <avr/io.h>
#include <util/delay.h>

void relay_init() {
    DDRB |= (1 << PB0);   // Set PB0 as output (Relay control)
    PORTB &= ~(1 << PB0); // Initialize relay as off
}

void send_command(const char *command) {
    uart_send_string(command);   // Send command via UART to ESP8266
}

void turn_on_appliance() {
    PORTB |= (1 << PB0);   // Turn on the relay (appliance on)
}

void turn_off_appliance() {
    PORTB &= ~(1 << PB0);   // Turn off the relay (appliance off)
}
```

```c
uint8_t read_sensor() {
    // Read sensor data (DHT11 temperature/humidity)
    return ADC;   //

 Placeholder for actual sensor reading
}

void monitor_conditions() {
    uint8_t temp = read_sensor();
    if (temp > 30) {   // If the temperature exceeds
30°C, turn on the fan
        turn_on_appliance();
    } else {
        turn_off_appliance();
    }
}

int main() {
    relay_init();
    uart_init();   // Initialize UART for communication
with ESP8266

    while (1) {
        monitor_conditions();   // Continuously monitor
conditions
        _delay_ms(1000);        // Wait before checking
again
    }
}
```

Expected Results

 The Wi-Fi-controlled system will enable remote control of appliances, with real-time monitoring of environmental conditions. For instance, the fan will automatically turn on when the temperature exceeds a certain threshold. Users can also manually control devices using a smartphone app or web interface.

Chapter 73: Weather Monitoring System

Weather monitoring systems play a crucial role in observing and analyzing environmental conditions, including temperature, humidity, pressure, and air quality. By leveraging AVR microcontrollers, we can build a cost-effective, real-time weather monitoring system that collects data from sensors and displays or transmits the data for further analysis. This system can be used in various applications, such as smart home automation, agriculture, and environmental monitoring.

In this chapter, we will explore how to design a weather monitoring system using an AVR microcontroller. We will cover the interfacing of sensors such as the DHT11 (temperature and humidity) sensor and the BMP180 (pressure and temperature) sensor. The collected data will be displayed on an LCD and can also be transmitted over a wireless communication module such as the ESP8266 for remote monitoring.

Key Concepts of Weather Monitoring System with AVR

Concept	Description	Example
Temperature and Humidity Sensing	Measuring the air temperature and humidity using sensors.	DHT11 sensor for temperature and humidity
Pressure Sensing	Measuring atmospheric pressure using a barometric pressure sensor.	BMP180 sensor for pressure and temperature
Microcontroller Interfacing	Interfacing sensors with AVR microcontrollers through communication protocols.	Using I2C or UART for sensor communication
Data Display	Displaying weather data on an LCD or OLED display.	Using an LCD to show temperature, humidity, and pressure
Wireless Data Transmission	Transmitting weather data over Wi-Fi, Bluetooth, or other communication	Using ESP8266 for remote monitoring

modules.	

Basic Rules for Weather Monitoring with AVR

Rule	Correct Example	Incorrect Example
Use proper sensor wiring and calibration	Connect DHT11 sensor to the correct microcontroller pins	Incorrect sensor wiring leading to inaccurate readings
Choose a reliable communication protocol	Use I2C for BMP180 and DHT11 for accurate data transfer	Using incompatible communication protocols
Display data in readable format	Display temperature in Celsius and humidity in percentage	Incorrect data formatting (e.g., raw values)
Implement sensor data filtering	Use averaging or smoothing techniques for more stable readings	Displaying raw, fluctuating sensor values without filtering

Syntax Table

SL	Operation	Syntax/Example	Description
1	Initialize DHT11 Sensor	`dht11_init();`	Initializes the DHT11 sensor for temperature and humidity readings
2	Initialize BMP180 Sensor	`bmp180_init();`	Initializes the BMP180 sensor for temperature and pressure readings
3	Read Temperature and Humidity	`dht11_read();`	Reads temperature and humidity from the DHT11 sensor
4	Read Pressure	`bmp180_read_pressure();`	Reads atmospheric pressure from the BMP180 sensor
5	Display Data on LCD	`lcd_print("Temp: 25°C");`	Prints the sensor data to an LCD
6	Transmit Data via Wi-Fi	`send_data_wifi("Temperature: 25°C");`	Sends data to a remote server or app via Wi-Fi (ESP8266)

Syntax Explanation

1. Initialize DHT11 Sensor

What does it do?

This function initializes the DHT11 sensor to read temperature and humidity. It prepares the microcontroller to receive data from the sensor.

Syntax:

```
dht11_init();
```

Example:

```
void dht11_init() {
    // Set pin direction and initialize communication
for DHT11
    DDRD &= ~(1 << PD2);   // Set PD2 as input (DHT11
signal pin)
    // Add any sensor-specific initialization if needed
}
```

Explanation:

- **DDRD &= ~(1 << PD2)**: Sets the PD2 pin as input to read the data from the DHT11 sensor.
- Additional initialization code may be required, depending on the sensor's requirements.

2. Initialize BMP180 Sensor

What does it do?

This function initializes the BMP180 sensor, which measures temperature and pressure. It sets up the communication protocol (I2C) to interact with the sensor.

Syntax:

```
bmp180_init();
```

Example:

```
void bmp180_init() {
    // Initialize the I2C communication for BMP180
    i2c_init();  // Initialize I2C
    bmp180_reset(); // Send reset command to BMP180
}
```

Explanation:

- **i2c_init()**: Initializes the I2C communication required by the BMP180 sensor.
- **bmp180_reset()**: Sends a reset command to the BMP180 to ensure it's ready to take measurements.

3. Read Temperature and Humidity (DHT11)

What does it do?
This function reads temperature and humidity data from the DHT11 sensor and stores it for further use.

Syntax:
```
dht11_read();
```

Example:
```
void dht11_read() {
    uint8_t data[5]; // Array to store sensor data
    if (dht11_request() == 0) {
        dht11_read_data(data);  // Read data from DHT11
        temperature = data[2];  // Store the
temperature value
        humidity = data[0];     // Store the humidity
value
    }
}
```

Explanation:

- **dht11_request()**: Sends a signal to the DHT11 sensor to start data reading.
- **dht11_read_data()**: Reads the sensor data, storing it in the data array. The temperature and humidity values are extracted from the data.

4. Read Pressure (BMP180)

What does it do?

This function reads the atmospheric pressure data from the BMP180 sensor.

Syntax:

```
bmp180_read_pressure();
```

Example:

```
void bmp180_read_pressure() {
    uint16_t pressure;
    pressure = bmp180_get_pressure();   // Fetch
pressure value from BMP180
    pressure_value = pressure;          // Store the
pressure value
}
```

Explanation:

- **bmp180_get_pressure()**: Communicates with the BMP180 over I2C to retrieve the atmospheric pressure data.
- The pressure value is then stored in the variable `pressure_value`.

5. Display Data on LCD

What does it do?

This function displays the sensor readings on an LCD screen, making the data available for real-time monitoring.

Syntax:

```
lcd_print("Temp: 25°C");
```

Example:

```
void lcd_print(const char *message) {
    lcd_clear();                // Clear the LCD screen
    lcd_send_string(message); // Send the message to
the LCD
}
```

Explanation:

- **lcd_clear()**: Clears the LCD display to make room for new data.
- **lcd_send_string(message)**: Displays the provided message (e.g., temperature or pressure) on the LCD screen.

6. Transmit Data via Wi-Fi

What does it do?
This function transmits the weather data over a wireless network (Wi-Fi) using the ESP8266 module.

Syntax:
```
send_data_wifi("Temperature: 25°C");
```
Example:
```
void send_data_wifi(const char *data) {
    esp8266_connect_wifi();  // Connect to Wi-Fi
    esp8266_send_data(data);  // Send the data to a
remote server or app
}
```

Explanation:

- **esp8266_connect_wifi()**: Connects the ESP8266 Wi-Fi module to the configured Wi-Fi network.
- **esp8266_send_data(data)**: Sends the provided data to a remote server or application for monitoring.

Real-life Application Project: Weather Station with Remote Monitoring
Project Overview
In this project, we will design a weather station using the AVR microcontroller to monitor temperature, humidity, and atmospheric pressure. The weather data will be displayed on an LCD for local monitoring and transmitted wirelessly using the ESP8266 Wi-Fi module for remote access.

Required Components

Component	Description
AVR Microcontroller	The main controller for the weather station
DHT11 Temperature and Humidity Sensor	Measures the temperature and humidity
BMP180 Barometric Pressure Sensor	Measures atmospheric pressure
LCD 16x2 Display	Displays the weather data (temperature, humidity, pressure)
ESP8266 Wi-Fi Module	Allows remote transmission of data to a server or app

Circuit Connection Table

Component	AVR Pin	Purpose
DHT11 Sensor	PD2	Reads temperature and humidity
BMP180 Sensor	SDA, SCL	Reads atmospheric pressure
LCD 16x2 Display	PD0, PD1	Displays the data
ESP8266 Wi-Fi Module	RX	TX	Sends data wirelessly to a remote server	

Project Code

```
#include <avr/io.h>
#include <util/delay.h>
#include "dht11.h"
#include "bmp180.h"
#include "lcd.h"
#include "esp8266.h"

void relay_init() {
    // Initialize relay control
}
```

```c
void uart_init() {
    // Initialize UART communication for ESP8266
}

void monitor_conditions() {
    uint8_t temperature = read_temperature(); // Read
temperature from DHT11
    uint8_t humidity = read_humidity();        // Read
humidity from DHT11
    uint16_t pressure = read_pressure();       // Read
pressure from BMP180

    // Display data on LCD
    lcd_clear();
    lcd_print("Temp: ");
    lcd_print(temperature);
    lcd_print("C Hum: ");
    lcd_print(humidity);
    lcd_print("%");
    lcd_print("Press: ");
    lcd_print(pressure);
    lcd_print("hPa");

    // Transmit data via Wi-Fi
    char buffer[50];
    snprintf(buffer, sizeof(buffer), "Temp: %dC Hum:
%d%% Press: %d hPa", temperature, humidity, pressure);
    send_data_wifi(buffer);
}

int main() {
    uart_init();  // Initialize UART for communication
with ESP8266
    lcd_init();   // Initialize LCD
    dht11_init(); // Initialize DHT11 sensor
    bmp180_init(); // Initialize BMP180 sensor
```

```
    while (1) {
        monitor_conditions();   // Monitor weather
conditions
        _delay_ms(1000);        // Wait before checking
again
    }
}
```

Expected Results

The system will display the current temperature, humidity, and atmospheric pressure on the LCD. It will also send this data via Wi-Fi to a remote server or app for real-time monitoring. The weather station will continuously monitor the environmental conditions and update the display and transmitted data every second.

Chapter 74: Smart Agriculture

Smart agriculture involves the use of modern technology to improve the efficiency and sustainability of farming practices. Through automation and real-time data collection, farmers can monitor and manage various parameters such as soil moisture, temperature, humidity, and light conditions. Using AVR microcontrollers, sensors, and communication modules, it's possible to design a smart agriculture system that can monitor crops, automate irrigation, and provide insights for better farm management.

In this chapter, we will design a smart agriculture system using an AVR microcontroller. The system will utilize sensors to measure soil moisture, temperature, and humidity. Based on sensor readings, the system will automatically control irrigation systems and send real-time data to farmers for remote monitoring via Wi-Fi using the ESP8266 module.

Key Concepts of Smart Agriculture with AVR

Concept	Description	Example
Soil Moisture Sensing	Detecting the moisture level in soil to determine irrigation needs.	Capacitive or resistive soil moisture sensor
Temperature and Humidity Sensing	Measuring environmental parameters that affect plant growth.	DHT11 or DHT22 sensors for temperature and humidity
Automation of Irrigation	Using sensors to trigger automatic watering based on soil moisture levels.	Relay or solenoid valve controlling water flow
Wireless Data Transmission	Sending real-time data over Wi-Fi to remote devices for monitoring.	ESP8266 Wi-Fi module for remote monitoring
Environmental Monitoring	Monitoring factors like light, temperature, and humidity to optimize conditions.	LDR (Light Dependent Resistor), DHT11, BMP180

Basic Rules for Smart Agriculture with AVR

Rule	Correct Example	Incorrect Example
Proper sensor calibration and placement	Properly calibrating the soil moisture sensor for accurate readings	Incorrect placement of soil moisture sensor causing inaccurate results
Set up automated irrigation logic based on sensor data	Turning on irrigation when soil moisture drops below a set threshold	Ignoring the sensor data and manually controlling irrigation
Use wireless communication for remote monitoring	Use ESP8266 module to send data to a cloud server or app	Not using any communication module for remote access
Power management and efficiency	Use solar panels or battery-powered systems for energy efficiency	Overusing power without considering energy sources like solar or battery

Syntax Table

SL	Operation	Syntax/Example	Description
1	Initialize Soil Moisture Sensor	`soil_sensor_init();`	Initializes the soil moisture sensor
2	Initialize Temperature and Humidity Sensor	`dht11_init();`	Initializes the DHT11 temperature and humidity sensor
3	Read Soil Moisture Level	`soil_moisture = read_soil_moisture();`	Reads the soil moisture level
4	Read Temperature and Humidity	`read_temperature_humidity();`	Reads the temperature and humidity from the DHT11

5	Control Irrigation (Relay)	`control_irrigation();`	Turns on or off irrigation based on soil moisture
6	Transmit Data via Wi-Fi	`send_data_wifi( "Moisture: 45% Temp: 25°C");`	Sends data to a remote server or app via Wi-Fi

Syntax Explanation

1. Initialize Soil Moisture Sensor

What does it do?
This function initializes the soil moisture sensor, which will be used to monitor the moisture level in the soil. The sensor could be a capacitive or resistive type, depending on the setup.

Syntax:
```
soil_sensor_init();
```
Example:
```
void soil_sensor_init() {
    DDRC &= ~(1 << PC0);   // Set PC0 pin as input to read from the soil sensor
    // Additional sensor-specific initialization code if necessary
}
```

Explanation:
- **DDRC &= ~(1 << PC0)**: Sets the PC0 pin of the AVR as an input to read data from the soil moisture sensor.
- Any sensor-specific initialization can be added, depending on the type of sensor being used.

2. Initialize Temperature and Humidity Sensor (DHT11)

What does it do?
This function initializes the DHT11 sensor for reading environmental conditions, such as temperature and humidity.

Syntax:
```
dht11_init();
```
Example:
```
void dht11_init() {
    DDRD &= ~(1 << PD2);   // Set PD2 pin as input to
receive data from DHT11
    // Optional initialization code for DHT11 if
required
}
```

Explanation:
- **DDRD &= ~(1 << PD2)**: Configures the PD2 pin as an input to interface with the DHT11 sensor.
- The DHT11 sensor may need further initialization, but basic configurations usually include setting up the I/O pins.

3. Read Soil Moisture Level

What does it do?
This function reads the current moisture level from the soil moisture sensor. Based on the moisture level, irrigation may be triggered.

Syntax:
```
soil_moisture = read_soil_moisture();
```
Example:
```
uint16_t read_soil_moisture() {
    // Read the value from the analog input connected
to the soil moisture sensor
    return ADC;   // Assume ADC is configured for soil
moisture sensor
}
```

Explanation:
- **read_soil_moisture()**: Reads the analog value from the soil moisture sensor and returns it. Typically, an ADC pin on the AVR is used to read the sensor output.

4. Read Temperature and Humidity (DHT11)

What does it do?
This function reads the temperature and humidity data from the DHT11 sensor and stores the values for later use.

Syntax:
```
read_temperature_humidity();
```

Example:
```
void read_temperature_humidity() {
    uint8_t data[5];
    if (dht11_request() == 0) {
        dht11_read_data(data); // Read data from DHT11
        temperature = data[2];  // Store the
temperature
        humidity = data[0];     // Store the humidity
    }
}
```

Explanation:
- **dht11_request()**: Sends a request to the DHT11 sensor to start sending data.
- **dht11_read_data(data)**: Reads the data sent by the DHT11 sensor into the data array. The temperature and humidity values are extracted from the array.

5. Control Irrigation (Relay)

What does it do?
This function controls the irrigation system by turning the relay on or off based on the soil moisture level. When the soil moisture is below a certain threshold, the irrigation system is activated.

Syntax:
```
control_irrigation();
```

Example:

```
void control_irrigation() {
    if (soil_moisture < 300) {  // If the soil moisture
is low
        PORTB |= (1 << PB0);  // Turn on the irrigation
relay (activate pump)
    } else {
        PORTB &= ~(1 << PB0);  // Turn off the
irrigation relay (deactivate pump)
    }
}
```

Explanation:

- **PORTB |= (1 << PB0)**: Turns on the irrigation relay by setting PB0 high.
- **PORTB &= ~(1 << PB0)**: Turns off the irrigation relay by setting PB0 low.

6. Transmit Data via Wi-Fi (ESP8266)

What does it do?

This function sends the sensor data (soil moisture, temperature, and humidity) to a remote server or app using the ESP8266 Wi-Fi module for remote monitoring.

Syntax:

```
send_data_wifi("Moisture: 45% Temp: 25°C");
```

Example:

```
void send_data_wifi(const char *data) {
    esp8266_connect_wifi();  // Connect to the Wi-Fi
network
    esp8266_send_data(data);  // Send data to a cloud
server or mobile app
}
```

Explanation:

- **esp8266_connect_wifi()**: Establishes a Wi-Fi connection using the ESP8266.
- **esp8266_send_data(data)**: Sends the weather data (soil moisture, temperature, humidity) to a remote server or app for real-time monitoring.

Real-life Application Project: Smart Agriculture System

Project Overview

In this project, we will design a smart agriculture system that monitors the environmental conditions of crops and automatically controls irrigation. The system will use soil moisture, temperature, and humidity sensors to collect data and will transmit this data wirelessly using the ESP8266 Wi-Fi module for remote monitoring. If the soil moisture level drops below a certain threshold, the system will automatically activate irrigation using a relay module.

Required Components

Component	Description
AVR Microcontroller	Controls the system and processes sensor data
Soil Moisture Sensor	Measures the moisture level of the soil
DHT11 or DHT22 Sensor	Measures temperature and humidity
**	

Circuit Connection Table

Component	AVR Pin	Purpose
Soil Moisture Sensor	ADC0	Reads soil moisture level
DHT11 Sensor	PD2	Reads temperature and humidity
Relay Module	PB0	Controls irrigation system
ESP8266 Wi-Fi Module	TX/RX (Pin 3/4)	Sends data wirelessly to a remote server

Project Code

```c
#include <avr/io.h>
#include <util/delay.h>
#include "dht11.h"
#include "lcd.h"
#include "esp8266.h"

void soil_sensor_init() {
    // Initialize soil moisture sensor
}

void dht11_init() {
    // Initialize DHT11 sensor
}

uint16_t read_soil_moisture() {
    // Read soil moisture value
    return ADC;
}

void control_irrigation() {
    // Control relay for irrigation
    if (read_soil_moisture() < 300) {
        PORTB |= (1 << PB0);   // Turn on irrigation
    } else {
        PORTB &= ~(1 << PB0); // Turn off irrigation
    }
}

void send_data_wifi(const char *data) {
    esp8266_connect_wifi();   // Connect to Wi-Fi
    esp8266_send_data(data);  // Send data over Wi-Fi
}

int main() {
    soil_sensor_init();
```

```
    dht11_init();

    while (1) {
        uint16_t soil_moisture = read_soil_moisture();
        control_irrigation();

        char buffer[50];
        snprintf(buffer, sizeof(buffer), "Moisture:
%d%%", soil_moisture);
        send_data_wifi(buffer);

        _delay_ms(1000);  // Update every second
    }
}
```

Expected Results

 The system will continuously monitor the soil moisture, temperature, and humidity levels. If the soil moisture drops below a threshold, the irrigation system will be activated. The environmental data will be displayed on the LCD and transmitted wirelessly to a remote server or mobile app for real-time monitoring.

www.ingramcontent.com/pod-product-compliance
Lightning Source LLC
LaVergne TN
LVHW052056060326
832903LV00061B/2913